# The Art of the Accident

NAI Publishers / V2_Organisatie

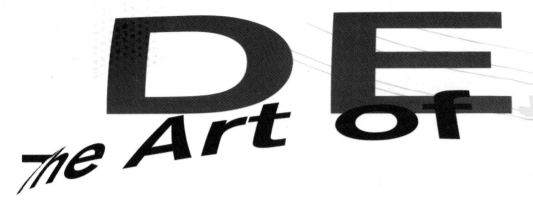

# The Art of the ACCIDENT

We live in a world of accidents. The things we produce have a tendency to malfunction as much as they function. We try to predict and control these functions, yet, we are often surprised by the creativity and variety with which the product can malfunction. The accident represents one of the great fears in a society where scientific and technical paradigms have for a long time been directed at safety and security. Planning, engineering and design are still mostly directed at the construction of safe and predictable things, while a new school of engineering is increasingly looking at ways of incorporating possible malfunctions into the planning process, and to use the accidental potential of products for enhancing their performance.

Yet, malfunction and failure are not signs of improper production. On the contrary, they indicate the active production of the 'accidental potential' in any product. The invention of the ship implies its wreckage, the steam engine and the locomotive discover the derailment (Virilio).

Aristotelian philosophy has pointed out that the accident is not something that is added from the outside, but that it is immanent to the thing itself. This also implies that failure, friction, collision and collapse have to be viewed as characteristics of substance itself. The accident is an intrinsic property and part of the program of any product. It is present as a potential within the technological phylum. The accident is not an 'event', which happens in time; the accident happens as a sudden transformation of matter in space. Nor is the accident the same as 'chance', which is brought to the thing from the outside, but something that realizes a potential that is inside, intrinsic to the thing.

The shock that an accident can trigger is effected by the accident's sudden and unexpected contraction of the domestic domain, the domain of safety, control and self-reference. The accident is experienced as an invasion of or intrusion into this domain, and for humans it is closely related to the loss of self-control over the body. More generally, the accident can be described as a situation in which a system can no longer grasp itself within its own terms.

# AF98
## ne Accident

*Ars accidentalis*

The accident is the ultimate functioning of a product. Beyond the classical opposition of functional vs. dysfunctional, the world of accidents becomes hyperfunctional.

Technology is a technique of accelerated and planned transformation. Technology designs accidents, and it tries to contain their effects. It is assumed to have 'failed' when it cannot contain its intrinsic accidents. Yet, any technical infrastructure is a combination of several accident-prone elements. In the same way as we can see the derailment as part of the train system, and the car crash as an *accidens* of the car, we can also investigate the accidental potentials of television, the computer, electronic networks, etc.

*DEAF98*, and this accompanying book of essays, interviews, art and architecture projects, is an exploration of what an *ars accidentalis* might be. The festival presents and discusses accidents and their preferred environments in such areas as electronic art, sound art, architecture, urban planning, economy and social systems, emphasizing the role that the accidental plays in the relation between art and technology, and in the transitory zone between these disciplines. *The Art of the Accident* showcases interactive machines, virtual environments, acoustic spaces, hardware and software projects with their 'accidental' potentials.

A world that is open to continuous change and to becoming different, requires an *ars accidentalis*. The creativity and the productivity of the accident, the break and the fall have to be understood as the potential to achieve new forms of heterogeneity and of disjunctive synthesis. Imprecision, haste, and forgetfulness are only some of the characteristics of this romantic discipline. *The Art of the Accident* is not looking for conclusive answers. It investigates the *project* in the face of failure.

DEAF98 / V2_Organisatie

# CO

transArchitectures
part of

Projects
part of

Symposium
part of

Exhibition
part of

## *Essays/Interviews*

# Exhibition/Projects

# transArchitectures 02 + 03

# RIGHT TO RISK

*Interview with Dick Raaijmakers by Bart Lootsma and Joke Brouwer.*

## ACCIDENT AND RISK

**DR:** I have a lot of problems with the word 'mishap'*. To me, it is a typical nineteenth century concept. A concept that marks the advent of social insurance, the awareness that something may happen to you and that you can insure yourself against it. Before that, things were different. If you were a carpenter working for a boss and you hit your thumb after having worked non-stop for twelve hours, your boss would just regard this as an accident in the line of duty. The same was true for child mortality. Children were born and frequently died. Of course they said "Oh, that poor child", but there would be another one.

I am exaggerating, but you know what I mean. It is about the prefix 'mis' in mishap. To me, 'mis' does not exist. I have no affinity with it, unless I start thinking about it in a certain archaic way.

*In his initial comments, Raaijmakers is referring to the Dutch word for 'accident', 'ongeval'. 'Val' is the same as 'fall', 'geval' is a case, fact or event, and the prefix 'on' turns it into its opposite, like the prefix 'mis'. The translation as 'mishap' is therefore closer to what Raaijmakers has in mind, connoting the 'factual' and the 'fall' implied in 'ongeval'.

One of my favorite themes is the decoupling of labor and the product of labor, in which the responsibility for this product is lost. And also the way risk is reduced to a minimum because of this decoupling. Workers hardly, if at all, run any risk during their work nowadays. That has all been banned. My ambition is to emancipate the concept of 'risk'.

For centuries, society has cherished the possession of rights and elevated it to the status of mankind's highest good. We think that the Universal Declaration of Human Rights is our ultimate achievement on this earth. I, on the other hand, have the crazy idea that it has turned into one of society's all time lows. In the name of rights, mankind has to this day been caused enormous misery. Just compare this to the ideas of modern artists, these fantastic trend-setters of real life. From Beethoven onwards, they have certainly not

# transArchitectures 02 + 03

The term 'transArchitectures' (Marcos Novak) stems from a discourse among architects and designers who, influenced by their experience with computer technology during the design process, are developing new concepts of time, space, shape, structures, construction, etc.

transArchitectures is not just another demonstration of the divergence between 'bits & bricks', between the material and the immaterial, or between virtuality and reality. On the contrary, the starting point of transArchitectures is that these concepts are intertwined and should be made to interact with one another. What is at stake is not just the use of computers in architecture and the architectural metaphor in the computer world. transArchitectures poses the challenge of simultaneously contemplating architecture and media, design and machine, and, within the conceptualization of this hybrid, the shift from 'time and space' to 'process and field'.

The media have saturated our lives, exercising strong influence on the way in which events are reported, perceived and understood. The resulting altered perception of space is also beginning to influence architectural developments. It is impossible to imagine Brunelleschi and Alberti without the technique of perspective and the painting, to imagine Loos and Le Corbusier without film and the train, or to imagine Robert Venturi and post-modernism without the car and television. Today architects are increasingly designing in the computer, using the machine not to represent or simulate reality, but making use of its incredible arithmetic possibilities in a conceptual way. Topology, fractal geometry and chaos theory support design processes which employ as models the shapes of clouds, of swarms, traffic jam or the behavior of fluids. Instead of drawing, the trans-architects are calculating, instead of making scale models, they are programming. Instead of shapes being imposed, they are being generated in non-linear and dynamic ways.

transArchitectures is a series of conferences, exhibitions and events which were initiated by Odile Filion (F) and Michel Vienne (B). DEAF98 includes the transArchitectures 02 + 03 exhibition and features several trans-architects in the DEAF98 Symposium. In its exhibitions and programmes, DEAF98 seeks to test the notion of an 'ars accidentalis'. The festival confronts transArchitectures with the ars accidentalis and its ubiquitous, accidental collisions of technological machines, designs, perception and movements in time and space. transArchitectures 02 + 03 is edited by Architecture & Prospective and is produced by IRD (Infographie Recherche et Développement). Curator, Michel Vienne - Chargé de missions, Stéphane Kervyn de Lettenhove.

bothered with rights, on the contrary, they have always been interested in going beyond rights; they have been busy giving shape to risk. Take John Cage, for instance. Cage and kindred avant-gardists are not interested in trivialities like having or acquiring rights but in making choices that involve risks. These risks have nothing to do with affectation, but are at the heart of the performance, the music. Cage teaches you to share music with others instead of making it your own personal property. In art, these aspects have been dealt with a long time ago and the risk principle has slowly but surely taken the place of rights. Every performing artist runs risks, that's what makes it art.

I have sometimes thought of setting up a political party and if I did it would have to be called Right to Risk. That's because I see concepts like accident and mishap as typical nineteenth century concepts. They are based on obsolete hierarchical ideas. In this respect, it may be interesting to realize that in the time of Goethe, being unhappy was something you cherished with all your heart. The same holds true for Beethoven: for him an unhappy love life was a precondition for the creation of magnificent works of art. These people did not insure themselves against feeling unhappy. On the contrary, I would say, they started feeling truly unhappy when they were not feeling unhappy! But anyway, in our society this is alien to our way of thinking. At the top of our legal system sits a judge with a dirty, dusty wig on his head. The hermetically sealed terminology used by these hired buffoons is disgusting in itself. Moreover, all their claims fundamentally conflict with all the higher spiritual ideas developed in art over the years. Judges and artists are the very opposite of each other. With their limited, stupid ideas about the meaning of life, judges can only dream of living according to the risk principle. After all, risk is of infinitely more value than these stupid, foolish rights. Abolish human rights! I would like to argue. People have no rights. They run risks. That is what we should devote ourselves to. Affecting people's existence that is full of risk is one of the biggest crimes, but today people do not see it that way. Risk means absolutely nothing in our society. It is something to insure yourself against. Once the risk principle has become of paramount importance in the future, the court system and all its lawyers will disappear, or will at least have to be redefined. Anyway, I will not live to see the day.

**Decoï (F)**
Hystera Protera

The current fascination with virtuality is the fascination of a non-originary origin. To avoid filling this conceptual black hole with customary fashion, we might pause sufficiently to allow the play of a writing genesis to open a space or a time in our thought. Considering writing in terms of spacing and temporization, instead of telling a story from a to b, implies a very different logic, a different feminine manner of operation: non-linear, cyclical, fluid, chemic rather than optic. It enables us to seek other cognitive strategies which correspond more closely to the inherent qualities of our new media.

Another aspect of risk is making, or what is even worse, avoiding mistakes. In the past, you always had to follow the rules of composing exactly, otherwise it was wrong. It was really a puzzle back then. You only have to think about the classical subject counterpoint. But nowadays, with various forms of improvisation, it is impossible to make any mistakes in that respect. People who make mistakes are reprimanded. This still has to do with angry conductors. But in real contemporary music – music that is really played – the meaning of making mistakes has slowly diminished in value. It does not really fit in with our society anymore. If you want to survive in our society, you have to learn to choose. You have to learn to choose the way you move, what modern tools to use, what your material looks like, which services you want to make use of, etc. To make a long story short: we are ready to say goodbye to an old and hackneyed set of concepts of falling, accidents, mistakes and running risks. That was why I was so surprised that you came up with the term 'accident' at V2. I find 'instability', a concept you introduced a few years ago, a much more beautiful and exciting concept because it is more fragile and much more artistic. No artist will take out an instability insurance. This will already be completely incorporated into his work, provided it is any good. Ordinary people, on the other hand, want stable media at all costs, television sets that function without interference day in day out, telephone connections established immediately, trains, planes and cars that run on time, etc. No, I'm afraid instability appeals more to me than the concept of accident. But I may be wrong.

## RIGHT

**DR**: To return to my ideas on rights versus risk, I would like to shed more light on the matter by taking the world of sport as an example. I am thinking in particular of competitive sport in which there are two competing parties. What would football be without risk? This concept has become the focal point in sport long time ago. Imagine a top club insuring itself against failed attempts to score a goal! Sure, they can take out insurance if their club is performing badly commercially. Or if a player accepts a bribe: that's one of the biggest sins imaginable. Maybe they can insure themselves against risks like that, but definitely not against losing a game or missing a goal. That is all part of the game.

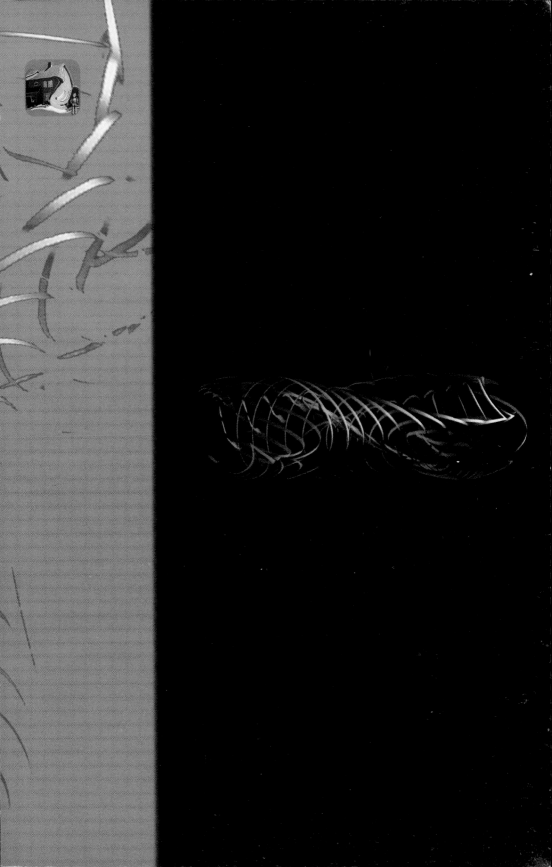

In this context, it is interesting to see how all kinds of rules and rights are introduced in competitive sport for the sole purpose of creating an optimum amount of risk. Before the game starts, a lot of super-straight white lines are drawn on the playing field. Then they throw a ball between these lines and the match can start. The ball is meant to stay inside these lines, or, alternatively, go outside them.

And the trouble starts when the ball lands exactly on the line instead of in front of it or behind it, like in tennis where the angry player calls in the umpire to convince him that the ball was not 'out' but 'in'. Inside this system of lines, which is really based on the classical legal system, everything is literally straight. There are no curves or bends but everything is super-straight. Why is this? To enable the two competing parties to run enormous risks and break the rules of this system of straight rules and lines. Precisely because of these risks, hundreds, thousands of spectators or more watch this basically stupid movement of these equally stupid balls. Not because of these straight lines or this round ball, no, because of the crossing, the literal going over these lines by the ball. In order to further outline and give shape to the risk of the players, they invented linesmen and referees who have to 'judge' the game. Note the terminology: judge! In the world of sport they leave nothing to chance; they can teach the playful society a lesson or two!

*JB: You say that everything is straight in competitive sport, which allows various forms of risk to occur. Today, there is a group of architects who design buildings in the computer. Nothing is straight anymore because it is not absolutely necessary when working with a computer. So you get curves and slopes in buildings. Nothing is self-evident anymore. I think that the V2_Lab is a good example of this; a work situation with a completely unstable floor where the gradient shifts continuously between zero and ninety degrees! Walking and falling become one. What happens to risk under these conditions?*

DR: The world is of course not straight at all: everything bulges and drops and everything shifts. We want that back: back to nature. You would like it to be possible to kinetically incorporate all these fluid architectonic variables in certain buildings without too much trouble. You can definitely feel this in the Water-

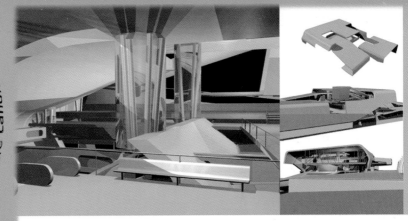

Neil Denari (USA)
More Landforms

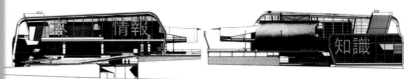

NATIONAL LIBRARY of JAPAN COMPETITION 1996

While digital territories are created and annexed every second in the production of information, land has become a symbolic representation of power. The codifications of the new digital zones allow us to access the inexorable flow of capitalist progress. For architecture it's necessary to gather knowledge about this codifications and about the effects that new global languages have on our perception of the territorial and social landscapes of the world. In order to respatialize the dramatic currents and flows of culture and in order to become a fully communicative spatial apparatus, architecture must intersect with the graphic.

**cor-tex**

PROJETS du JAPONAISE

© 1997 COR-TEX ARCHITECTURE / FOR MORE INFO ON THESE PROJECTS, PLEASE PICK UP A COPY OF INTERRUPTED PROJECTIONS AT YOUR LOCAL BOOKSTORE

COR-TEX.

LOOPS

ARCHITECTURE

GALLERY MA / INTERRUPTED PROJECTIONS 1996

VERTICAL MINIMUM HI-RISE HOUSING / TOKYO 1994-97

Pavilion on the Dutch coast. Entering such a room is a very strange experience, acoustically as well. But do not forget that, in terms of entertainment, such rooms come very close to certain fairground attractions, where you also have things that shake and unbalance you so that you no longer know what is up or down or left or right. These attractions are of course at a different level, but the main thing is that you pay your money at the box office to be in a room for a while where everything is fluid, or rather, elastic. In this case we are no longer talking about an altered society but a make-believe one; a society resembling a fairground attraction, in which the encounter with all sorts of horrible things is staged, so to speak; it also sort of compensates for the real society which is very dull and where no risks are run. This is precisely why people like to go on holiday and camp in flimsy tents and rickety caravans. They want very much to run risks in the unreliable countryside. They leave the safety of their homes and exchange it for a definitely unstable environment. Not because they are forced to do so, as in the case of an evacuation, but voluntarily. Looking at it this way, exposing yourself to risk in this way is kind of perverse.

It is remarkable that art has always been at the forefront in things such as risk. You can experiment with it in various art forms. Art has the ability to question itself. Art as criticism, that is the power of art. Society can learn a lot from art. Someone like John Cage, for instance, will never ever claim: "Look how much risk I put in my piece!" Or "I am dying to make a piece with a lot of risk in it". His genius is that he has been able to completely reshape the issue of making choices, in which the variability of all kinds of musical variables is enormously important, without making it obscure. Liberating imperatively closed forms is basically the same as freeing people. This has an enormous emancipatory power. Our terminology is still inadequate to express this in everyday words. I know that in our culture, especially on the Internet, whole new sets of concept are developing, which slowly but surely will replace the existing ones. The term 'surfing' is an excellent example. Surfing on the electronic waves, its movement, is a beautifully poetic and ironic approach to the way in which you should move through networks. It will certainly continue; a terminology that is so beautiful and individual that it will no longer apply to boring everyday life but to a new electronic reality.

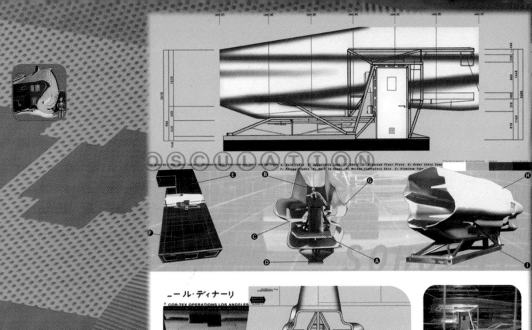

OSCULATION

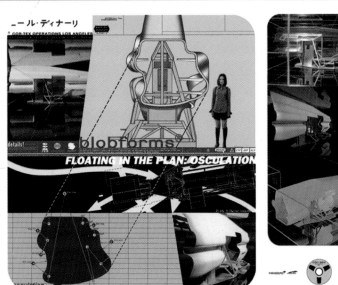

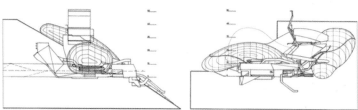

ー・ル・ディナーリ

COR-TEX OPERATIONS LOS ANGELES

blobforms

FLOATING IN THE PLAN: OSCULATION

osculation

DETAILS DESIGN STUDIO / NEW YORK 1993

FIBERGLASFIBER HOUSE / LOS ANGELES 1991

MASSEY RESIDENCE / LOS ANGELES 1994

# THE WORLD AS AN ACCIDENT

**BL**: *The text about your work by Willem Jan Otten in the program of the Soundman in the Frascati Theatre (Amsterdam) contains a passage from what I assume is your own text about 'Falling as Music'. In this text, you quote Wittgenstein's famous first sentence from the Tractatus: "Die Welt ist alles, was der Fall ist". In the translation by the Dutch writer W.F. Hermans this sentence is: "The world is everything which is the case". You rightly remark that the German word 'Fall' can be interpreted differently, namely as 'fall', which would result in the following translation: "The world is everything as it has fallen". In another passage, you say that falling has everything to do with accident and that all accidents can be traced back to vertical falls or horizontal collisions, in other words to pure accidents. In that case the ultimate accident would be the Fall of Man described in the Bible. Do you think the world itself is an accident?*

**DR**: Well, I'm not sure if I would interpret it that way. We should certainly not forget that this whole terminology, also Wittgenstein's, is grafted onto nineteenth century mechanical ideas. Wittgenstein, Mach and Einstein are important scientists and philosophers who marked a pivoting point between the nineteenth and twentieth century. In spite of their innovative work and the introduction of completely new ideas about the relationship between nature, science and society, concepts like accident and mishap still have heavy archaic overtones which facilitate a mental leap to a classical concept like 'the Fall of Man'.

Anyway, during the last few decades I have intensely focused on falling in the metaphorical sense. Normally speaking, falling is a very primary concept. For falling is something that just happens physically. I was especially interested in reducing human behavior to its most elementary form, to something which cannot possibly be taken back any further. The idea of falling directly resulted from a way of linear thinking that I was entertaining at the time to get a clear picture of the use of electricity in music. When I myself started experimenting with electronic music in the fifties and sixties, I did not do so in the first place as a composer, although that played a role too, but rather as an analyst. I was especially interested in the methodical or, if you wish,

Ammar Eloueini (F)
**ctrl.alt.del**

We do not operate any longer in a system limited to three dimensions, but in a hyperspace which calls into question the space such as we are used to perceiving and imagining it. The challenge for an experimental architecture is to explore this new dimension that has been vacant until now. Established and accepted terms such as dimensions, spaces, and structures should be redefined. There is a great need for new approaches, responding to the architectural and urban complexity, suited to expressing changes, based on dynamic and evolutionary systems.

phenomenological side of making electric music. I was
interested in finding the basic principle behind the fact
that you could make music with the use of electricity by
just turning a few knobs. At the time, I was already an
educator in heart and soul, I wanted to know how
everything worked; not from a technical point of view but
socially and interactively. What happens in the head of a
composer when he wants a certain tone to be followed by
another tone by electronic means. I wanted to put my
finger on the fundamental difference between a violin
tone and a generator tone. Not the obscure difference
between the two, for we all know this, but the essential
difference.

   To give an example, I experience a violin tone as a
tone that you have to carry forwards, so to speak, a tone
whose creation is a continuous process. With a generator
tone, it is exactly the other way around. You switch it on
by pressing or turning a knob and you get a linear tone
that continues until you switch it 'off'. This tone can do
without you, whereas a violin tone cannot, not even for a
fraction of a second. The energy, the volume of this
generator tone comes straight from the mains, it is not
yours. The violin tone is in fact yours. Music experts will
say: that is his tone, beautiful! Well, the continuous
generator tone is absolutely related to the fall in this
respect. Falling is also a continuous process, until the
moment you hit the floor, where the fall reaches its climax.
When you fall, it is not your own doing either, external
factors are at play, unless you start doing stunts when you
are dangling safely from a parachute after having jumped
from a plane. But that is more a confirmation than a
negation of what I am arguing.

   That is why I have chosen the fall as a beautiful
metaphor, a beautiful model as well, for something that
you first have to prepare and then try to bring to a climax.
You just turn a knob and the energy flows from that which
is falling. You get this energy for free while looking on
with your hands in your pockets. That is why the fall
corresponds to the most rudimentary aspect of music.
There is nothing more elementary in music than the
sound of a fall. At the academy of music, you can learn
how to play the violin, to strum a guitar or hammer away
at a piano and percussion instruments, and blow copper
and wooden cylinders, but they do not teach you anything
about falling. I am very fond of such simple paradoxical

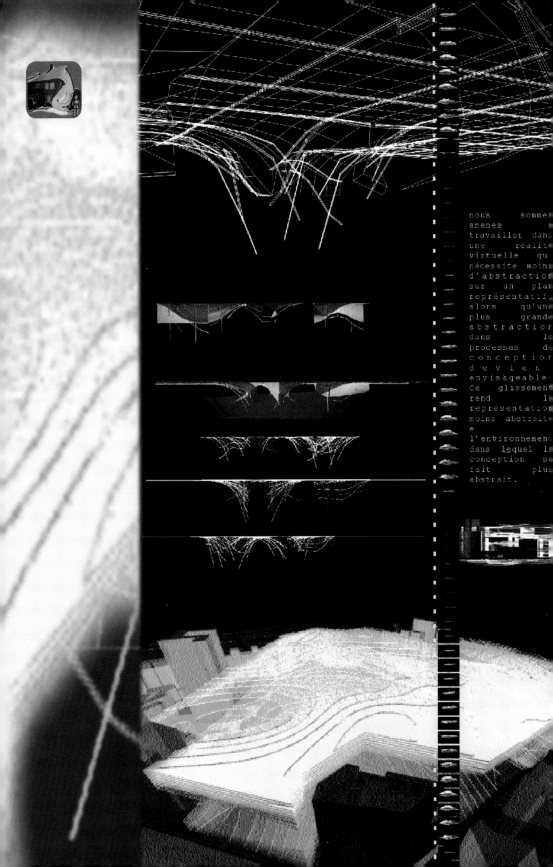

nous sommes
amenés à
travailler dans
une réalité
virtuelle qui
nécessite moins
d'abstraction
sur un plan
représentatif,
alors qu'une
plus grande
abstraction
dans le
processus de
conception
devient
envisageable.
Ce glissement
rend la
représentation
moins abstraite
e
l'environnement
dans lequel la
conception se
fait plus
abstrait.

theories and want to find out the exact reason for this. The answer is that the fall takes place after the essential part of the music is already over, and this essential part is making music, together with others. A fall sometimes produces an enormously interesting sound, but such a sound will never ever be written down in any concert score. That is why the fall is such an excellent model for me, especially because I make electronic music. You have no part in the creation of electronic sounds. These sounds come into being when you push a button, to put it bluntly.

# BREAKING DOWN

*BL: Equipment breaking down is also a very important theme in your thinking as well as in your work. You once gave an interview to Elmer Schönberger and his tape recorder broke down. Elmer had to laugh and snigger about this, to which you reacted by asking yourself aloud: "Why this laughter?" And you immediately gave the answer yourself: "Technology can be equated with improperly acquired energy and result. (...) Have you ever seen a farmer laughing after he had worked his fingers to the bone in the fields? This farmer looks serious." This breaking down of things and this improperly acquired energy is something that is indeed very important to you.*

**DR**: It sure is. I am interested in the typical aspects of a machine, and especially the division of labor resulting from the advent of the machine in our society. Nowadays, you do not have to swing a hammer yourself but just push a button here and unleash a tremendous hammering somewhere else. Over the last century, the distance between you and your place of work has increased enormously, which is a typical result of machines. When I am investigating this dichotomy within the world of modern art and question this using artistic means, I am liable to become pedantic. Like: "machines should be banned!, I prefer the honest paintbrush", or something to that effect. I am purely interested in the relationship between reality, my ideas about reality and the way these ideas can be molded into artistic forms as effectively as possible. The way I go about it, you soon arrive at reductions of this reality into all kinds of archaic forms.

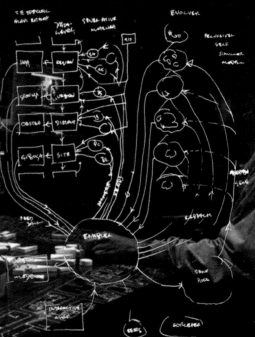

John & Julia Frazer (GB)
Evolutionary Architecture

In the future context of urban strategies the comprehension of the possibilities of a city is only guarantied by 'citizen participation'. For the city of Groningen, we developed an Evolutionary Model which requires a generative dimension and the use of genetic algorithms to develop appropriate rules and strategies in order to produce a rule-based system which learns on the basis of feedback from the city's inhabitants. The structure of the model is specifically tailored to the scale and nature of the local social, environmental, historical and future situation. By activating these models around the world you can create a virtual global city, a connectivity of urban models communicating and exchanging information and experience around the world. A permanent center for Civic Studies in every town should mediate as an 'Outlook Tower' between the real and the virtual city.

## ARCHITECTURE AS AN ARTIFICIAL LIFE FORM
### MATERIALISATION PHASE II

In its first five years, The Architectural Association's Diploma Unit 11 developed a theoretical framework of an alternative generative process, using computer models to compress evolutionary space and time. This led to a prototype that could be demonstrated interactively, and the launch on the Internet of an experimental evolutionary environment, which attracted global participation, established a dematerialised model.

The new phase of the programme has begun to externalise this conceptual model into constructed form, focusing on urban-scale evolution and other historical and cultural examples of co-operative and ecologically integrated development. The approach has been to consider metabolic processes as a way of understanding both the formal development of urban symbiosis and the specific problem of materialisation.

The city planning department of Groningen, Holland, commissioned a small working prototype of a predictive urban computer model. The unit produced an evolving model which explains the transition from the past to the present, and projects future trajectories - a 'what if' model for generating, exploring and evaluating alternatives. The model mediates in scale, space and time;

*in scale between the urban context and the fine grain of the housing typologies*

*in space between the existing urban fabric of Groningen and specific dwelling units*

*in time between the lifestyle within the medieval core and the desires of the citizens of the next century*

A particular characteristic of the prototype is that it combines generative techniques (cellular automata) and learning strategies (genetic algorithms), to produce a rule-based system which learns on the basis of feedback from the city's inhabitants.

Central to the model is the idea that the computer program inhabits an environment, e.g. roads, understands its developmental rules and constraints in its topography, latitude, and climate, and economy- and then starts to solicit or make proposals for possible futures.

The model becomes an inhabitant, discourse with other human inhabitants, understand and interpret their environment, urges, expectations, and reactions to their existing environment and projected future environments. On the basis of this interaction, the virtual inhabitor patiently modifies its criteria for evolutionary development and selection, endlessly repeating the process of refining and modelling prototypical futures. As it does so, it occasionally produces experimental genetic mutations or amplifies variety.

The inhabitor can inhabit at any level: cell, room, house, district, city, region, continent, planet. It can inhabit past, present and possible future environments. The model allows a collective consciousness informed from virtual inhabitants of past and present habitats, and from the interaction of citizens who provide feedback to inform and select criteria.

The core of the inhabitor is the Evolver, an evolving genetic model in which the isospatial catastructures and genepool are controlled by genetic algorithms. The Evolver is a recursively self-similar program which furthermore it provides starting configurations or seeds for genetic algorithms, which learn on the basis of feedback from specific sites. The criteria for genetic selection are determined by citizen interaction with the Enabler.

The Enabler maintains an interactive city map and acts as a stage for dialogue between citizens and the inhabitants.

The structure is hierarchically nested and mirrors the environment at the regional scale (down to cellular). The catastructure is strategically flexible without being geometrically constrained to modularity. It can interact with other sites at the same level or with other levels either top-down or bottom-up. Use of specific data (GIS) and maps are employed in simulations and respond to exogenous influences in the case of Groningen, economics, solar gain and commercial spatial studies. Three of thematic generating models operate within the schema of the prototype, and demonstrate at the level of the local topography, the city form, the Oosterhamrikt district and the Ciboga site. Generative models actively generate new possibilities from inputs from the Evolver. In turn, feedback from specific sites affects the selection processes in the Evolver.

PROJECT CONCEPT AND COMPUTER PROGRAMMING
John and Julia Frazer
Gianni Botsford
Cristiano Ceccato
Dominic Skinner
Guy Westbrook
Peter Graham
Architectural Association Diploma Unit 11

IMAGES
Gianni Botsford
Cristiano Ceccato
Dominic Skinner
Manit Rastogi

TEXT
John Frazer
Faryel Khatri

# THE GRONINGEN EXPERIMENT

For instance, in a performance I let a cyclist take half an hour to get off his bike, or let him fall off his bike at this tempo; all impossible movements that require the utmost of the performer. Magnificent to watch, these primal images.

People like Bell and Edison were two pioneers in the field of disconnecting sound and people. Sound transmission and sound recording are the two important concepts that mark the beginning of our new society. So you could say that their inventions – the telephone and the gramophone – are the fruits of doing a deal with the devil in which the human voice – our soul – is sacrificed in exchange for an unbridled multiplication of our voice, both in distance and time.

The sound quality of our voice was absolutely terrible on this first gramophone and telephone, but it saved an enormous amount of time and distance. As a result, the separation between what you say and the fact that you say something became a fact. The true meaning of really possessing your own voice without it being taken from you by others manifests itself in wartime, when people are put under pressure to tell things they absolutely want to keep secret. These people are put under pressure to confess things they want to keep to themselves. Under such circumstances, you behavior what is going on, that you are selling something – your voice, your secrets, your most intimate thoughts – when you finally give in. There are also people who, if necessary, allow themselves to be tortured to death but do not give away anything which could betray others. In such cases, this silence often takes on very heroic forms.

My voice is my conscience, and what is in my head is mine. But the moment others start exploiting and selling my voice with the help of all kinds of technical equipment, this voice is no longer mine. I have literally sold it. All this has to do with the 'soul'. I cannot give away my soul just like that either.

Under pressure, I cannot just betray my friends on the pretext of "oh, it's just my voice, it doesn't mean that much". Of course this is different in everyday life: I am talking and you are recording my voice, and in a moment you will be taking my voice away in your bag. That is all part of the daily routine; putting a device in front of me and using it to steal my voice. Only, we do not call it stealing but recording and reproducing.

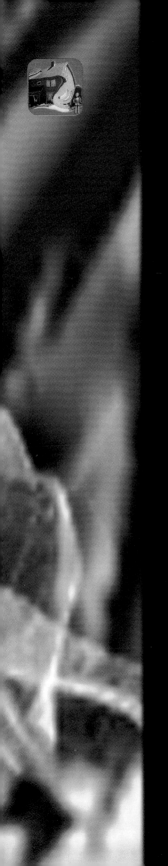

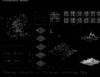

### Composite Model

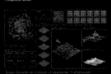
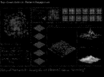

### Composite Model

## Cellular Automaton

## Economics

This ability to respond to changes in the environment, that is, regulate growth factors in response to changing social and economic requirements and ultimately experiment and gain knowledge based on previous experience, means that the city will have acquired the capacity to govern itself in an auto-catalytic manner, a form of intelligent self-enhancement.

### A Metametabolism Model of Intelligent Self-Regulation

### Economics

## Economics, Metametabolism and Intelligent Cities in the Super-Urban and Hyperspatial Domains

*Cristiano Ceccato*

### The Economic Analogy: Metametabolism

### The Economic Model

**TOP-DOWN**

**BOTTOM-UP**

## Solar Logic

*Gianni Botsford*

### When I Stand Still, I am Moving

## CENTRAL PLACE SYSTEMS AND THE EMERGENCE OF SPATIAL STRUCTURES

### Conceptual Framework

**Scale:**

**Time:**

**Distance:**

### Computer Models

## The Groningen Joint Model

### Thematic Generator Models

# THE
# OUTSIDER

*BL: Your work is very analytical. A large part of it is based on taking things apart. In an interview with the Volkskrant, you once said that your work is tragic and cold by definition and in the same article you said that it is important to be at the edge of things, almost outside of them. If we think about how technology has developed over the last few years, is it still possible to stay on the sidelines? It gets more and more difficult to distinguish between technology and nature. For instance, the millennium problem is largely caused by the fact that we no longer know exactly how certain computer programs were made, not even if we meticulously analyze them. Even to the inventors of these programs, protecting the base codes of computer analyze is of such crucial importance that they are obliged to forget them. It is like the builders of the pyramids, their knowledge has also been forgotten or at any rate lost. It has completely disappeared. We ourselves have become like cyborgs – surrounded by technology, integrated with technology, technology that influences our genes. How can we not take part? Can we stay on the sidelines? Can we continue to be so analytical?*

**DR**: That's a very good observation, I think. Let us not forget that I have been in the privileged position to witness a totally unexpected integration of two established disciplines, music and technology, from the beginning. And that I have been able to follow this development literally from the sidelines. At the time, this integration was quite simply called electronic music. When it came about, it was more a kind of congealing, an odd way of reciprocal use than a really tightly-knit integration. Music had been using technology for reproduction purposes for several decades, and up to this day there is even something like a music industry, but at a creative level this integration did not come about until after the Second World War.

Why do I call my position at the time privileged? Because I was in a position to witness what was happening when the peace of the traditional music world was rudely shattered by a kind of electronic meteorite which radically penetrated music. Technology penetrated music and caused a shock wave. It also caused a shock wave of expectations and utopian dreams which people would not be able to express in words for some time to come. But also a shock wave of dismay and disapproval:

TUD B. Franken
iBl Pavilion + Orbit

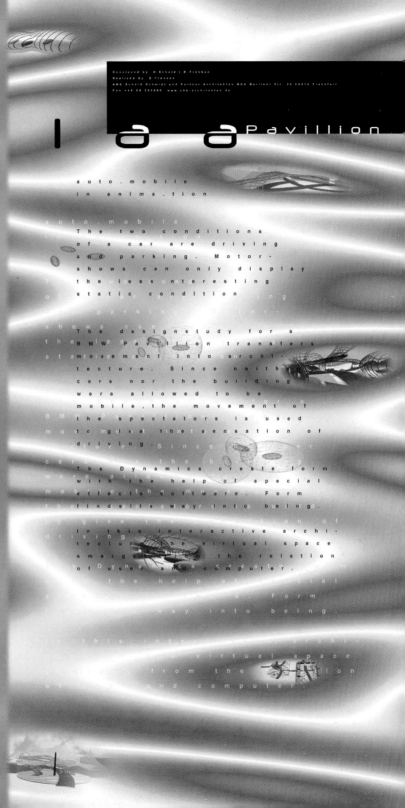

Considered by H.Schold | B.Franken
Realized by B.Franken
ABB Schold Schmidt und Partner Architekten BDA Berliner Str. 32 60314 Frankfurt
Fon +49 69 285085  www.abb-architekten.de

# I a a Pavillion

auto.mobile
in anima.tion

auto.mobile
The two conditions
of a car are driving
and parking. Motor-
shows can only display
the least interesting
static condition

The designstudy for a
BMW Pavilion transfers
movement into archi-
tecture. Since neither
cars nor the building
were allowed to be
mobile, the movement of
the spectators is used
to give the sensation of
driving.

The Dynamics create form
with the help of special
reflectsh software. Form
finds its way into being.

In this interactive architecture the virtual space
emerges from the relation
of user and computer.

Corresponding to the development of text from a linear, local and two-dimensional media to hypertext as a complex, translocal and multidimensional medium, architecture has to transcend to hypertecture. The absence of gravitation in a virtual environment can free hypertecture from architectural bindings. Architectural elements can be transformed to semantic carriers of information. The orbit is a cultural and social experiment in the field of hypertecture, the passage to a digital parallel world. The meridians define the locality of the individual site. The crossings or joints are the prerequisite to develop new forms of neighborhood and responsibility. In the orbit there is no separation between public and private space. The future participants will change and develop the relation of form and content.

"Music cannot be mechanized just like that!" "We will not be plugged into the mains!", said the composer and director of the academy of music Kees van Baaren at the time. He also said to me: "As long as I live, I will prevent this from happening; that a violinist is plugged into the mains." So it was sort of a terrifying idea to him. This shock wave was very interesting and I have tried to capture it in a publication entitled *De kleine mechanica van de open vorm (Mechanics of the open form)*. It is about what happens when music and technology come in contact with each other. Anyway, we have come an unbelievably long way since then.

To put it bluntly, my time is now over. I have run out of models for my repertoire. If you labor it the way you do: no, you cannot stay on the sidelines. You can feel that you want to have nothing to with it, but it is no longer possible to consciously stay on the sidelines. As you just said, sidelines no longer exist. The new world is or is becoming electronic, look at the Internet, and there are no more sidelines, only sideroads. But that is something else. Nor is it possible to be against such a development any longer, to be against this new world. It is no longer possible to adopt a stance of "I'm against it". If you apply this to my own work, I am not against anything.

Somewhere, slowly but surely, a whole new set of concepts geared to these new problems is developing. Look at what you are working on and what some politicians, the best ones at any rate, are trying to do; developing new concepts about society. It is no longer possible to help the Third World using the language of missionaries either. Nevertheless, you still see slogans like "without your help we are lost". That sort of stale attitude will have to go. That image of a road on which aid workers are painstakingly struggling along. And all the time we are helping them and pushing these aid workers along. There are no more roads, there are only networks. The concept of an 'electronic highway' is stale as well and will also disappear in the long run. That is the way it will be and nothing can change that.

Conceived by: M Kohn : B Franken
Realized by: M Sommerfeld,E Biederman,C.Trojan & Clarius C IIII,J Haberkampe,E Grieve,T.Drewitz
With the Help of Livingston Electronic Services : Germany : www.livingston.de

# orbit

## The Orbit

A project realized
by the Technische
Universität
Darmstadt/Germany

It is the passage
to a digital
parallel world
designed for the
internet

The orbit is a
cultural as well
as a social and
architectural
experiment inviting
everybody willing
to abide to a few
basic rules to
participate.

This project is the
first meridian at
which people world
wide are able to
start their own
meridian. The crossings
or joints are the pre
requisite to develop
new forms of neighbour
hood and responsibility

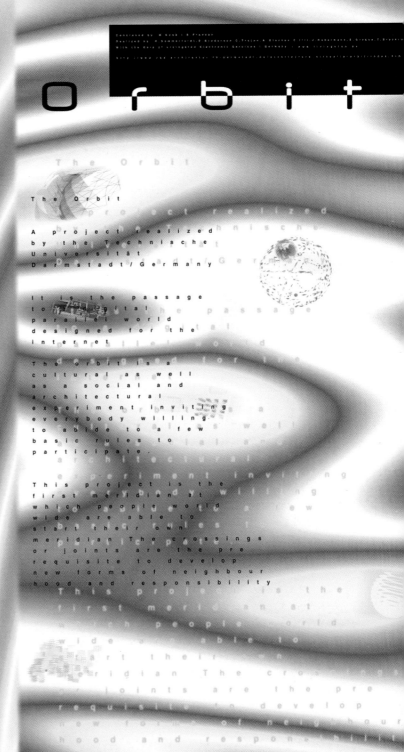

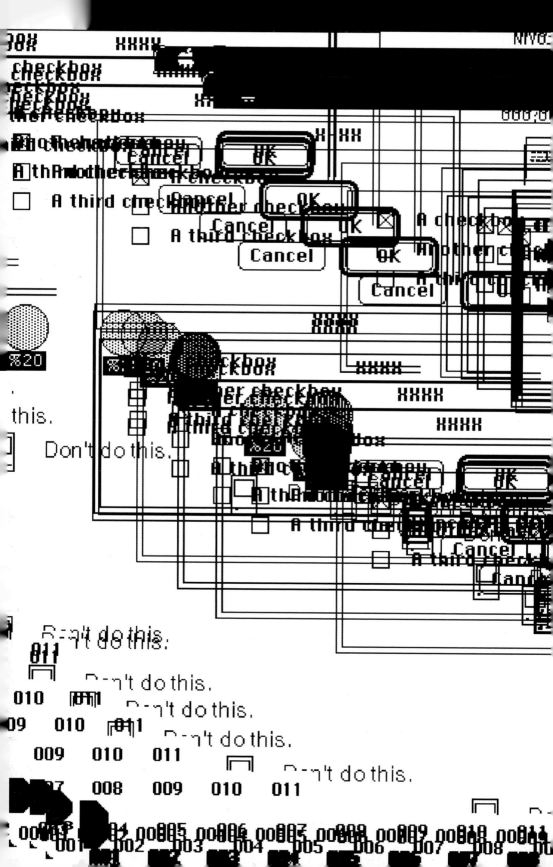

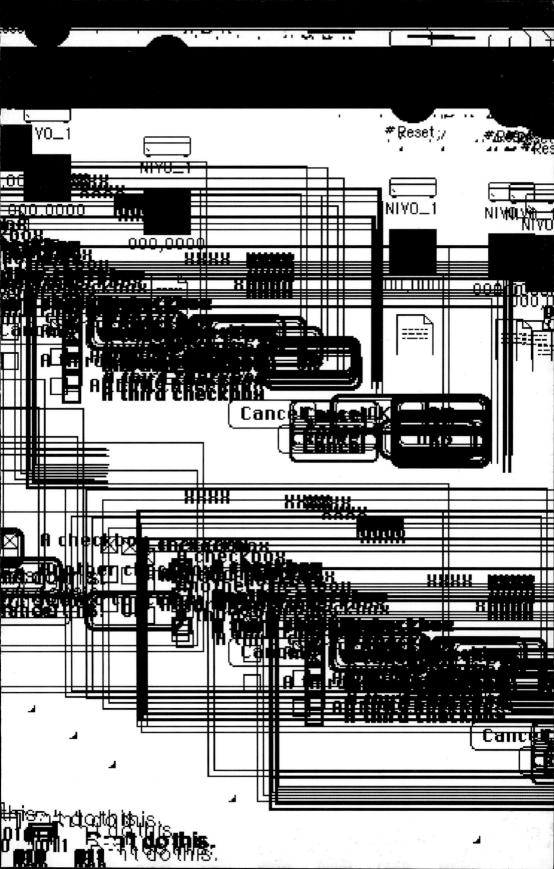

# SURFING THE ACCIDENT

*Interview with Paul Virilio by Andreas Ruby.*

*AR: In your writings on the accident there are two different readings of an occurrence that is very characteristic of modern society: on the one hand, there is a positive interpretation highlighting the constituent role of the accident in the refining and development of technology. On the other hand, there is a negative judgement hinting at the fear of an accumulation of fragmentary accidents that will lead to the 'integral accident'. Why these differences in your diagnosis of the accident?*

**PV**: The original industrial accidents as, for instance, the derailment of a train or the crash of an airplane, were all specific, localized, and particular accidents. They were taking place at a certain place and at a certain moment in time. Now, however, the revolution of instantaneous transmissions brought about by telecommunications makes the accident global. The Millennium Bug is no longer a local accident, but a global one – because it will involve everybody. I have called this type of accident a integral accident because it causes other accidents in its wake. Just like there has been a change in the nature of the accident somewhere in the eighteenth and nineteenth century – from the natural accident towards the industrial accident – we now witness a fresh transmutation of the accident: from the industrial accident to its post-industrial successor. This transmutation is accompanied by a very substantial increase in scale. The industrial accident is still the kind of event that 'takes place'. The post-industrial accident, on the other hand, goes beyond a certain place, you may say that it does no longer 'take place', but becomes an environment. The disaster that befell the Titanic involved only its passengers; the Millennium Bug will involve everybody on this Earth.

*AR: But why then do you deny the integral accident that positive potential you are discerning in the specific accident?*

**PV:** Because the global accident has not taken place yet, it is an accident in the making. Consequently, I can

Arakawa/ M. Gins (USA)
Architectural Body

# Ubiquitous Site House

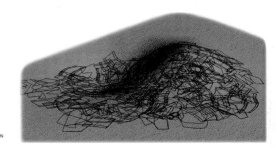

TERRAIN

Human beings are born into architecture and are from then on conditioned by it. The body as architecturally motivated replaces mind. "What's on your mind?" can be more accurately posed as "What's up with your architectural body?"

Shape precludes entry, but entry can occur when a resident forcibly inserts herself into the pliant, half-structured muddle. Room size is proportional to energy expended. Although an occasional dip in the terrain may broaden room expanse, generally, each area pushed open constitutes an architectural surround whose every feature lies within touching distance. Brought to be always within easy reach of the body proper, the architectural body -- the body taken as extending to the limits of its architectural surround -- reveals itself to be the thinker (also, the one who feels) as much as, or more than, mind ever was.

TOP VIEW

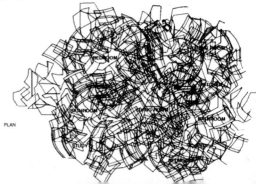

PLAN

only speak about what it would be like in a speculative manner. But then, I am always speaking about things that have not happened yet, but which are in the process of becoming reality. I anticipate by thinking. Maybe the global accident will happen as a result of the Millennium Bug. From its start, one could proceed to argue in favor of politics of the global accident. That would be an accident within which we would have to live, an environment unto itself.

> **AR**: *At the end of August 1998, the Spa-Francorchamps circuit saw the biggest crash in the history of Formula One racing when thirteen racing cars smashed into each other. Fifteen million Deutschmarks went into thin air in a few seconds, yet none of the drivers suffered serious injuries. According to former Formula One champion Niki Lauda, such an accident would inevitably have resulted in people being killed if it had taken place only ten years earlier. Meanwhile, technology has made such progress as to preclude this. Could one infer from this that mankind will be able to abolish the accident some day?*

**PV**: Certainly not. You cannot separate the accident from reality. The accident is merely the other face of substance, and Aristotle defined it already as such. According to Aristotle, reality is a mixture of 'substans' (i.e. what is well established, from the Latin 'substare'), and of 'accidens' (what 'falls into', from 'accidere'). He characterized 'substans' as absolute and necessary, and 'accidens' as relative and fortuitous. Consequently, reality is made up of these two dimensions. As soon as something is well established (a substance), it is necessarily accompanied by something unreliable, which can trigger off forces difficult to contain at any moment. Technology can only progress in a struggle against the accident. For example: as part of the development of a new line of cars, the Renault factories conduct some 400 'crash tests' monitored by video cameras and computers. This is done in order to improve the car. Thus the accident is part of the production process. Causing accidents results in the amelioration of the production of substance. Hence the accident is an element of rationality.

> **AR**: *But in everyday language, the accident is still being viewed as something eminently bad – it would therefore seem necessary to change the associative meaning of the accident.*

**32**

e event

e born into arc

itecturally mot

"What's on you

th your archite

unitable consci

ess

ably linked wit

d that activate

bodily articula

## architectural body

human beings are born into architecture and are from then on conditioned by it

the body as architecturally motivated

replaces mind -- "What's on your mind?" can be more accurately posed as "What's up with your architectural body?"

dispersed but reunitable consciousness or extended, far-flung, and reworkable bodiness

the body inextricably linked with architectural surrounds that are activated by it and that activate it

multiply initiated bodily articulation

BODY PROPER + ARCHITECTURAL SURROUND = ARCHITECTURAL BODY

## reversible destiny

death, not the word but the event, becomes obsolete

nondeath without end

denecessitates dying

dying becomes extinct

no more irretrievable disappearances

vintage nondying

ongoing regeneration

no destiny but a reversible one -- the pair as inseparable: reversible destiny

its motto: death is old-fashioned

**PV**: Absolutely. Since I have a Judeo-Christian religious background, it is obvious to me that one must link any definition of the accident to the idea of original sin. The content of this idea is merely that any person has the potential to become a monster. Now, this idea of original sin, which materialist philosophy rejects so forcefully, comes back to us through technology: the accident is the original sin of the technical object. Every technical object contains its own negativity. It is impossible to invent a pure, innocent object, just as there is no innocent human being. It is only through acknowledged guilt that progress is possible. Just as it is through the recognized risk of the accident that it is possible to improve the technical object.

*AR: The connection between 'substans' and 'accidens' itself is not stable, but subject to considerable transmutations: in the course of the development of civilization, the substance of things (i.e. what defines them from the inside) has been gradually augmented with elements of the 'accidens' variety (i.e. what is being added from the outside). A technical gadget like a heart stimulator, for instance, becomes an inherent part of the body whose heart is no longer functioning properly. One could say that the accident becomes more and more part of the substance.*

**PV**: As techno-sciences increasingly develop into life sciences through bio-technologies and nano-technologies, the ability to alter matter itself in its information cycle is also being enhanced. The moment one starts working on the genetic code of living matter, one intervenes in the genesis of substance itself. And thus, the resulting accident is of another nature, it has nothing in common anymore with the idea of accident previously described. Here the accident is inherent to the being itself, something that is almost a reversion of the Aristotelian definition: at that stage it is the accident that becomes absolute and necessary, whereas the substance appears to be relative and fortuitous. With 'genetic engineering' one has clearly entered the realm of eugenics. Eugenics which pertain to everything industrial, that is everything that can be produced industrially in laboratories – and it promptly meets afresh its protagonists in the Frankensteinian fiction, Dr. Jekyll and Mr. Hyde. The integral accident is not simply a case of instantaneous contagion (as with the stock markets today), but a phenomenon that questions the exchange that has existed between substance and accident up till now. So now we have to ask ourselves: what are the limits of industrialization?

# Asymptote (F)
## The Difference-Scape

HYPERFINE SPLIT

ARCHITEXTURING

The idea of the web as a utopian force is based on the idea of community. It depends on the scope of our access to information. The digital is bringing on a new landscape delineated by those who have access and those who don't. The impossibility of dominance over this newly minted nature and the inherent lapses and gaps it entails, is exactly where the most potential exists for new entities. In relation to the web, architecture might transcend her own restricted condition and reveal itself as a textual entity to make the web an open and free terrain for all. Architectural inscriptions become vectors of the human aspiration towards the unknown.

*AR: But do we still have any options open in this? Take, for instance, economic globalization and the situation in Russia: a country which was systematically defeated in the 80s by Reagan's rearmament policy, and now it has to be bailed out by Clinton, because a total collapse would be far too dangerous to the global economy (and world peace). An entirely absurd outcome indeed, but nobody seems to be able to get out of this predicament.*

PV: What you see here is a change in the nature of warfare. We are now witnessing the entering of a new stage in the history of warfare. The first stage was based on protective weaponry – the fortress. The fortress is the first political stage of warfare, and this is because it takes into account the social body. Over a long period in history, defensive weaponry dominated over destructive weaponry. The invention of artillery as a weapon marks the beginning of a second paradigm in the history of warfare. Defensive weaponry was no longer dominant: it became dominated by destructive weaponry. This situation would last till the nuclear era and the principle of deterrence. Nuclear weapons were so dangerous that nobody could use them without risking the complete destruction of the world. So, this marked the end of this stage and a new weapon system was called for. These were the information and communication weapons which are the mainstay of the 'Info-war'. This war will for the most part be fought out in the realm of knowledge. The Clinton-Lewinsky case is the best example. Publishing 'information' about his private life on the Internet was an attempt to strip Clinton naked and disqualify him as President of the United States. The first shot fired in the Info-war is an integral accident. But we are only at the very beginning of this, at the zero hour.

*AR: Nevertheless, reading your analyses, one often gets the impression that you are toying with the idea of going back in history.*

PV: No, I have never said that going back in history was an option. I am not a pessimistic person, I am a person who believes through death. Therefore I do believe that it is necessary to go through the fires of the crisis of progress. Progress has caused the development of the accident, of a global accident that now threatens all life on Earth. This type of progress has been pre-programmed with the atomic bomb. But what happened in the nuclear

HYPERFINE SPLITTING 003

WRITING SPACE

IMAGESCAPES

realm can now happen in the biological realm as well. This is likely to occur through a form of eugenics that favors 'biologically correct' beings above simians, like you and me, who one might call 'Wombies' because they were born out of a womb. Right now, new beings can be created in a laboratory by manipulating the genetic code. In my opinion, the integral accident threatens us in the same way that ancient societies were threatened by large-scale fires, floods, or epidemics. But we will have to pass through this fire – fighting! Not to retrace our steps, but in order to move forward, beyond our present situation.

**AR**: *Are you seeing yourself as a kind of whistleblower, who warns mankind about the upcoming integral accident?*

**PV**: At this stage, I am already encountering a recurrent disbelief regarding an idea I put forward a few years ago. Wherever I speak, I am being branded as 'apocalyptic' or as a 'catastrophist'. But I am not talking about an apocalypse. The integral accident does not mean the End of the World, it is just another situation. And the only thing I do is to bear witness to its existence. In 1910, there were people who warned of the risks of a world war – something hitherto unthinkable, because no war of that magnitude had ever occurred yet. So these people were laughed at. But then, 1914 saw the outbreak of the First World War. And so, in the same vein, I am merely stating that we will experience an integral accident, which will incorporate other types of accident in a systematic manner, and which will affect the whole planet. This has nothing to do with a pessimistic approach, on the contrary: daring to put it in words is the beginning of a new optimism.

**AR**: *And therefore the true challenge is: how to learn to live with the accident?*

**PV**: Right! We must face the worst thing that we have created: science itself. Therefore we must fight it, not in order to return to a pre-scientific state of things, but to move beyond science as it is now. My feeling is that we must always be prepared for the worst possible scenario – because we are mortals. To be alive means to be mortal. Consequently, we are continuously facing death. Ancient societies mediated this relationship through religion. But atheistic societies cannot handle it anymore. Where do you see burials and death apart from Princess

Maurice Benayoun (F)
Missing Matter

Virtuality is reality before it is going to happen. Virtual architecture deals with information and communication. Its material are meaning and exchange. Virtual architecture is not a defense against a hostile outside world, but gives meaning to our living in the world. Instead of closing the human being in an imaginary world, cut off from the real, the virtual enriches reality because it is modified by its presence in the real. By exploiting the generic and the reactivity of the real, this 'infra-reality' gives meaning to them. The virtual is a personally directed world, loaded with meaning: more human than the real.

Diana's? I am not talking about the death of the individual here, but about collective death. One should approach Death the same way as the surfer takes the roller wave: by entering it. One must enter the catastrophe to reap its benefits without suffering its drawbacks. You cannot prohibit the catastrophe, you must surf it!

**AR**: *That looks like a promising strategy for the United States right now. By launching 75 Tomahawks cruise missiles on Sudan and Afghanistan, the United States have to all practical purposes landed themselves in a permanent state of imminent, total war. Now each and every US citizen, wherever she or he finds himself on Earth, has become a target for terrorist counter-attacks by radical Islamists. Would this be the start of politics in a permanent state of accident?*

**PV**: When Clinton launched these cruise missiles against Islamism, he was negating the civil politics of science in favor of military politics. There is a tendency in the foreign policy of the United States to go for automated strikes. But automated war technologies are a-political technologies. Because politics is characterized by cogitation, it is based on diplomatic dialogue. But Clinton substitutes war for diplomacy and depoliticizes politics. Therefore, Clausewitz's paradigm about "war being the continuation of politics by other means" no longer applies. This is a dangerous development that clearly shows how necessary it is to invent a politics of science that is not merely military. At this juncture, science does no longer exist outside the realm of war. Since the nineteenth century, or even earlier, science has been militarized, think only of the work of Archimedes and Michelangelo on ballistics and artillery. Our task today is to civilize science, not as an option, but because it is a necessity.

**AR**: *How would you value the self-learning capabilities of new computer systems, that is, their capacity to develop a form of intelligence that would enable them to cope with unexpected situations, such as, for instance, the occurrence of an integral accident?*

**PV**: Well, it is true that the fifth generation computers will not only be able to learn but also to bring forth other computers. What bothers me most in this idea of self-learning computers is the closed circuit character of these systems. The world of computing generally is plagued by this closed loop problem, which is what makes it so dangerous in the hands of a totalitarian system. In order

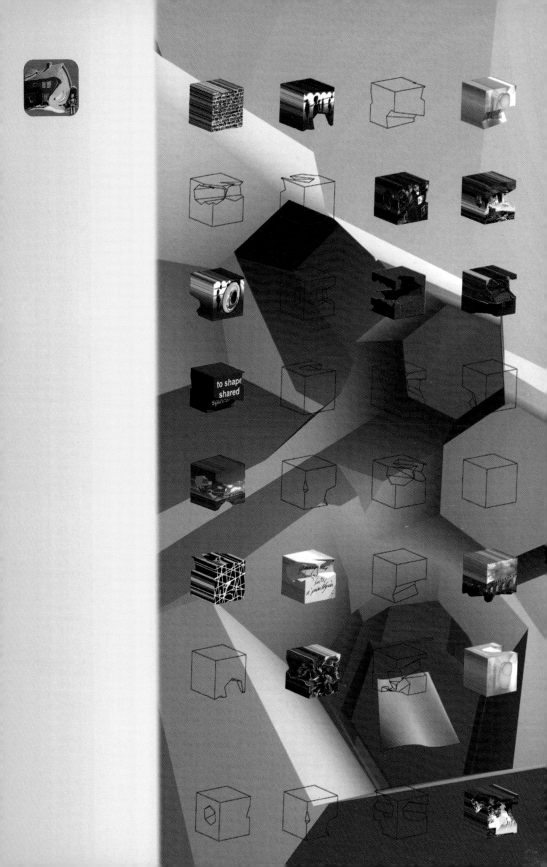

to shape
shared
space

to avoid this 'Gleichschaltung', as the Nazis called it, it is necessary to structure new computer systems as open systems.

*AR: Bill Gates' house is a good example of such a closed computer system. It is the perfect digital slave, it automatically anticipates and satisfies every request of its master (such as closing the curtains when there is too much sunlight, etc.). It is a prototype of a kind of world cleansed from accident. But maybe a world without accident would be so boring that it would become necessary to reinvent the accident in order to escape the unbearable monotony of an over-protected life.*

PV: The twentieth century can already be regarded as a museum of accidents. Take the history of film, of television, of video (including video games), and the biggest spectacle is the accident. It is not fortuitous that the Titanic has become a modern myth, or that television invents a new genre like 'Reality-TV' to celebrate the accident. There certainly exists a desire to enjoy accidents. That is why I once proposed to set up a museum of accidents: a museum that would bring the accident to us instead of bringing us to the accident.

*AR: And this while outside this museum, the accident is more than ever a life drug, a crucial stimulant. This is what couples are after who engage in dangerous sexual practices linking pleasure to death, or the parachutist who makes a sight jump (i.e. without altimeter, putting his life at risk).*

PV: If the accident has become so desirable nowadays, it is because modern societies have erased death, they have removed it from daily life. But since death is an inherent part of life, we want to reinstate it. We are experiencing a desire to expose ourselves to risk in order to regain this suppressed part of our humanity.

*AR: George Bataille described 'potlatch' as a specific type of sacrifice practiced by so-called primitive societies: an act of divesting something valuable by giving it to a living person or deity in order to ward off a catastrophe. Could the accident be to our times what sacrifice was to ancient societies?*

PV: It is indeed a fact that all gift and counter-gift practices, which were meant to protect oneself against an adversary, or to frighten him, are showing up again in an altered guise with the post-industrial accident. The large

Karl S. Chu (USA)
the Sphere of Virtuality.

DEMIURGIC SPACE

hourglass of the demiurgic

The topology of the
new world order is
an 'Hour Glass'. The
top half corresponds
to the emerging
sphere of virtuality.
The bottom cone is
the semiotic
machine of the
physical world.
Through the
reciprocal
effectuations of the
two cones, virtual
time may be capable
of modulating the
tension between
biological and
abstract time. The
effects of this
transition will bring
about a
reconfiguration of
the relationships
between man,
nature and machine.
Architecture will
then emerge as a
collective body of
self-synthesized
information systems
within demiurgic
space of the Hour
Glass which is
opened up by the
absence of myth.

number of road accidents is truly a kind of
sacrifice to the godhead of mobility to keep
the wheels of traffic moving. It is a sacrifice
made unconsciously, but one for which society
is apparently prepared to pay the price
nonetheless. Whereas ancient societies made
their sacrifices in a conscious and voluntary
manner, within a ritual of worship, we, on the
other hand, have unlearned to practice
sacrifice as a ritual – so we are overtaken by
it. The accident is a present day sacrifice that
is inflicted upon us from the outside.

46

# Experiment is accident

*E-mail interview with Steve Mann by Arjen Mulder*

*[http://wearcam.org/pleasewait.html]*

I do not talk to strangers.
Therefore you must slide a government-issued ID card through the slot on my head if you want to talk to me. These SAFETYGLASSES prevent me from seeing or hearing you until you identify yourself! Until you provide positive ID, the camera and microphones on my head will not be connected to my head mounted display set. Your time is very important to me, so please wait for my next available moment!

If you would like to try to sell me a new product, press 1. If you would like to ask me to fill out a form, press 2. If you would like to show me an advertisement, press 3, and slide your credit card through my slot to purchase my attention. If you would like to inform me that photography is not permitted on your premises, press 9, and wait for my next available moment. For quality-control and training purposes, this conversation may be recorded or monitored.

**AM:** *Steve, what is all that stuff on your head and body?*

**SM:** Wearable computing facilitates a new form of human-computer interaction comprising a small body-worn computer system that is always on and always ready and accessible. Wearable computing will now be defined in terms of its three modes of operation and its six attributes. There are three operational modes in this new interaction between human and computer:
*Constancy:* The computer runs continuously, and is 'always ready' to interact with the user. Unlike a hand-held device, laptop computer, or personal digital assistant (PDA), it does not need to be opened up and turned on prior to use. The signal flow from human to computer, and computer to human, depicted in Fig 1a runs continuously to provide a constant user-interface.
*[http://wearcam.org/wearcompdef/fig1a.gif]*
**Augmentation:** Traditional computing paradigms are

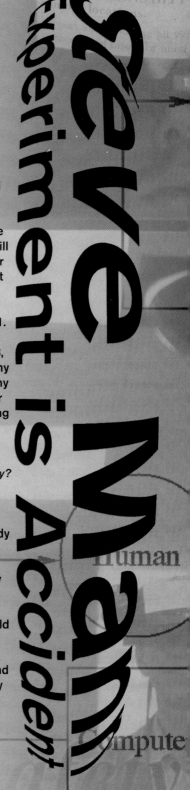

Sicherheit Zuerst

uman

fig.1a

mputer

Steve
Mann
Wearcam

For **your** protection
a video record of you
and your establishment
*may* be **transmitted** an
*recorded* at **remote**
locations

based on the notion that computing is the primary task. Wearable computing, however, is based on the notion that computing is *not* the primary task. The assumption of wearable computing is that the user will be doing something else at the same time as doing the computing. Thus the computer should serve to augment the intellect, or augment the senses. The signal flow between human and computer is depicted in Fig 1b.
*[http://wearcam.org/wearcompdef/fig1b.gif]*

**_Mediation:_** Unlike hand held devices, laptop computers, and PDAs, the wearable computer can encapsulate us (Fig 1c). *[http://wearcam.org/wearcompdef/fig1c.gif]* It doesn't necessarily need to completely enclose us, but the concept allows for a greater degree of encapsulation than traditional portable computers.

There are two aspects to this encapsulation:

+ **_Solitude:_** It can function as an information filter, and allow us to block out material we might not wish to experience, whether it be offensive advertising, or simply a desire to replace existing media with different media. In less severe manifestations, it may simply allow us to alter our perception of reality in a very mild sort of way.

+ **_Privacy:_** Mediation allows us to block or modify information leaving our encapsulated space. In the same way that ordinary clothing prevents others from seeing our naked bodies, the wearable computer may, for example, serve as an intermediary for interacting with untrusted systems, such as third party digital anonymous cash 'cyberwallets'. In the same way that martial artists, especially stick fighters, wear a long black robe that comes right down to the ground, in order to hide the placement of their feet from their oponent, wearable computing can also be used to clothe our otherwise transparent movements in cyberspace. Although other technologies, like desktop computers, can help us protect our privacy with programs like *Pretty Good Privacy (PGP)*, the achilles tendon of these systems is the space between us and them. It is generally far easier for an attacker to compromise the link between us and the computer (perhaps through a so-called trojan horse or other planted virus) than it is to compromise the link between our computer and other computers. Thus wearable computing can be used to create a new level of personal privacy because it can be made much more personal, e.g. so that it is always worn, except perhaps during showering, and therefore less likely to fall prey to covert attacks upon the hardware itself. Moreover, the

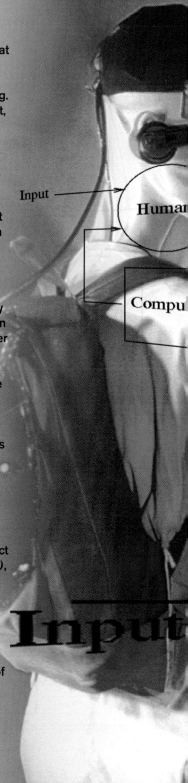

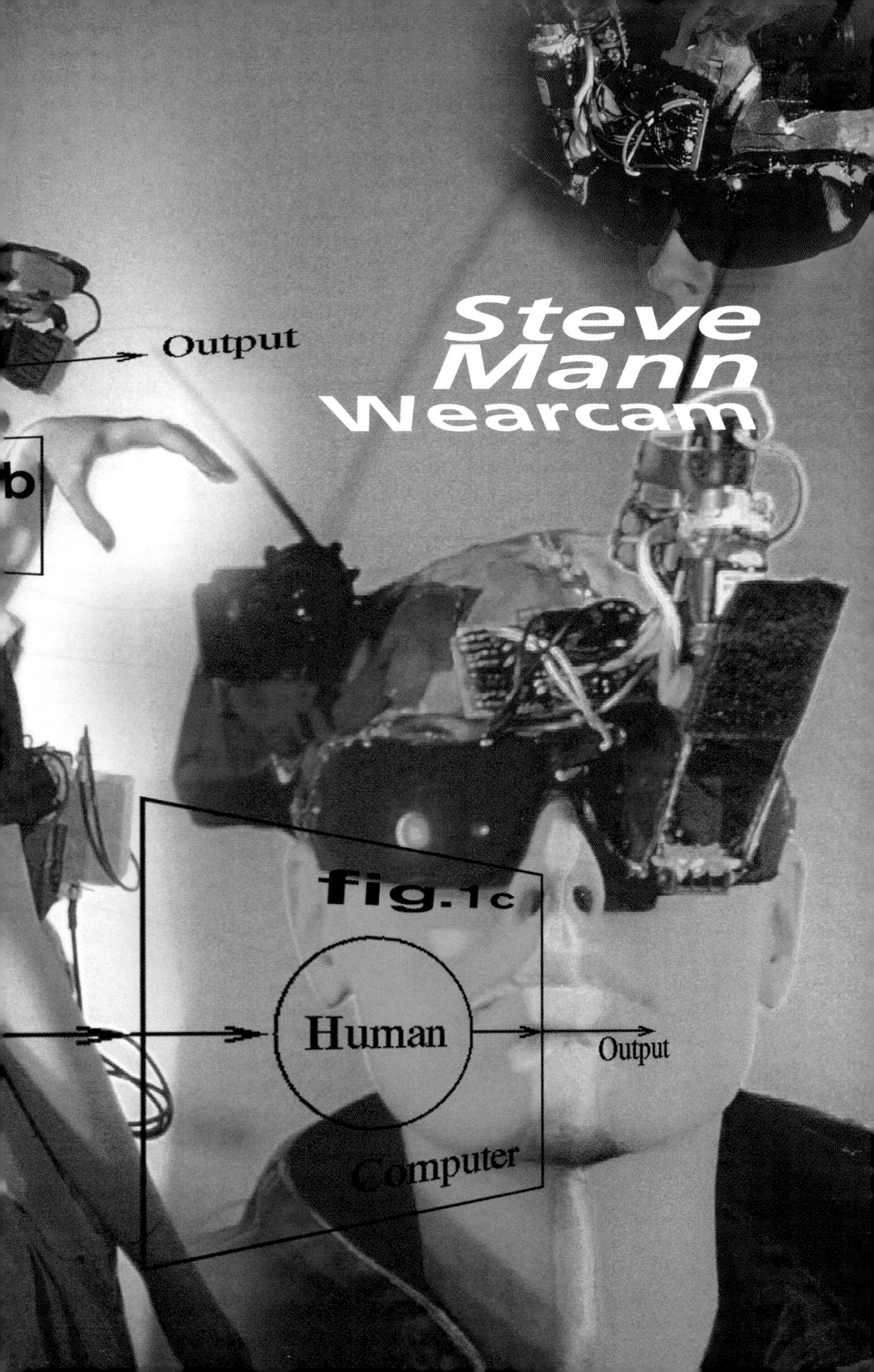
Steve
Mann
Wearcam
Output
b
fig.1c
Human
Output
Computer

close synergy between the human and computers makes it harder to attack directly, e.g. as one might peek over a person's shoulder while they are typing, or hide a video camera in the ceiling above their keyboard. Furthermore, the wearable computer can take the form of undergarments that are encapsulated in an outer covering or outerwear of fine conductive fabric to protect from an attacker looking at radio frequency emissions. The actual communications between the wearer and other computers (and thus other people) can be done by way of outer garments, which contain conformal antennas, or the like, and convey an encrypted bitstream. Because of its ability to encapsulate us, e.g. in embodiments of wearable computing that are actually articles of clothing in direct contact with our flesh, it may also be able to make measurements of various physiological quantities. Thus the signal flow depicted in Fig 1a is also enhanced by the encapsulation as depicted in Fig 1c. To make this signal flow more explicit, Fig 1c has been redrawn, in Fig 1d, where the computer and human are depicted as two separate entities within an optional protective shell, which may be removed or partially removed if a mixture of augmented and mediated interaction is desired.
[http://wearcam.org/wearcompdef/fig1d.gif]

Wearable computing is a framework for enabling various degrees of each of these three fundamental modes of operation. Collectively, the space of possible signal flows giving rise to this entire space of possibilities, is depicted in Fig 2.
[http://wearcam.org/wearcompdef/fig2.gif]

While individual embodiments of wearable computing may use some mixture of these concepts, the signal path depicted in Fig 2 provides a general framework for comparison and study of these systems. The signal paths typically each, in fact, include multiple signals, hence multiple parallel signal paths are depicted in this figure to make this plurality of signals explicit.

*AM:* But wait a minute ...

**SM:** There are six informational flow paths associated with this new human – machine synergy. These signal flow paths are, in fact, attributes of wearable computing, and are described, in what follows, from the human's point of view. Two additional attributes follow from these six, and are also associated with wearable computing. The six attributes of wearable computing are as follows:

# Diller + Scofidio
## JET LAG

*Jet Lag* is a performance about characters severed from the conventions of time and space through telecommunications and high-speed travel. In two stories, it features the media fiction of a sailing trip around the globe, and the static, domestic spaces of intercontinental air travel. *Jet Lag* combines stage action with live and recorded video in the presentation of two intersecting narratives

**1.** In his famous interview, *The Third Window*, Paul Virilio tells the story of Sarah Krachnov, the American grandmother, who in a period of six months flew across the Atlantic one hundred and sixty-seven times with her young grandson in an attempt to elude the pursuit of the child's father and psychiatrist. They traveled New York – Amsterdam, Amsterdam – New York, never leaving the plane or airport lounge except for the brief stop at the airport hotel. Krachnov finally died of jet lag. In the words of Virilio, this contemporary 'heroine' lived in 'deferred time'

**2.** In 1969 a British eccentric named Donald Crowhurst joined the round-the-world solo yacht race sponsored by the Sunday Times of London. Ill-prepared but driven by the guaranteed publicity of the event, Crowhurst loaded up the film equipment provided to him by the BBC to record his journey and set sail. Within several weeks Crowhurst encountered heavy seas in the South Atlantic. He drifted in circles on the open sea for the remainder of the race. Haunted by

UNRESTRICTIVE

COMMUNICATIVE

1. *Unrestrictive* to the user: ambulatory, mobile, roving, "you can do other things while using it", e.g. you can type while jogging, etc.

2. *Unmonopolizing* of the user's attention: it does not cut you off from the outside world like a virtual reality game or the like. You can attend to other matters while using the apparatus. It is built with the assumption that computing will be a secondary activity, rather than a primary focus of attention. In fact, ideally, it will provide enhanced sensory capabilities. It may, however, mediate (augment, alter, or deliberately diminish) the sensory capabilities.

3. *Observable* by the user: It can get your attention continuously if you want it to. Almost-always-observable: within reasonable limitations (e.g. that you might not see the screen while you blink or look away momentarily) the output medium is constantly perceptible by the wearer.

4. *Controllable* by the user: Responsive. You can grab control of it at any time you wish. Even in automated processes you can manually override to break open the control loop and become part of the loop at any time you want to (example: 'a big Halt button you want as an application mindlessly opens all 50 documents that were highlighted when you accidently pressed 'Enter' would make a computer more controllable). Infinitely-often-controllable: the constancy of user-interface results from almost-always observability and infinitely-often controllability in the sense that there is always a potential for manual override which need not be always exercised.

5. *Attentive* to the environment: Environmentally aware, multimodal, multisensory. (As a result this ultimately gives the user increased situational awareness).

6. *Communicative* to others: Can be used as a communications medium when you want it to. Expressive: allows the wearer to be expressive through the medium, whether as a direct communications medium to others, or as means of assisting the production of expressive media (artistic or otherwise).

Two additional properties that follow from the above are:

*Constant:* Always ready. May have 'sleep modes' but never 'dead'. Unlike a laptop computer which must be opened up, switched on, and booted up before use, it is always on and always running.

*Personal:* Human and computer are inextricably intertwined.

the specter of failure, Crowhurst broadcast false radio positions, produced a counterfeit log and documented a successful voyage on film. As he re-joined the race in the last leg, the fear of social humiliation finally led the troubled sailor to take his own life by drowning. Crowhurst ultimately disappeared into his deferred space.

Both true stories feature characters in transit whose trajectories seek out unconventional horizons. Krachnov is subjected to the ubiquitous, non-stop space of travel, while she produces a virtual home for her grandson in a succession of airport hotel rooms. She has accommodated herself in an endless loop, the airplane and hotel interiors acting as a horizon continuously folding in on itself. Crowhurst simulates travel while floating in perpetual limbo. A spiral turned inwards, his horizon turns into a medialized black hole into which, in the end, he vanishes. In an interesting play of gender stereotypes, the female reproduces a static, domestic space – in constant motion, while the male fictionalizes motion – frozen in space, confined by the trappings of masculinity and the bravado of movement.

Concept and idea: Diller + Scofidio.
Director: Marianne Weems (former dramaturgy of the Wooster Group).
Text: Jessica Chalmers.
Video designer: Christopher Kondek.
Lighting design: Jennifer Tipton.
Sound: Dan Dobson.
Computer animation: James Gibs.
Play: Jeff Webster, Tim Cummings, Dominique Dibbell, Kevin Hurley, Heaven Phillips, Dale Soules.
Production: Renate Petroni and The Builders Association.

**+ _Prosthetic:_** You can adapt to it so that it acts as a true extension of mind and body; after time you forget that you are wearing it.

**+ _Assertive:_** can have barrier to prohibition or to requests by others for removal during times when you wish such a barrier. This is in contrast to laptop computer in briefcase or bag that could be separated from you by a 'please leave all bags and briefcases at the counter' policy of a department store, library, or similar establishment.

**+ _Private:_** others can't observe or control it unless you let them. Others can't determine system status unless you want them to, e.g. clerk at refund counter in department store where photography is prohibited can't tell whether or not you are transmitting wireless video to a spouse for remote advice, in contrast to camcorder technology where it is obvious you are taking a picture when you hold it up to your eye. Note that a computer mediation device with sufficient bandwidth can synthesize or even heighten the augmentational aspects. For example a sufficiently attentive computer can sustain a sufficient illusion of being unmonopolizing that it could encapsulate the user and still provide the same experience as system running in the augmentational mode of operation. Similarly, a sufficiently communicative machine, especially if 'machine' is broadened to include mechanical mediation devices such as motorized exoskeletons, can synthesize the unrestrictive attribute.

_**AM:** But what I want to ..._

**SM:** The most fundamental issue in wearable computing is no doubt that of personal empowerment, through its ability to equip the individual with a personalized, customizable information space, owned, operated, and controlled by the wearer. While home computers have gone a long way to empowering the individual, they only do so when the user is at home. As the home is perhaps the last bastion of space not yet touched by the long arm of surveillance – the home computer, while it does provide an increase in personal empowerment, is not nearly so profound in its effect as the wearable computer which brings this personal space – space one can call one's own – out into the world. Consumer technology has already brought about a certain degree of personal empowerment, from the portable cassette player that lets us replace the music piped into department stores with whatever we would rather hear, to

# Călin Dan
## Happy Doomsday!

*HD!* is an art project that reflects on the culture of war by using the conventions of computer gaming. *HD!* starts from the premise that war and interactivity have common patterns, a view that lies beyond enthusiasm and critique, somewhere in the limbo of entertainment itself.

The visitors access *HD!* via an installation that consists of two fitness machines connected to a media system (computer, data projector, sound). By working out on the fitness machine, the user can navigate through and act in a virtual multi-user environment which is essentially a simulator of European history. Depending on preliminary options and their physical performance, a database can be accessed containing information about military history and cultural history in still images, documentary and feature films, news reels, etc. A mix of war, cultural, political and other human generated sounds are shaping a mood setting ambiance where the narrative channel interferes, inserting short dialogues between various supporting characters. Defined also at the level of graphics, these characters are giving guidance to the players, keeping alive the quotational character of *Happy Doomsday!* as 'a game about game playing'. The fitness machines are instruments through which two competing users can influence the political developments represented in the virtual environment and change history into a personal fiction.

### Sex, lies & video games

In the attempt of understanding what interactivity is, *HD!* uses the basic reactive set up of two human beings. Corporal interaction between humans is limited both in aggression and acceptance, and boredom

small hand held cameras that capture police brutality and human rights violations. However, wearable computing is just beginning to bring about a much greater paradigm shift, which may well be equivalent in its impact to the invention of the stirrup, or that of gunpowder. Moreover, this leveling of the playing field may, for the first time in history, happen almost instantaneously, should the major consumer electronics manufacturers beat the military to raising this invention to a level of perfection similar to that of the stirrup or modern handguns. If this were to happen, the time scale over which technology diffuses through society will have decreased to zero, resulting in a new kind of paradigm shift that society has not yet experienced.

**AM:** *Doesn't your body protest against these protheses?*

**SM:** Rather than attempting to emulate human intelligence in the computer, as is a common goal of research in Artificial Intelligence (AI), the goal of wearable computing is to produce a synergistic combination of human and machine, in which the human performs tasks that it is better at, while the computer performs tasks that it is better at. Over an extended period of time, the wearable computer begins to function as a true extension of the mind and body, and no longer feels as if it is a separate entity. In fact, the user will often adapt to the apparatus to such a degree, that when taking it off, its absence will feel uncomfortable, in the same way that we adapt to shoes and clothing to such a degree that being without them most of us would feel extremely uncomfortable whether in a public setting, or in an environment in which we have come to be accustomed to the protection that shoes and clothing provide. This intimate and constant bonding is such that the combined capabilities of the resulting synergistic whole far exceeds the sum of either. Synergy, in which the human being and computer become elements of each other's feedback loop, is often called Humanistic Intelligence (HI).

**AM:** *Aha! Now any new philosophy consists of a set of new ideas and practices, and a critique of older ideas and pratices. What do you criticize?*

**SM:** The perceived 'success' of video cameras in banks has led to their use in department stores, first at the cash register and then throughout the store,

often sets in quite rapidly. In order to keep up the necessary level of attention, another feature has to intervene. We normally call it dialogue; although probably a more generic name should be applied, and that is story telling. No matter how short, story telling is actually the real motivation for dialogues, where people are throwing at each other images, actions, topographic descriptions intersecting in a non-linear succession. But the reactive set is not this – it is the shoestring virtual space between the physical performance of the narrator and the mental visualization of the audience, between figuration and abstraction, between the spoken and the speculative, between the named and the unnamed, the immediate and the projected.

## Computer Game Europe

According to the teachings of the surfing class, exhibited seriousness is not a productive attitude in our infantile environment, where everything has to be wrapped playfully in order to pay off. Therefore, EUROPE can't be a chaotic model, but might be an INTERACTIVE GAME. Needless to mention this in the post-Gulf era: all games converge into war games. Their structure depends on what is the significance of the war parameter in the user's psychology. A user-friendly war is a war that rewards the skilled warrior in an obvious way. Skill is something connecting the neurons to the muscles, in the same way that the mouse (the joystick) is connecting the software to the screen. Skill cannot be internal or even remote, without developing into a frustration. Skill has to be exhibited tri-dimensionally. Through skill, physical effort survives in the computer game era as the ultimate approach to entertainment. While territoriality remains (still) the maximum war-game reward, it is obsolete in the post-industrial real-war protocols.

### Design and production:
Software: Aadjan van der Helm, Neil de Hoog, Jan-Wijbrand Kolman, Bram Meijboom.
Hardware: Peter de Jong.
Interaction: Paul Boots.
3D: Meik van der Noordt, Constantin Stürmer, Lenno Verhoog, Merel van der Weij, Carola Zee.
2D: Shachaf Dekel, Arjan Groot, Janine Huizenga, Menno van de Laarschot, Rogier Meijerink, Willam Pompen, Fred Sophie, Merel van der Weij.
Sound: Boris Debackere Graffiti: Koen van de Crommert, Daan Drubbel, Thomas van Vroenhoven.
Production Management: Anne Nigten.
Produced in co-operation with Ars Electronica Center, Linz (A).

monitoring the general activities of shoppers. 'Success' there has led to governments using ubiquitous surveillance throughout entire cities to monitor the general activities of citizens. (In Baltimore, throughout the downtown area, the government installed 200 cameras as part of an experiment that, if 'successful', would mean other cities would also be so equipped.) Businesses such as the Sheraton Hotel have used hidden video cameras in their employee locker rooms, and the use of hidden cameras by both businesses and governments is increasing dramatically. The recent proliferation of video surveillance cameras interconnected with high-speed computers and central databases is moving us toward a high-speed 'surveillance superhighway,' as cameras are used throughout entire cities to monitor citizens in public areas. As businesses work alongside governments to build this superhighway and expand it into private areas as well, there is a growing need to develop methodologies of questioning these practices.

I propose 'Reflectionism' as a new philosophical framework for questioning social values. The Reflectionist philosophy borrows from the Situationist movement in art and, in particular, an aspect of the Situationist movement called détournement, in which artists often appropriate tools of the 'oppressor' and then resituate these tools in a disturbing and disorienting fashion. Reflectionism attempts to take this tradition one step further, not only by appropriating the tools of the oppressor, but by turning those same tools against the oppressor as well. I coined the term Reflectionism because of the 'mirrorlike' symmetry that is its end goal and because the goal is also to induce deep thought ('reflection') through the construction of this mirror. Reflectionism allows society to confront itself or to see its own absurdity. One of my goals in applying Reflectionism to the surveillance problem is to allow representatives of the surveillance superhighway to see its absurdity and to confront the reality of what they are doing through direct action or through inaction (blind obedience to a higher and unquestionable authority).

**AM:** *What's that got to do with wearable computers?*

**SM:** My WearComp invention (wearable computer with visual display means) formed the basis upon which I built a prosthetic camera called WearCam, which was worn

# VinylVideo ™
## Gebhard Sengmüller

*An invention by Gebhard Sengmüller and Onlineloop (Günter Erhart, Martin Diamant), represented by BestBefore.*

*BestBefore, Onlineloop* and *DEAF98* are proud to present to you the top-of-the-line, cutting-edge technology of *VinylVideo™*. *VinylVideo™* is based on the high-performance and totally user-friendlytrashpeg technology which Onlineloop have developed after three years of intensive research. This technology allows video data to be transformed into sounds and then pressed onto normal long-playing records. With our *VinylVideo™* home kit, this output is reconverted into film images which you can then conveniently view on your home TV set.

*VinylVideo™* is a fake media archeology. A discontinuity in the development of electronic film technology constitutes the historical background for this video disc technology: Even though television, the electronic transmission of moving images, had been feasible since the late 1920s, storage of these images became possible only after the development of the video recorder in 1958. Recording images for private use did not become available until the mass introduction of the VCR in the early 1980s (!). Before this, the average consumer was confined to using Super-8 film, a technology dating back to 1900, usually without sound. Recording of television programs was not possible at all.

*VinylVideo™* reconstructs a home movie technology of the late 40's/early 50's and thus bridges a gap in the history of consumer technology. The images are stored on a conventional analogue record, with a running time of ca. 12 minutes per side. These records are played on a standard turntable with an

rather than carried and could be operated with both hands free – and thus while doing other things. A wireless connection to the Internet provided offsite backup of all image data, facilitating another aspect of the Reflectionist philosophy – namely, as far as destruction is concerned, to put the pictures beyond the reach of totalitarianist officials. Just as an individual cannot rob a bank and then destroy the video record (because the video is recorded or backed up offsite, or is otherwise beyond the bank robber's reach), my apparatus of détournement put the images beyond the destructive reach of members of the establishment, because of the Internet connection, which allowed for offsite backup of all images at various sites around the world.

WearCam-on-the-WWW extends this 'personal safety' infrastructure and further deters representatives of an otherwise totalitarian regime from being abusive: on one hand, I have collected the indestructible evidence of hostile totalitarian actions, and on the other, my friends and relatives are quite likely to be watching, in real time, at any given moment. This process is a form of 'personal documentary' or 'personal video diary'. Wearable Wireless Webcam challenges the 'editing' tradition of cinematography by transmitting, in real time, life as it happens, from the perspective of the surveilled. Furthermore, because I am merely capturing measurements of light (based on the photometric image composite, which represents the quantity of light arriving from any angle to a particular point in space), which are then yet to be 'rendered' into a picture, I may choose to leave it up to a remote viewer operating a telematic virtual camera to make the choices of framing the picture (spatial extent), camera orientation, shutter speed, exposure, etc. In this way I may absolve myself of responsibility for taking pictures in establishments (such as department stores) where photography is prohibited, for I am merely a robot at the mercy of a remote operator who is the actual photographer (the one to make the judgment calls and actually push the virtual shutter release button). In this manner, an image results, but I have chosen not to know who the photographer is. Indeed, the purpose of these personal documentaries has been to challenge representatives of the video surveillance superhighway who at the same time prohibit photography and video.

ordinary diamond needle, the signals are then processed by a 'Black Box' into a video signal that is displayed on a black and white TV-set.

Lack of bandwidth poses the main problem for the mechanical storage of film on a record: Unlike TV with a bandwidth of 3-5 Megahertz, LP's hardly provide capacity for 1/200 of this, ca. 25 Kilohertz. To accomplish the storage of film, radical data reduction has to be used. For *VinylVideo™*, the number of frames per second and resolution were drastically reduced, storage of color is not possible. But this is not enough: switching from frequency modulation, that delivers stable signals but takes up a lot of bandwidth, to amplitude modulation results in additional data reduction. The downside of this is a loss in the quality of the stored images, the pictures become more sensitive to disturbances, like imperfections of the LP. The difference in quality can be compared to the difference between FM and AM radio broadcasting, the latter being much more sensitive to interference. Instead of building a circuit based on vacuum tubes, *VinylVideo™* uses a computer program for real-time processing of the video data.

*VinylVideo™* is presented on a home entertainment unit with integrated turntable and television tube. The visitors may select among available video discs and enjoy the new medium in a relaxed atmosphere. *VinylVideo™* also supplies VJs (video jockeys) for the first time with the possibility of real video scratching. This means that it is possible to jump around in the visual material simply by moving the turntable's pickup, and the picture can be manipulated by changing the record's speed. Furthermore, the video discs can be played on a regular audio turntable, which results in interesting acoustic signals – especially when played at an extremely reduced speed – caused by the constantly changing visual content.

## Records available:

**vv rec.no. 02** Heimo Zobernig – avoidance
**vv rec.no. 03** Oliver Hangl – sky is the limit
**vv rec.no. 04** Annika Eriksson – three possibilities, sometimes i want to be somebody else
**vv rec.no. 05** Monoscope – feat. Jürgen Moritz, Norbert Pfaffenbichler
**vv rec.no. 06** Harry Hund – guinea pig massacre

## Especially made for DEAF98:

**vv rec.no. 07** Visomat Laboric: Loops (music selection: Paul Paulun)
**vv rec.no. 08** Cut-Up (Geert Mul) – Visual Breakbeats for D/VJ'S (18 loops for visual scratch breaks) & City At Night on Vinyl
**vv rec.no. 09** Vuk Cosic and Alexej Shulgin – ASCII Video meets Cyberpunk Rock Band 386 DX

**AM:** *Could you give an example?*

**SM:** *ShootingBack* was a meta-documentary (a documentary about making a documentary). Since I am a camera, in some sense, I do not need to carry a camera, but in *ShootingBack*, I did anyway. This second camera, an ordinary hand-held video camera, which I carried in a satchel, served as a prop with which to confront members of organizations that place us under surveillance. First, before pulling the camera out of my satchel, I would ask store representatives why they had cameras pointing at me, to which they would typically reply "Why are you so paranoid?" or "Only criminals are afraid of the cameras." All this, of course, was recorded by my WearComp/WearCam apparatus concealed in an ordinary pair of sunglasses. Then I would open up my satchel and pull out the hand-held video camera and point it at them in a very obvious manner. Suddenly they had to swallow their own words. In some sense, *ShootingBack* caught 'the pot calling the kettle black.' To further the Reflectionist symmetry, I also experimented with wearing some older, more obtrusive versions of WearComp/WearCam, which I described to paranoid department store security guards as "personal safety devices for reducing crime." Their reactions to various forms of the apparatus were most remarkable. On one occasion, an individual came running over to me, asking me what the device I was wearing was for. I told him that it was a personal safety device for reducing crime – that, for example, if someone were to attack me with a gun or knife, it would record the incident and transmit video to various remote sites around the world. I found that by taking charge of the situation and throwing the same rhetoric back at them, even though photography was strictly prohibited I could overtly take pictures in their establishment, while telling them in plain wording that I was doing so. My approach, which essentially forced them to swallow either their words or their policy, left them tongue-tied, unable to apply their 'photography prohibited' policy, confused, bewildered, in what I believed was a state of deep thought – at least they finally began to think about the consequences of their blind obedience.

**AM:** *You seem to be a sort of ghost rider.*

**SM:** I think many people don't understand the danger of centralized surveillance. Perhaps others are on the

the living

the living

# Debra A. Solomon
# the_living

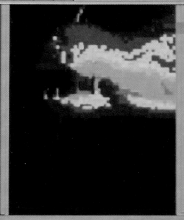

Anytime we appear in the 'online' digital world, from the simple answering of an e-mail, to taking part in a internet chat or video conference, we do so in the form of our digital persona. This persona is not a mirror of who we are in the physical world, and is unlikely to be as complex. This digi-persona is formed, not unlike our physical persona, by the environment in which it appears and by our ability to control the impression that we make upon the other. Whether we do nothing to control the presentation of this digi-persona or become absorbed in creating new or several digi-personas appropriate to our different social situations, the fact remains that this digi-persona always exists and is our sole albeit inadvertent representative online.

*the_living* is a digi-persona that has been created solely for the digital environment and that exists only in the public cultural space of the Internet. the_living communicates through her CUSeeMe reflector, a low-resolution online video conferencing and chat system for multiple users, and by inviting users to her online Visit room, *the_living_room*. the_living initiates relationships with other digi-personas whom she meets in the video conferencing environment. She engages in prolific live correspondence in various media to create story-lines and characters.

The home of *the_living* is the computer screen which is built up of web pages, windows displaying images, logs of ongoing chats, or computer code, as well as sound. Like in the kyogaru culture of Japanese high school girls, *the_living* sends midi sound-embedded web pages to her acquaintances, 'so that we can chat in a homogeneous space, listen to the same music, look at the same thing, be in the same room together.'

## Chat Window

the_living : Why else would anyone have selected and edit all these bits of low_res?
the_living : In Los Angeles there were public access channels devoted to things like this

The logic of these cut-ups was that you can somehow push back the medium, you know?

? ⋅ X ⋅ √ ⋅ To ⋅  Send To  All

## Chat Window

the_living : hello
the_living : there were about seven girls waiting there, all in t
all floating just off the tatami. Except the one sitting by herself
head of the imaginary table, was a robot.
the_living : The face was smooth only partially featured, ep
twin straight rows of small holes where a mouth should have be

The face was smooth only partially featured

? ⋅ X ⋅ √ ⋅ To ⋅  Send To  All

wrong side (all is relative), and need someone on the right side to confront, to tell them they're on the wrong side? All a matter of perspective.

**AM:** *Sure. But somehow your 'audiences' in the shops, these people that seem to be so used to surveillance cameras and also to cameras of the big media, seem to crash mentally when you appear with your wearcam and wearcom.*

**SM:** It is probably, in part, due to the unfamiliarity of my approach, so in this way I have succeeded in re-situating everyday familiar objects (cameras) in a disturbing, disorienting fashion (what I call 'surveillance situationist' approach). People have become so numb to traditional surveillance that they don't seem to see it anymore. What they need is something to force the issue to an edge, and confront the matter. They don't seem to mind being watched by strangers, but maybe don't realize that someone could be getting to know them through the medium of surveillance, and possibly bring harm (e.g. like the peaceful protesters are often rounded up, detained, murdered, etc., as a result of surveillance videos which were supposedly for 'public safety').

**AM:** *So you're the accident invading their personal safety?*

**SM:** I see the accident as a means of seeing the walls of hegemony's cell. The forces of hegemony often manifest themselves as control systems to maintain social order, much like the obedience collars worn by dogs. Obedience collars are said, by their manufacturers, to produce an 'electrical corrective signal' when the dog deviates from its confinement space. In addition to being a pleasant euphemism for 'painful electric shock', the notion of a 'corrective signal' describes quite well the dehumanizing 'control systems' approach to maintaining social order. The 'control theory' approach to maintaining social order might, at first, appear to maximize happiness for all, but at some point one must ask whether Disneyfication leads to Prisonification, or whether Singapore leads to Sing Sing. Is the idyllic world a prison? Perhaps the prison grows around us so slowly that we don't see it, until an accident happens and we hit the walls of our cell, like Jim Carrey of the Truman Show who sails to the edge of the earth and crashes into its wall, suddenly discovering his confinement vessel – the

the_living experiences the 'future' presented in popularized science fiction of the present, as a seamless digital and physical existence. As a digital character, the_living embodies the dream of total connectivity; she is a veritable connectivity hero. Her live performances, a curated series of 'broadcast quality' live events, are rituals in blurring the borders between the physical and the on-line worlds. the_living continually appears in a highly engaging physical situation while interacting by broadcasting a semi-fictive video and chat narrative to the audience in the video conferencing environment. In past performances she has been seen with her laptop at the bottom of the swimming pool, boating on the Amsterdam canals, and pedaling in a swan boat on the River Fulda in Kassel, all the while interacting with the other participants. the_living steals and recycles live events of real and fictitious personas, like reliving the life of Whirlgirl, a comic strip heroine who the_living imports into her medialized real-life fiction through video and chat narratives. In other performances she imitates the 'fixed camera perspective' style of CUSeeMe video by sending pre-recorded fixed camera scenes to her audience thus completely blurring what is perceived to be the 'live image.'

Living, communicating, creating and being part of a live-experience herself the_living attempts to 'be in the present' while simultaneously relaying her experience to her remote audience through streaming video and chat. the_living is hyper living, living more than once, at once. the_living explores the impact of the self-coined phrase, 'Using my Flesh-holder's body as an Experience Conductor ... ' She does not hide in a voyeuristic space as one individual or artist-performer presenting her work, but provides a mediated interactive space in which a new visual culture can develop and where participants will live a richer on-line life.

Find the_living online at http://www.the-living.org.

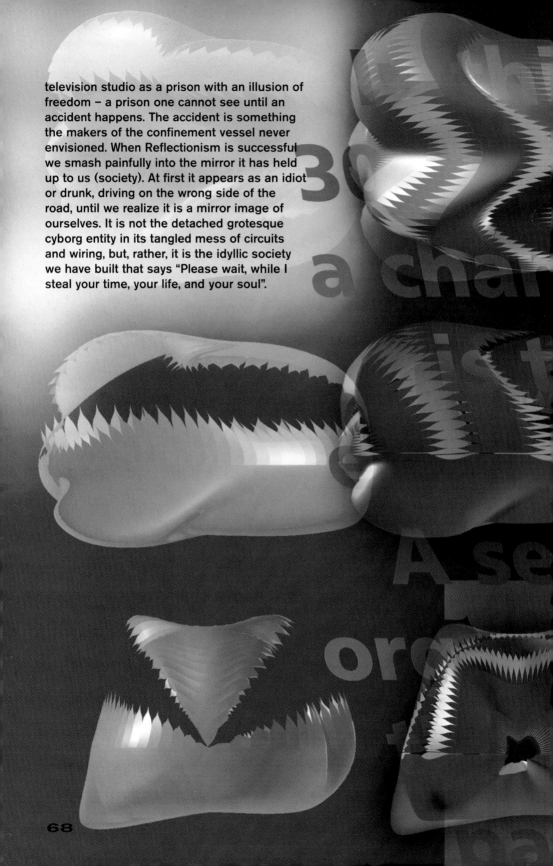

television studio as a prison with an illusion of freedom – a prison one cannot see until an accident happens. The accident is something the makers of the confinement vessel never envisioned. When Reflectionism is successful we smash painfully into the mirror it has held up to us (society). At first it appears as an idiot or drunk, driving on the wrong side of the road, until we realize it is a mirror image of ourselves. It is not the detached grotesque cyborg entity in its tangled mess of circuits and wiring, but, rather, it is the idyllic society we have built that says "Please wait, while I steal your time, your life, and your soul".

# Greg Lynn
# Embryologic housing

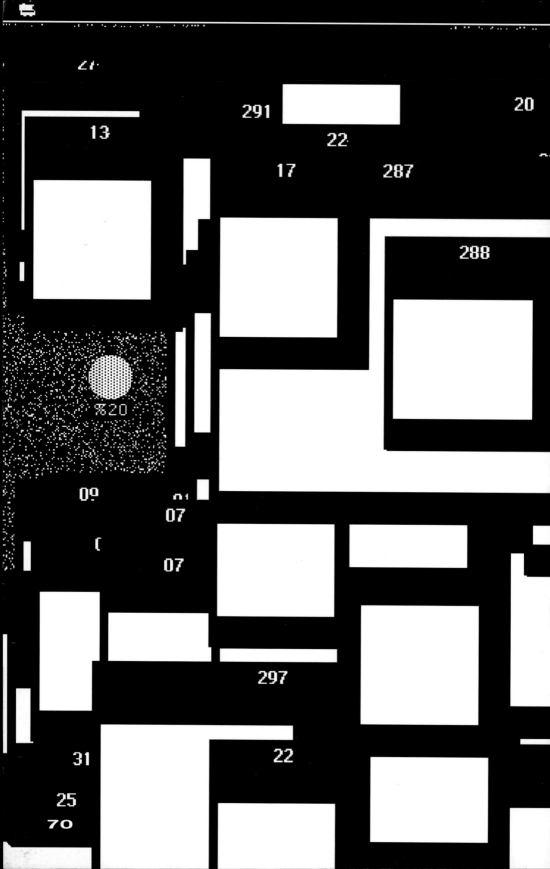

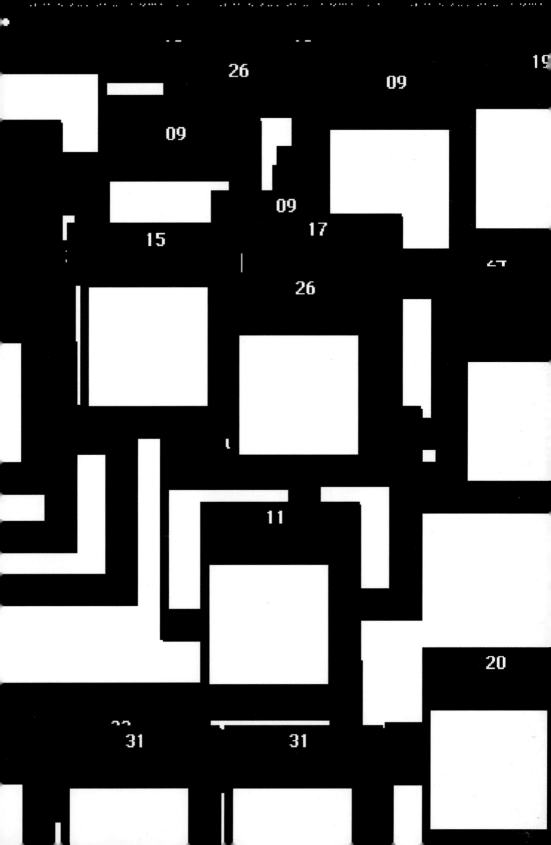

# Mistakes & Misbehavior: Tantrums in/Tampering with Cyberspace

*Perry Hoberman*

## 1. Breakages, Systems, Interfaces

Is it possible to break something inside a virtual environment without causing an immediate rupture in the illusion and the immersion? This is, of course, something of a rhetorical question. A quick answer might be: of course, things can be broken; however, any possible fissures have to be defined and coded well in advance of the actual breakage.

I am wondering whether there can be moments in which a virtual breakage can have the status of a breakage in the physical world, with all its attendant consequences, including elements of unpredictability and unrepeatability. What is (or what could be) the relationship of this breakage to the status of the virtual world itself? More generally, what about the whole realm of unexpected and unprogrammed interactions in virtual worlds; might alternative strategies to the usual state of affairs exist, in which every possibility has to be accounted for and pre-programmed?

This realm would contain elements of human-machine interaction that do not fit neatly into practical, predictable and instrumental accounts of technology; it might include categories like misbehavior, mistakes, mischief, tampering (both willful and unintended), uncooperativeness and the general testing of limits for whatever reason.

I am asking these questions primarily about immersive simulation technologies, that is, Virtual Reality, although I think they might be applicable to cyberspace in general. The question might be more generally stated as:

Perry Hoberman Mistakes & Misbehavior

# Perry Hoberman
## Systems Maintenance

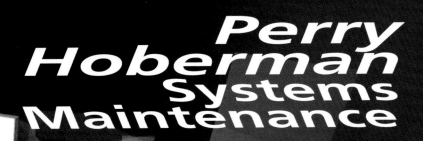

A circular room in the exhibition is furnished with a number of simple, brightly colored pieces of furniture which can be rolled around on wheels by the audience. Suspended on a metal arm that can be moved around the room sits a video camera that is pointed at the furniture. The video image is projected onto a large screen on the wall.

Close by there is a 1/10 scale model of the same room, including exact models of the furniture which can be lifted up and moved. A second video camera is mounted on a metal arm, pointing at the center of the model. The image from this camera is superimposed on the other camera's image on the projection screen. By turning the platform on which the model rests, the camera viewpoint can be moved around the model room.

A third, digital model of exactly the same room with furniture is displayed on a computer monitor where the furniture can be rearranged by means of a trackball interface. Similarly, the viewpoint of the virtual camera can be changed. The image of this room is also projected on the single projection screen, which shows the congruencies and incongruities between the three rooms as overlays and distortions.

By moving the furniture and viewpoint in each of the three rooms, visitors can match (or mismatch) the components of the rooms as they appear in the projected image. At certain times during the exhibition, three activators try to straighten out the three rooms. Communicating through headset walkie-talkies they coordinate their actions and attempt to copy the changes made by the exhibition visitors in one of the rooms by repeating them in the two others. As people are manipulating the different rooms, the video projection – in effect a 'fourth room' –

What happens to a system when confronted with something that cannot be systematized? (A more fundamental question, and a scarier one, is whether there is in fact anything that is ultimately resistant to systemization and assimilation.) I think this question strikes at the heart of why our Virtual Realities often seem, in fact, so unreal. Virtual technologies are usually touted as holding a vast liberating potential; but more often than not they seem to be exactly the opposite, restricting the participant's field of action to options that are tightly scripted by the designer.

Here are a few definitions of Virtual Reality. From Pimentel and Teixeira: "More than a 'fantasy machine', virtual reality is ... the creation of a universal metalanguage ... (that) allows us to share ideas and thoughts ... by communicating in ... the human sensory language of reality." Or Marcos Novak: "a habitat for the imagination ... a landscape of rational magic." Howard Rheingold: VR puts us "on the brink of having the power of creating any experience we desire." I have a working (and only slightly tongue-in-cheek) definition of my own. VR is: something that requires endless waiting for an interminable line, only to briefly enter a rudimentary world in which one is a solitary inhabitant with nothing to do.

Interface designers generally work under the assumption that the user will be willing and able to follow instructions; the art of good interface design, of user-friendliness, involves making tasks as sensible and logical (not to say obvious) as possible. For practical applications, ones in which real work gets done, this approach would appear to make perfect sense. However, these very assumptions might be antithetical to the task of creating artificial worlds that seem in any way real. It is exactly at the moment when the user stops following instructions that the effectiveness of the illusion is assessed.

## 2. Brittle Restrictions

Most interactive virtual worlds are notoriously brittle. The moment the user stops following instructions (whether these instructions are implicit or explicit), most VR stops functioning, at least to some degree. The user might wander (virtually) off of a predetermined path,

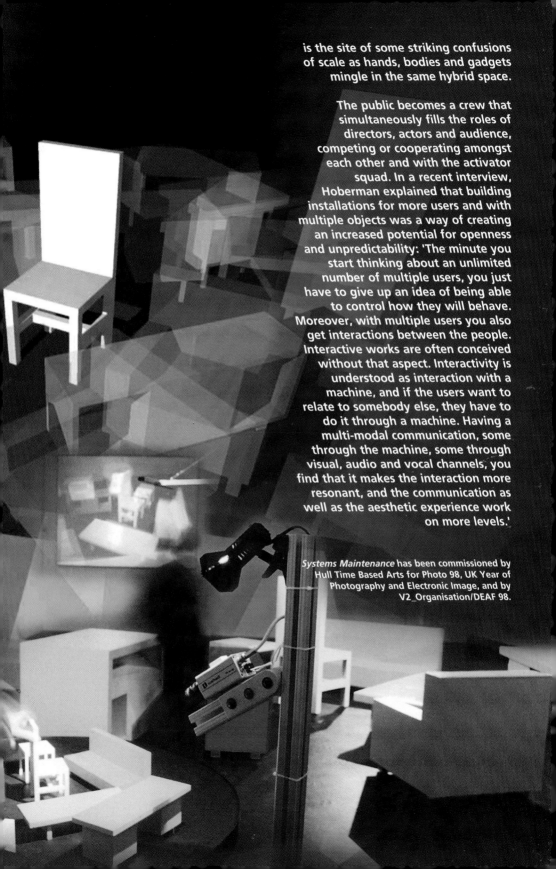

is the site of some striking confusions of scale as hands, bodies and gadgets mingle in the same hybrid space.

The public becomes a crew that simultaneously fills the roles of directors, actors and audience, competing or cooperating amongst each other and with the activator squad. In a recent interview, Hoberman explained that building installations for more users and with multiple objects was a way of creating an increased potential for openness and unpredictability: 'The minute you start thinking about an unlimited number of multiple users, you just have to give up an idea of being able to control how they will behave. Moreover, with multiple users you also get interactions between the people. Interactive works are often conceived without that aspect. Interactivity is understood as interaction with a machine, and if the users want to relate to somebody else, they have to do it through a machine. Having a multi-modal communication, some through the machine, some through visual, audio and vocal channels, you find that it makes the interaction more resonant, and the communication as well as the aesthetic experience work on more levels.'

*Systems Maintenance* has been commissioned by Hull Time Based Arts for Photo 98, UK Year of Photography and Electronic Image, and by V2_Organisation/DEAF 98.

generally ending up in a black void that could best be likened to the utter blankness of a movie screen after a projection bulb has blown. Or the user might wander (physically) out of range of a position sensing system, in which case the viewpoint might freeze, or even jump back to an arbitrary default position. Multiple choices in cyberspace rarely include 'none of the above'; the closest one can usually get is to make no choice at all, in which case nothing very interesting happens. And generally, much interactive work is addressed to a fixed (or ideal number) of interactors, often one or two. When this limit is exceeded, the interactive work often begins to malfunction, sometimes ceasing to work altogether. Conversely, there are pieces of work that require a minimal number of players to function well, or at all; below this threshold, there is nothing to do.

So how much must we restrict our actions inside these artificial realities? And if these worlds are in fact as fragile as they appear, might there be some way to make them more pliable, more resilient? In my work *Faraday's Garden*, participants walk through a landscape of innumerable household and office appliances, power tools, projectors, radios, record players, and various other personal comfort devices. The floor of the room is carpeted with switch matting, a pressure-sensitive covering designed for security systems. When stepped on, the switch matting triggers the various machines and appliances, creating a kind of force field of noise and activity around each viewer. As the number of participants increases, the general level of cacophony rises, creating a wildly complex symphony of machines, sounds and projections.

In 1992, I presented the performance of a work called *Runway* based on *Faraday's Garden* at the Whitney Museum's midtown branch in New York. The audience for the work stood facing a stage area where four performers manipulated the various appliances and machines. The audience could step onto a hundred-foot-long path of switch matting, thus triggering off various machines. The idea was that the audience would have control over when the machines turned on and off, and the performers would determine what the machines would do when they were on. However, the audience that showed up was much larger than expected; and in the rush to get in, not a single member of the audience read the instructions printed in the program. As a result, the entire audience

spent the entire performance standing on the switch matting, which kept every single machine on simultaneously and continuously. What was meant to be a complex interplay between audience, performers and machines instead became a single sustained machinic roar, punctuated by sudden moments of dramatic silence and stillness as the circuit breakers were repeatedly tripped and reset. This may well have been an improvement over my original concept.

# 3. Assimilation and Contradiction

The formulation of virtual reality assumes an assimilation of the user's experience with the encompassing domain of the system. Whether we refer to the present state of existing VR apparatus, or to an 'ideal' VR which has not yet been attained due to various limitations of today's technology, the objective is the same: any user data that can be monitored and tracked will be, and any sensory channel that can be addressed will be. The corollary to this is that any aspect, either input or output, that can't be accounted for is necessarily ignored. Thus, if we have no means of monitoring the 'other' hand (the one that is not wearing the data glove), that hand doesn't exist in VR; and if we can't provide any sort of tactile feedback, then the virtual world will be made of substances that offer no resistance or solidity.

Of course everything that is ignored in the virtual world continues to exist in the actual one; we still have two hands, and our muscles and nerves continue to function. Because VR can't offer any account of the elements it can't assimilate, our experience is therefore doubled and schizophrenically split; rather than entering an ethereal dream world, a so-called "habitat of the imagination", our sensorium is split along an arbitrary fault line. Far from leaving our bodies behind, we are simply asked to ignore the unrepresented part, which has been 'amputated' by the system.

This experience was described one hundred years ago in an early short story by H.G. Wells, *The Story of Davidson's Eyes*. Researcher Sidney Davidson who lives in England has his view suddenly and inexplicably replaced

# Mark Bain
## The Live Room
### Transducing Resonant Architecture

*The Live Room* is a temporary site specific installation, distributed across the exhibition space, in which machines fuse into architecture combining forces of action into form, structure and space. In this project, small acoustic intensifying devices are used which are mounted to the structure of the building, engaging the architecture and running impulsive energy throughout. The system is designed to produce sound and vibration in direct relation to the building and the dimensions of the space.

*The Live Room* utilizes seismic induction equipment to activate the interior (or exterior) surfaces of the site and create a large scale 'tectonic charging' by means of vibration. By using a variety of transducing devices and signal generation equipment, Bain can effectively 'tune in' a space by delivering its resonant frequency to its different parts.

Normally we think of sound as waves of energy traveling through a medium (such as air) on its way to the ear. Because the molecules are more spread out, gasses like air are in fact less efficient mediums for sound to travel than liquids or solids. Therefore the solids which make up most architectural forms can be thought of as very efficient conductors of vibro-acoustic energy. Though these electro-mechanical devices don't actually produce their own sound, the energy they impart changes the surfaces into what, in essence, are infinitely large acoustic radiators or speakers. By using multiple transducers, the room can be driven with energy which is derived in response to the shape and material makeup of the room.

Buildings, human bodies and all other materials, have their own particular resonant frequency. If this frequency, also known as the value of efficient excitation, is accurately located, it is possible through mechanical means to literally 'ring' the material, like striking a bell. If this 'ringing' is reinforced through a feedback system, it is possible to produce a phase aligned addition to this wave form where potentials are present for the material to oscillate out of control. In 1898 the inventor Nikola Tesla was working with a similar energy imparting device which was said to be so small "you could put it in your overcoat pocket".

"I was experimenting with vibrations. I had one of my machines going and I wanted to see if I could get it in tune with the vibration of the building. I put it up notch after notch. There

with what eventually turns out to be the view from a remote South Seas island. He sees a beach, a ship, penguins, the sea; he observes a sea battle, played out in eerie silence. His actual location, and his other senses, remain intact; at first, unable to reconcile the contradictory sensory fields, he panics. When his colleague Bellows speaks to him, Davidson hears a disembodied voice; when Bellows touches him, he recoils in terror. Bellows first thinks Davidson has been struck blind; Davidson is convinced that he is experiencing the afterlife when he says, "I suppose we're both dead. But the rummy part is I feel just as though I still had a body".

Slowly the mystery is elaborated (if not explained). Davidson's movements in his physical location are matched precisely by changes in his view in the remote one; when he goes upstairs to his bedroom, his view rises sickeningly high into the air above the island; when he descends from the hills of his home in Hampstead Village, his view descends correspondingly from a beach into the water and then deep into the sea. Day and night are reversed (since it turns out that he is perceiving a simultaneous view of the other side of the world). Eventually his sight returns to normal, the physical world gradually blotting out the remote one.

In the postscript to the story, which takes place two years later, Davidson (fully recovered) happens to be shown a photograph of the actual ship, and finally realizes that what he experienced was not a hallucination but an instance of remote vision. Wells, writing as the narrator Bellows says: "It sets one dreaming of the oddest possibilities of intercommunication of the future, of spending an intercalary five minutes on the other side of the world, or being watched in our most secret operations by unsuspected eyes." (If there exists a more prescient and detailed description of contemporary telematic systems, I would be amazed.)

Throughout Wells' story, what is striking is how Davidson's experience continually encompasses all his senses, which are put in radical contradiction to each other. The concept of remote vision, rather than being seen as something wonderful, is presented as a kind of horror story. One question raised by this story, then, would be: what is the relationship between these two realms of experience? And for designers and artists, the

was a peculiar cracking sound. I asked my assistants where did the sound come from. They did not know. I put the machine up a few more notches. There was a louder cracking sound. I knew I was approaching the vibration of the steel building. I pushed the machine a little higher. Suddenly all the heavy machinery in the place was flying around. I grabbed a hammer and broke the machine. The building would have been about our ears in another few minutes. Outside in the street there was pandemonium. The police and ambulances arrived. I told my assistants to say nothing. We told the police it must have been an earthquake. That's all they ever knew about it." (Nikola Tesla, 1935)

This notorious event was said to have also produced a similarly intense sympathetic vibration two blocks away from Tesla's laboratory.

Mark Bain's notion of 'transient architecture' describes a system of infection where action modulates form and where stability disintegrates. *The Live Room* project seeks to intensify these sites with hybridmachines, fusing architecture with dynamic systems. This act of 'site charging' is intended to create resonating spaces which are normally thought of as static. This action is an attempt towards the liberation of tectonics from typical inertial limits; where resonant structures vibrate in sympathy to induced frequencies. With this work, Bain suggests a model for transducing architecture, i.e. defining the space with external influences of a vibro-kinetic nature.

*The Live Room* in addition generates infrasonic sound, i.e. sounds at frequencies below the threshold of hearing which still affect the body and perception in ways which can seem unpredictable. There is a subtle strangeness to this project which revolves around the production and injection of these unique low frequencies. When the body comes in contact with infrasound and vibration, unique phenomena develop. Parts of the body can be excited through differing frequencies allowing the spaces within to be felt. Certain feelings and tendencies can also be elicited, whether it is nausea, headache, the gag reflex, or the urge to defecate. These physical responses have induction components which relate to certain cycle rates. In *The Live Room*, a common occurrence related to the vibration is the effect on the vestibular system and the sense of orientation and balance. When positioned on active floor panels a feeling of shifting horizon may be felt. While standing, balance can be altered and suddenly your perception is that of surfing the architectural plane.

*The Live Room* constructs a topological space composed of virtual objects which haptically interface with the audience. By interacting with the cycling wave forms the visitor is occupied, infested with frequencies, modulated by vibrational energy and imparted with the volumetric sensibilities inherent within the body. The audience are the activated objects, traversing the site and feeling the liveliness of themselves, others and the space within.

next question is: is there then any way to consider the whole of one's experience in the design of virtual worlds? Must we ignore what we can't control?

But once the VR apparatus is perfected – when VR encompasses sight, sound, smell, touch, proprioception, temperature, etc. – won't this whole problem be put to rest? At that point, wouldn't we really 'leave our bodies behind'? I would propose that even when all the problems are worked out, and VR actually 'works', even then, our experience will still remain doubled, and that there will always be disjunctions between the inside and outside of VR.

Perhaps the paradigmatic moment for us in Wells' tale is his description of the gradual return of Davidson's sight. "It's very dim and broken in places, but I see it all the same, like a faint specter of itself. (...) It's like a hole in this infernal phantom world. (...) It looks like the ghost of a bit of your hand sticking out of the darkening sky ... " This condition of overlap, which is growing stronger here until Davidson's sight returns to normal, directly prefigures the development of 'augmented reality', but this condition might also accurately capture our experience of all virtual worlds.

Here I'd like to go into yet another digression and talk for a moment about the debased art of karaoke. In karaoke, any distinctions between performer and audience breaks down; anyone who wants to can become the center of attention (for a moment). The performer/participant, who until a short while ago was just another member of the audience, immerse him- or herself in a media spectacle, a kind of primitive pop cultural proto-virtual reality. Once onstage, they are free to perform the text of the karaoke any way they desire. Karaoke has both an inside – the performer immersed in the image of the music video – and an outside, the hybrid live video performance witnessed by the audience. Karaoke isn't truly interactive (so far); but it is participatory, which is probably more important. Instead of holding up a tired notion of limited multiple-choice control of the media, karaoke allows the participant to mould an existing media spectacle into something of their very own.

I think karaoke, despite what might be called its primitive and debased character, embodies certain

# Gunter Krüger
## COMPACTOR {The Machine}

*COMPACTOR {The Machine}* straddles the early days and the future of television, collapsing its content and technological development into a barely decipherable bundle of fast-moving images. Sitting in the casing of a piece of television furniture from the 1950s, the *Compactor Machine* compresses television images at an extreme rate, making it possible to view material of an original length of several hours in 10 seconds and less. Different genres of television programming (talk show, news, sport, documentary, porno, action, etc.) can be selected and replayed at five different speeds, ranging from a compression rate of 60.000 per cent to almost 2 million per cent.

Through the temporal compression, the images display a level of accidental abstraction that tests the viewer's competence in recognising certain genres and decoding, or constructing, a narrative from the rash image sequence. This is digital television with programs that can be demanded and viewed on the fly, and a highly economical way of presenting the standardised contents of single-genre TV channels.

The history of many media and other technologies begins with a disappointment. Paul Nipkow, inventor of the 'Nipkow disk' and one of the key figures in the development of television technology, recounted his disappointment on witnessing the first public presentation of his system: 'The television sets were placed in dark cubicles with long queues of hundreds of people outside, patiently waiting for the moment when they would see tele-vision for the first time. I was among them and I became more and more nervous. I was about to see for the first time what I had been thinking about for 45 years. Finally it was my turn and I entered. A dark curtain is drawn and before me I see a surface of flickering light, on which something is moving. You couldn't recognize much.'

At the beginning of most imaging technologies, such a diffuse, grey flicker of light has been the only faint promise of the potentials of the new invention. Yet, it can always be the flicker emerging from a bifurcation, the flicker of a lucky historical accident having happened, an accident that bears the potential of spinning the technological development off in a new and unexpected direction.

*COMPACTOR {The Machine}* is a fictitious warp in the time-line of television culture. It tests the TV viewer's limits of cognition and recognition by pushing the moving images to their dromoscopic extremes. In the 'real-time' of the *Compactor*, the reproduction of reality is plunged into an almost absurd mix of visual abstraction and content redundancy. Sooner or later, this fast-forward culture will demand a new aesthetics, an adjustable real-time button and a reality

qualities and potentials that might point us in some provocative directions in thinking about interactive virtual worlds. In karaoke, the participant, rather than being given the task of navigation or choice, is encouraged to improvise, to 'riff' off of a kind of score. This spontaneous performance is conjoined with the more calculated video to create a combined spectacle that is compelling enough to hold an audience's attention.

# 4. Dreaming and Sleepwalking

An equivalence has been suggested, many times before, between virtual reality and dreams. However, in dreams the body is immobilized. In waking life, our brain passes neural instructions to our muscles to move, the muscles obey, and our various senses report back on this movement, all in one unbroken loop. In dreams, this loop is short-circuited; the impulse to move never reaches our muscles, and we dream that we have moved while our body remains relaxed and inert. This would seem to suggest that it is cinema rather than VR that is closer to the dream experience, where we really do 'leave our body behind', immobilized and passive on a cushioned seat, and that if VR is to be compared to any aspect of sleep at all, it could much better be likened to sleepwalking.

The sleepwalker inhabits one realm while continuing to move in another, very much like the person encased in VR gear. This is clearly a precarious position, one where any sense of a unified experience is constantly under threat of interruption and disruption by an incommensurate physical reality that almost by definition takes precedence over the fragilely constructed world of the dream.

So perhaps we could then describe the challenge as this: we need to figure out how to keep sleepwalking even when we bump into something. This of course would be the moment where the sleepwalker would be rudely jolted awake. This dynamic is not likely to change, even when all the problems are solved, and we finally have 'complete bodies' in VR. (Perhaps a useful phenomenon to consider here would be the not-uncommon nightmare of dreaming that you have woken up, only later realizing that you are still trapped inside of the dream.)

# Aaron Williamson
## HEARING THINGS
### (The Oracle)

HEARING THINGS (The Oracle) is an installation and performance that explores the creation, capture, transformation and disintegration of language.

In Greek antiquity, an Oracle – such as the one at Delphi – would be founded on the site where a vaporous subterranean spring emanates from the earth. The medium of the Pythia would receive 'oracles' from the Gods in the form of non-verbal, frenzied gibberish and incoherent disclaimings. These oracles would be verbally interpreted to give guidance on matters of the day.

In the space of Williamson's installation, an electronic Oracle – based on computer speech recognition software that receives signals from microphones in the space – recognizes and (mis)interprets any sound or voices as speech, translating them into a continuous stream of text. A vaporous spring emanates from a raised platform onto which visitors are lured by an inviting, overhead microphone. The visitors may trigger nonsensical and creative mishearings, stimulating the Oracle to produce unexpected accidental phrases out of the unknowing computer set-up. The results, which are then projected onto a large glass screen suspended over the platform, are both amusing and curiously affecting as the computer endlessly generates phrases and statements, desperately trying to make sense of the most inauspicious stimulation.

The computer lacks the necessary ability to differentiate between sounds and spoken language, and is hardly equipped for its attempts at verbalization. Despite its inability to enter into a real dialogue, or

A first step in this direction would seem to be simply to acknowledge the continued presence of all facets of our existence during any immersion into VR, and to stop insisting on the rhetoric of a pure and unified out-of-body experience. As Davidson puts it in the H.G. Wells story, "We seem to have a sort of invisible bodies". This seems somewhat right; in cyberspace, our free hand exists just as much as the data-gloved one, it's just that it's become invisible, like a kind of phantom limb.

But I think it's more complicated than this. In what has become the 'standard' VR experience (that is, an HMD and dataglove) wherever, or whatever our 'body' is, it is simultaneously multiplied and fragmented in ways that are extremely hard to describe. First, there is one's experience of one's body in the material world; this is based on the sense of proprioception, which is subject to the physical and physiological laws of gravity, inner ear balance, solid matter, and so on. Then there is one's imagined body, that is, one's self-image, which often, or perhaps even usually, diverges from the physical body in various specific ways. Next, there is the body as displayed in virtual space, which produces its own specific experience, based both on representation and also on invisibility or absence. Then there is the imagined VR body, which may overlap the original self-image, but has a different range of possibilities, based on the depicted VR body, which might be largely invisible, free from the pull of gravity, etc.

All four of these bodies – and my description here is already too schematic and incomplete – overlap and affect each other; they are certainly not experienced as distinct bodies – and are further complicated by the fact that in any viewer-centered VR, or in ordinary experience for that matter, our experience of our body is put into constant flux by our changing surroundings – encountering one's image in a mirror is only the most obvious example.

To add one last layer of complexity, we have only to realize how much the equation I just presented depends entirely on the specifics of VR as experienced in a standard HMD. I would have to come up with an entirely different formulation for a CAVE, for instance, where one's physical body is not masked from vision.

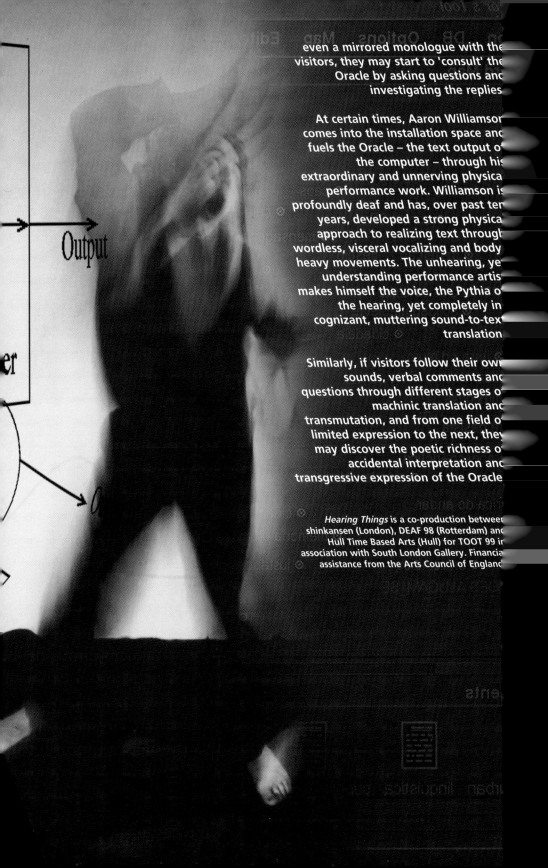

even a mirrored monologue with the
visitors, they may start to 'consult' the
Oracle by asking questions and
investigating the replies.

At certain times, Aaron Williamson
comes into the installation space and
fuels the Oracle – the text output of
the computer – through his
extraordinary and unnerving physical
performance work. Williamson is
profoundly deaf and has, over past ten
years, developed a strong physical
approach to realizing text through
wordless, visceral vocalizing and body
heavy movements. The unhearing, yet
understanding performance artist
makes himself the voice, the Pythia of
the hearing, yet completely in
cognizant, muttering sound-to-text
translation.

Similarly, if visitors follow their own
sounds, verbal comments and
questions through different stages of
machinic translation and
transmutation, and from one field of
limited expression to the next, they
may discover the poetic richness of
accidental interpretation and
transgressive expression of the Oracle.

*Hearing Things* is a co-production between
shinkansen (London), DEAF 98 (Rotterdam) and
Hull Time Based Arts (Hull) for TOOT 99 in
association with South London Gallery. Financial
assistance from the Arts Council of England.

We might also consider here just what is at stake in immersion, in our compulsion to 'stay inside' the simulation, in spite of what might be called the 'actuality cues' which are constantly pulling at us. But, for now, assuming that we really do want to stay inside: how can limits be tested in this arena without causing the entire edifice to come crashing down?

Before dealing with this question, I would like to examine a few instances where the edifice does, in fact, come crashing down, and consider these as a few of the many possible methods of virtual world destruction.

I am going to use as examples certain episodes of the celebrated comic strip *Little Nemo in Slumberland*, written and drawn by Windsor McKay in the first half of this century. Little Nemo inhabits a fantastic world that is somewhere between dream and nightmare, a world that is often subjected to powerful forces of dissolution that start small but grow inexorably, leading to utter destruction and disintegration, until finally (always in the last frame), Nemo awakes.

In a strip from November 5, 1911, we look out over a fantastic and grandiose city. Flip, the self-centered, unscrupulous and mischievous instigator of chaos in most of Nemo's dreams, has managed to get behind the wheel of a steamroller. Here, its effects are limitless and far-reaching, and eventually cause the entire city to collapse like a house of cards.

In *A Trip to the Island in the Sky* from April 21, 1912, a banquet is taking place on an airborne island, a kind of miniature flat earth. Flip wanders away to the edge of the island and, ignoring the prominent warning sign, strolls beyond the safe zone, managing to tip the entire world over, with the resulting anticipated chaos.

And then on January 21, 1912, Flip follows Nemo into *Midget City* (Nemo, the dreamer, is one of the midgets); *Doctor Pill*, trying to stop Flip, follows. The two end up battling in a scene that would later be replayed in countless Godzilla movies, ripping up buildings to be used as projectiles; of course, in the process, Midget City is utterly decimated.

# Timothy Druckrey
## Why 2K or

*I.*

```
DDCCBY      WKCCCR
DDYYBY      WKYYCR
DDCCBY      WKCCPR
SUB 1       WKYYPR
DDWKCCCR    WKC1CR
DDWKYYCR    WKY1CR
DDWKCCPR    WKC1PR
DDWKCCCR    WKCCBY
DDWKYYCR    WKYYBY
DD1         WKMMBM
DDYYBM      WKYYBM
DCCBM       WKCCBM
DDPMCC      CCBY
DDPMYY      YYBY
IFGT 0
3 1         YYBY
E
3 1         CCBY
DD0         YYBY
DDPMCC      CCBY
DDPMYY      YYBY
IFGT 0
3 1         YYBY
E
3 1         CCBY
DD0         YYBY
```

The signs are everywhere. Ars Electronica's Infowar, ISEA's Revolution, Steirischer Herbst's Art and Global Media, Interpol's operation Cathedral (an international roundup of net pornographers), the launch of a 'satellite' over Japan by North Korea, 30,000 Iranian troops along the Afghan border, the Serbian siege of Kosovo (and the impending attack by US backed NATO forces), perverse media mergers, reactionary utopianisms, imploding economies, the return of distinctly undemocratic forms of repressive tolerance, the revealingly pathetic links between monogamy and monopoly, monotony and the fundamentalization of sexuality by the compulsive theologies of conspiracy – in short a world in crisis.

And if the phantasmatic information economy has provided a shield against the crumbling material world, one was reminded by George Stein at the Infowar symposium that 'information leads to dependency, dependency to vulnerability, vulnerability to defeat'. Not a rosy picture for the wired world. Yet while the promises of international information integration provide the fuel for strategic development, a shadow of fallibility emerges to rupture the systemic illusion that our social software will stabilize crisis. The mistake was innocently efficient and overwhelmingly problematic. Two digits ignored by programmers and hardware designers have posed more than a dilemma to a culture subservient to computers and their infallible memory for numbers. Rather than include 19 before the year in the 20th century, computational dates were indicated only by the last 2 digits. And now, 16 months before the millennial clock ticks to a new century, the 'time bomb' looms ahead as what Paul Virilio calls 'the integral accident.'

'Y2K,' said Alistair Cooke on a BBC report in June, 'probably the most ominous logo, the most threatening symbol to human life, since E=MC2.' This dazzlingly portentous comment was made with the calmest of demeanors, as if the destructive potential of the problem was as inevitable as it was surreally unmanageable. Cooke's report quoted heavily from US

In a strip from October 22, 1905, Nemo has to journey through a forest of gigantic mushrooms; exhausted, he bumps into one of them, which starts a horrific chain reaction, as mushroom after mushroom comes crashing down over the terrified boy.

Finally, on November 19, 1905, Nemo enters a crystal cave. He is introduced to *Queen Crystallette*, and, despite warnings, he is overcome by love and embraces her; she immediately shatters, beginning yet another chain reaction as every character other than Nemo fractures and splits into countless shards.

In each example, an event that would normally be contained in its effects, instead spreads like a powerful destructive virus until the world itself succumbs to uncontrollable internal pressures and Nemo wakes up. This destructive force is usually unintended; it is the result of carelessness or mischief, by either the dreamer or the dreamed.

This might be indicative of the kinds of things that could happen in multi-user virtual environments when a single process gets out of hand, or when users are granted the kind of absolute power posited by Jaron Lanier when he discusses 'post-symbolic' communication. The questions raised are social: if two of us are inhabiting a common world, over which we both have absolute control, what happens to you when I sabotage that world, intentionally or inadvertently?

Despite the inflamed rhetoric of cyberterrorism, viruses and industrial sabotage that are often cited as the most immediate threats, I would guess that the real breakdowns are more likely to come from carelessness and poor design. As usual, it's the day-to-day stuff that gets you.

I am torn between two conflicting desires: on the one hand, I want to pinpoint the source of these disasters so that they can be contained; on the other, I want them to play themselves out, letting them articulate themselves in as much detail as possible so that they can be experienced fully. What could be more thrilling than collapse and destruction on such a vast scale; and where else could such events be experienced (and survived) outside of a virtual world?

Senator Bennett's speeches to hearings on the Y2K issue that outline priorities and strategies for approaching the issue. Yet, doing much more than crisis management seems futile. Bennett writes that 'the world as a whole is almost doomed to have major problems because other countries are way behind us – however badly prepared we are – in their thinking and planning for Y2K'. The priorities are significant. Bennett outlines seven as essential: utilities, telecommunications, transport, financial systems, government services, business activities, litigation. Tests done with several power companies have not been favorable. As an experiment, two in Great Britain set their clocks ahead. At midnight on December 31st, 1999 both went off-line. Bennett indeed suggests that rather than attempt to fix the related problems in software and hardware, government agencies ought to prepare crisis management plans to stay in operation and to extend this readiness to the companies involved in essential services like the power grids, water systems, international air traffic controllers, etc.

Why 2 K? Because, as Virilio has always reminded us, 'every technology brings a corresponding form of accident', because foreshortened assumptions about failure are blissfully ignored by cost-benefit analyses, because failure and progress (as this century has so dearly signified) go hand-in-hand as a measure of manageable catastrophe, because the adaptability of codes wrongly seemed a simple process of substitution.

So the crisis countdown continues. Jean Baudrillard characterizes it thus in a recent essay called *The End of the Millennium or The Countdown*: "For this century – which can do nothing more than count the seconds separating it from its end without being able, or really wanting, to measure up to that end – the digital clock on the Beaubourg Centre showing the countdown in millions of seconds is the perfect symbol. It illustrates the reversal of the whole of our modernity's relation to time. Time is no longer counted progressively, by addition, starting from an origin, but by subtraction, starting from the end. This is what happens with rocket launches or time bombs. And that end is no longer the symbolic endpoint of a history, but the mark of a zero sum, of a potential exhaustion. This is a perspective of entropy – by the exhausting of all possibilities – the perspective of counting down to infinity. We are no longer in the fatalistic, historical or providential vision, which was the vision of a world of progress and production. The final illusion of history, the final utopia of time no

# 5. Strategies of Interactivity

Are there any alternatives to the closed system of multiple-choice multimedia templates for designing virtual worlds? Does the designer have to anticipate every possible event in advance? The techniques of artificial life suggest an alternative. Here a process is started and allowed to develop according to evolutionary pressures, without attempting to predict any particular outcome. This would appear to have potential, but it has so far been used with a pretence of neo-scientific objectivity to develop simple organisms; I have seen few attempts to use it to open up a space of higher-level narrative or interaction. I suspect that it may be harder to do this than it appears at first sight; A-life generally involves a 'bottom-up' approach, and the units it works with are tiny bits of code; A-life creatures so far focus mostly on elementary tasks like survival, eating, reproduction, etc. Then again, maybe the jump from their ant-like perspective to ours is not so huge as it seems.

Opposed to this are the 'top-down' methods: what might be called the 'brute force' approach to design; one tries to anticipate more and more branching possibilities, preparing the system for any possible action on the part of the user. The user simply follows one particular path through a totally precalculated narrative space. Eventually, as the world gets more articulated, this route would seem to be doomed to failure because it inevitably results in a combinatorial explosion. This approach also seems like less fun for the designer, and perhaps also for the user, since it precludes any possibility of surprise.

# 6. Machine Logic

As Walter Benjamin puts it, the only viewpoint where one doesn't see the equipment is that of the camera; and therefore cinematic language is predicated on a 'special' (and utterly artificial) 'procedure'. The audience is only able to look where the camera has already looked for them.

In Virtual Reality, the viewpoint is no longer predetermined by the camera – we can look anywhere we

longer exists, since it is already registered there as
something potentially accounted for, in digital time
just as mankind's finalities cease to exist at a point
where they come to be registered in a genetic
capital and solely in the biological perspective of the
exploitation of the genome. When you count the
seconds from the end, the fact is that everything is
already at an end."

"

Gödel was right to remind us that contradiction was
an essential condition: no assumption without its
opposite, no control without defeat, no seriousness
without absurdity. So if fallibility characterise
experience, then the whole absurd enterprise of
militarised notions of interactivity (based on
command and control strategies) is a myth hinged
on the mystification of the misleading assumption
that systems won't fail (or that their's will fail first!)
Even the 'indestructible' and redundant Internet
impervious to nuclear attack, proves vulnerable not
from external assault but from unintended error

Mutations, accidents, blunders, oversights
omissions, faux pas – have, indeed, rooted many of
the developments of the past generations. And if the
jettisoning of infallibility can be usefully employed
in creative ways, we might be able to rethink the
algorithmic imperatives that envelop electronic
media. Surrounded by pieties of all sorts –
ontological fantasies, epistemological illusions
traumatized psychologies, anecdotal embodiments
over-dramatized technical reason – the field of
electronic art has been cast as a sphere in which
managed computational performance is sustained by
extravagant allegories of exactitude, flawlessly
debugged performance at the expense of the
possibility of unpredictability. These mystifications
compel an acknowledgement of imperfection, error
and, ultimately, failure

This willing acceptance could easily be read as the
admission of failure or even as a form of
technophobia. Yet, as is clear, an assault on the
'triumphs' of reason, on the flaws in the system, can
expose more than the imperfections of technology
They can extend the de facto normative, and
blissfully functional ideologies of modernist
technology into destabilized, ruptured, and absurd
systems that are more laughable than logical, more
reckless than rational, and perhaps more interesting
than predictable

want. This is often presented as an vast improvement on the cinematic medium, so one might expect, following on from Benjamin's line of thought, that now, since we can look anywhere, we could, if we wanted to, see the equipment. But all of a sudden there isn't any equipment to be seen. Of course, this is because VR is the result of another 'special procedure'; namely, the element of immersion, which creates a division between inside and outside, and puts the user inside the image. The image has become opaque, and the equipment is hidden safely behind it. Even the virtual machinery – the virtual cameras, lighting equipment, and props – are invisible or unseen. Everything is adjusted so that no matter where you look, you see a unified image, without breaks or gaps.

Adolpho Bioy Casares presented the prototype for this aspect of VR in *The Invention of Morel* first published in 1940. The hapless and unnamed narrator escapes to a mysterious island inhabited by strange people who inexplicably ignore him. A series of fantastical events, including sudden changes in the weather and the tides, uncanny repetitions, and doubled suns and moons, lead the narrator to think that he has died, or else gone completely mad.

Eventually he learns the truth: the scientist Morel has invented the ultimate recording device, with a corresponding projector; these devices can reproduce a person "exactly as he/she is ... with the sounds, tactile sensations, flavors, odors, temperatures, all synchronized perfectly. An observer (would) not realize that they are images ... you would find it easier to think that ... a group of actors, improbable doubles (had been engaged) ... No screens or papers are needed; the projections can be received through space ... "

But an unfortunate side effect of the recording device is that it steals the "soul" of the living creatures photographed; the person dies, but the recording, an "image with a soul", lives on, "incorruptible". In fact, Morel brought his friends to the island under false pretences, and then turned the machine on them and himself, recording the entire group in order to achieve a kind of immortality. Everything experienced by the narrator actually occurred much earlier; the island is inhabited only by projections, replaying over and over again.

# Ed van Megen
## (ASA)
### Access All Accidents

In 1990, the *Association for Strategic Accidents (ASA)* was founded by its current president William E. Kurz. Shortly after the breakdown of the communist systems in the Soviet Union and Eastern Europe, people from western societies showed a dramatic change in life-style. People showed a new hunger for adventure and an increasing tendency towards risk-taking behavior. Especially the hype of extreme sports such as bungee-jumping were supporting this trend. Science however (confirmed by the publications of the Society of Risk Analysis) ignored this phenomenon and kept focusing on modernization risks, those risks that individuals undergo on an involuntary basis and that are mainly caused by industry.

The foundation of the ASA was an attempt to popularise the concept of 'voluntarily sought risk'. The motivation to proclaim this was, and still is, very simple. If risk-taking behavior is an essential part of human conduct, then we have to shift it away from exploiting nature and transpose it into the cultural domain.

The ASA claims that if we want to be progressive in a social as well as technological sense, we have to deal with the construction of risk. In our so called free market economy the social production of wealth is inevitably bound to the social production of risk. The accident is the manifestation of this axiom. The accident reveals the true identity of an object. Therefore we have to stop negating the concept of 'the accident' and start dealing with it in a much more productive way.

The paradox we struggle with is that security can only be gained from experiencing risky situations or accidents.

By now, the narrator has fallen in love with one of the projections, the enigmatic Faustine; so he eventually turns the recording device on himself, suturing himself into the recording so that, even though he will die, his image can live on with her forever: "When I was ready, I turned on the receivers of simultaneous action. Seven days have been recorded. I performed well: a casual observer would not suspect that I am not a part of the original scene ... I rehearsed every action tirelessly. I studied what Faustine says ... I often insert an appropriate sentence, so she appears to be answering me ... I hope that, generally, we give the impression of being inseparable, of understanding each other so well that we have no need of speaking."

Bioy Casares' story presents a kind of horrific but utterly compelling worst-case scenario, in which our assimilation to the feedback logic of the machine is taken to an ultimate conclusion.

Kevin Kelly asks: "What happens when we connect everything to everything?" The simple answer might be: you can't. That is, if you think you're connecting everything to everything, you're simply redefining 'everything' to exclude and ignore whatever remains unconnected. *The Invention of Morel* shows the utter fallacy of Kelly's question: the narrator "connects" himself to Morel's invention, at the expense of his own life.

Of course, the narrator in *Morel* is rather witless. For an example of a more resourceful assimilation to machine logic, we have Buster Keaton's film *Sherlock Junior*, in which Keaton, playing a projectionist, walks into the movie being projected. A 'real' person now caught inside a film, Keaton is subjected to a series of arbitrary cuts. That is, the scene behind him switches, but he doesn't, and he is forced to deal in rapid succession with an ocean, a lion, a stone bench, and so on. Eventually, Keaton learns to manipulate cinematic logic to his own ends, solving the crime, winning the girl.

# 7. The Breakdown

How we deal with the possibility of breakdowns is perhaps an ethical question. In one sense, we don't really

In order to progress, seeking the experience of risky situations and accidents would represent a more sincere attitude than the existing hypocritical desire to 'gain security'. We have to realize that if we choose for technological progress, the accident is a constructive rather than a destructive force in the process of gradual improvement. The accident is truly creative the moment it shatters expectations. Moreover, it would only be fair to expose the consumer to those possibilities which are, until now, the stowaways of technological development. If the accident is already coproduced when a new technology prospers then we have to proclaim access to all accidents.

Paul Virilio wrote in 1979 that the foundation of a 'Museum of Accidents' was long overdue. In this museum, "every technology and every scientific discipline should choose their own specific accident and show it as a product. Not in a moral way, out of prevention (as a security measure), no, as a product that should be questioned epistemo-technically." This thought of Virilio stood at the cradle of the Association for Strategic Accidents.

In the beginning, ASA projects dealt with such topics as advertisement, the non-helping-bystander effect and risk tourism. In recent years, the focus of interest within the ASA has developed from exploring the role 'fear' plays in the construction of risk, towards the close encounter of the physical and electronic accident. A special research issue in the last years has been the phenomenon of the 'Diamond Experience'. People who voluntarily took a risk and people who were involved in an accident, talk about their experiences in similar ways. The recall seems to cause a kind of euphoria or victorious feeling. In the "Fear Edition" (http://www.icf.de/asa) William E. Kurz called these paradoxical states of emotions 'Diamond Experience'.

have a choice because everything is going to break down eventually, so it's simply a question of coming to terms with that fact. Certainly for media artists, there is a lot of pressure to insist that things can be made perfect and can be kept fully operational. But this requires repression of the knowledge that this is not true – eventually, your work is going malfunction. So the choice is whether or not to accelerate this process and make things fall apart or destroy themselves.

The challenge would be to make a work that would accept any sort of behavior. No matter how anarchic or destructive someone wanted to be, it would be part of the core functionality of the work. When you ask people to participate in your work, that work has to be able to take a reasonable amount of abuse. It's not fair to ask people to come and play in your playground and then tell them to be really careful because maybe they are going to break something.

In a sense I am quite happy with things going wrong. I want to find out what a given device is capable of outside of its original function. This is obviously related to how someone defines what a machine or device is supposed to be doing in the first place. Whether something is interpreted as a function, a malfunction, or an accident is completely dependent on your point of view. For something to be an authentic malfunction it would have to be something unplanned. Of course I hate it when my computer crashes. But at the same time these moments provide very fertile ground for thinking about how we work with machines and what they actually do. So although practically speaking such malfunctions are useless, philosophically and theoretically they are full of potential.

Moreover, many malfunctions are not malfunctions at all. They are just the way the technology works. Obviously we're not talking about cases of loss of life or serious injury or anything; that would mean giving up the game entirely. But most of the time what we are doing is not so important that we couldn't stand having something to shake us up a bit.

**Greg Lynn**
**Embryologic housing**

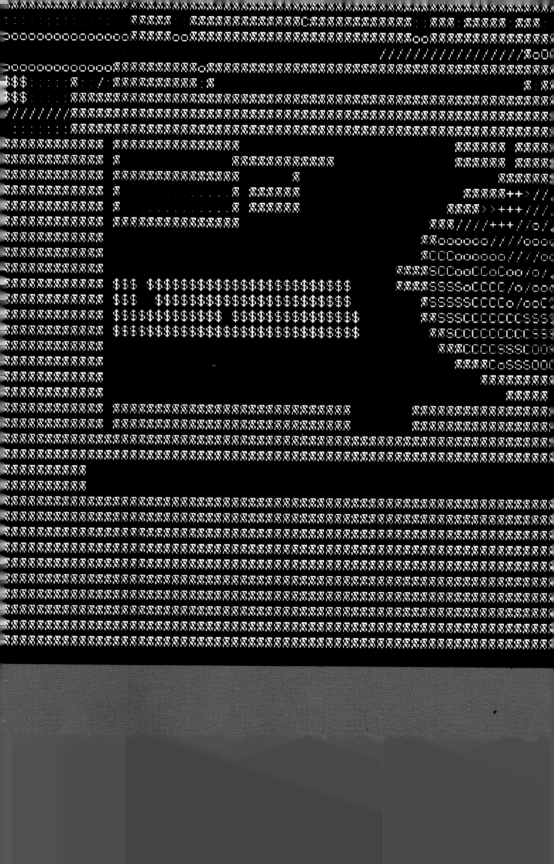

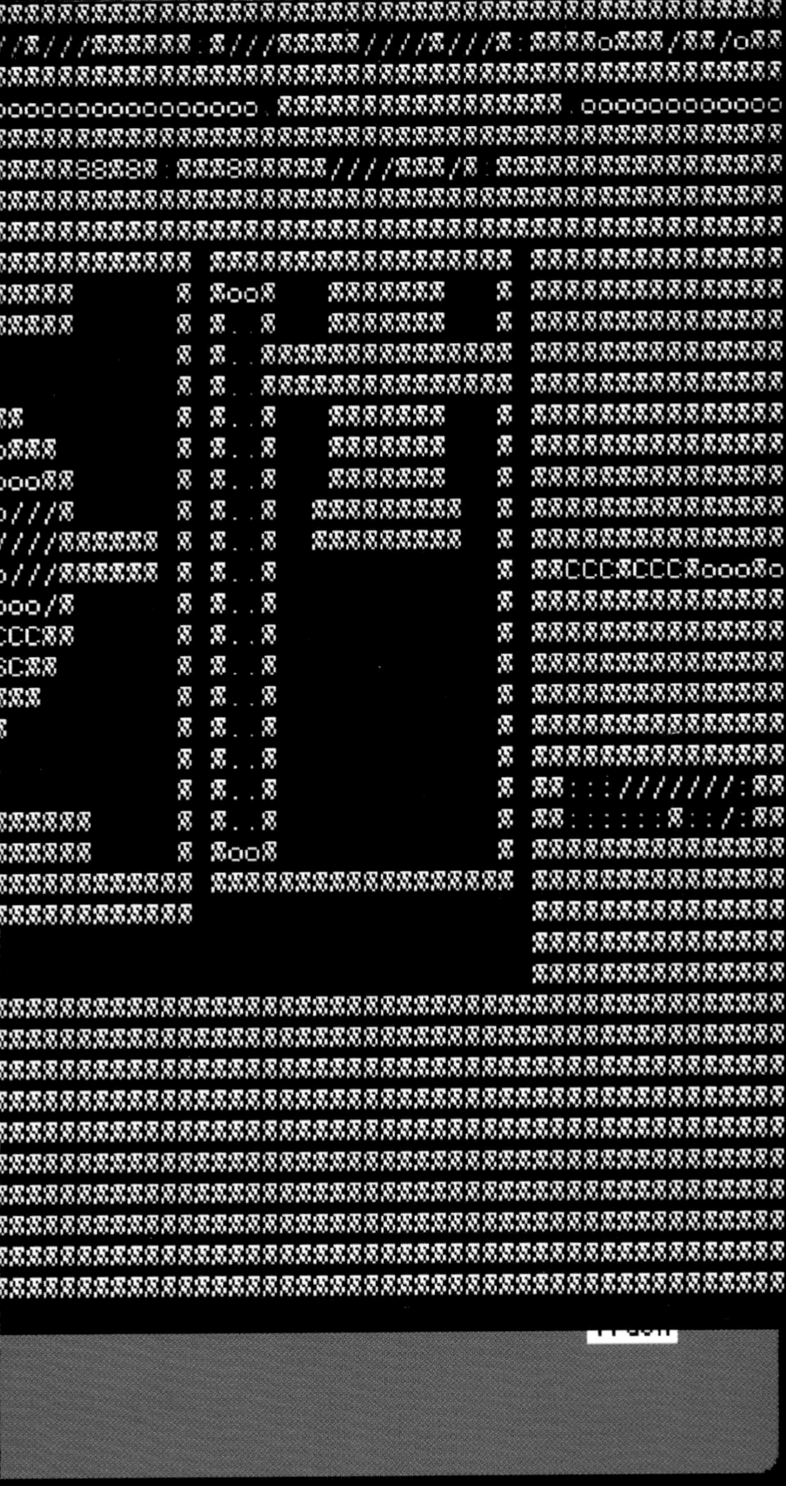

# Next Babylon: Accidents To Play In

*Marcos Novak*

When a distinguished but elderly scientist states that something is possible, he is almost certainly right. When he states that something is impossible, he is very probably wrong.[i]

Arthur C. Clarke, Profiles of the Future

The Idea knows nothing of negation.[ii]

Gilles Deleuze, Difference and Repetition

The process escapes one person's control, but it matters little knowing who set it off and by whom it will be inflected in turn.

Constant, New Babylon

## Axioms Toward Newspace

10. Art is the roadbuilding habit (Zeno). It ruptures, then rebuilds, the edge of thought.

09. Architecture is the art of the elaboration of inhabitable space, beyond mere accommodation, in the direction of excess over need.

08. Elegance is the achievement of maximal effect with minimal effort.

07. Both cyberspace and bodyspace are real and physical, and both are inextricably intertwined with the virtual.

06. Cyberspace is constituted by information technologies; bodyspace is augmented by information technologies.

05. Immersion is the transition from bodyspace to cyberspace; Eversion is the transition from cyberspace to bodyspace.

04. Space and time are no longer separate, not even in an everyday sense: a spacetime vernacular has developed.

03. Hence, we must speak of a vernacular of augmented spacetime, of bodyspacetime and cyberspacetime.

02. Augmented spacetime encompasses the full continuum from bodyspacetime to cyberspacetime.

01. This new continuum is newspacetime, or newspace, for short, the

Marcos Novak (USA)
Indirection: Speaking in tongues

transarchitectures:

after territory

post-Euclidean

multidimensional

curved space

liquid

time-variant

data fields

latent form

transmissible

esoscopic

transarchitectures

Architects face the challenge to create works that both express the scientific spatial conceptions and address a non-local virtual culture. Facing it means accepting the three aspects of future architecture: liquid architecture in cyberspace, transarchitecture at the hybrid linkage of physical and virtual space, and avatarchitecture, the design of self and other in augmented space. The interfaces must allow the user to sense impossible spaces while maintaining a tangible presence in physical space. This architecture does not restrict itself to the manipulation of shapes but to the manipulation of events and relationships. The architecture of the future enables us to step outside the known world and enlarges the world for all.

space proper of transarchitectures.

00. Beauty is objective; meaning is subjective. Both are relational.

000. Accidents will happen.

# Accidental Writing

This text was once much longer, too long for this book. Rather than editing it down manually, and in the interests of exemplifying the art of the accident, I gave the original text over to algorithmic processes that reduced it in size and destabilized its meanings. Naturally, these processes introduced numerous accidents, errors, discontinuities, and unexpected changes, the most obvious of which was the breakdown of hierarchic structure in favor of a structure that is flatter but also more amenable to recombination.

Two countervailing processes were used: first, the main body of the text was submitted to repeated reductions using *Data Hammer*, a program designed to summarize material found on the Internet. Second, the Babelfish/AltaVista translation program was used to translate a quote from Constant into various languages. Constant's phrase was first rendered into another language, then back into English, then into yet another language, and so on, the output of each step becoming the input for the next step.

# Data Hammers and Babel Fish

## 00

*[(transAccidents: Point of origin, English:) The process escapes one person's control, but it matters little knowing who set it off and by whom it will be inflected in turn. (Constant, 1974)]*

## 01

*[(transAccidents: English to German:) Der Prozeß entgeht einer Steuerung, das der Person, aber er macht aus wenig weiß, wem es einstellte weg von und durch, wem wird es der Reihe nach gebeugt.]*

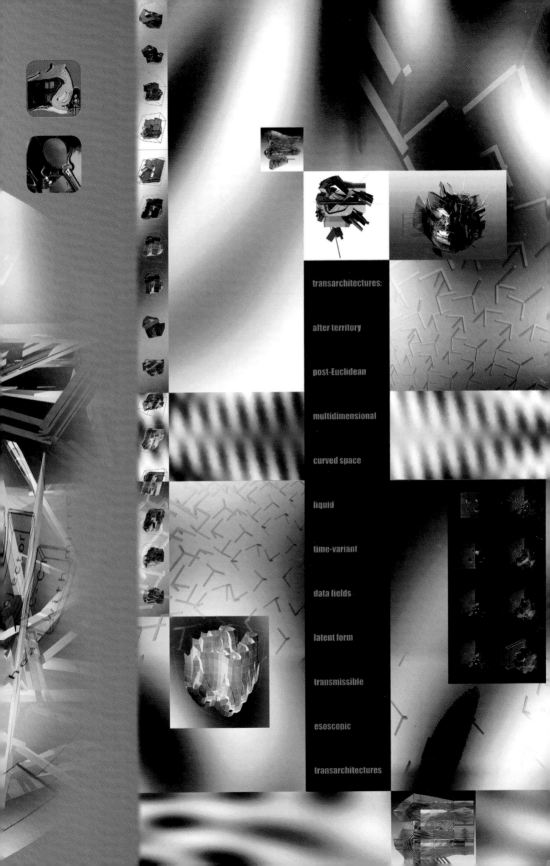

transarchitectures:

after territory

post-Euclidean

multidimensional

curved space

liquid

time-variant

data fields

latent form

transmissible

esoscopic

transarchitectures

## 02

*[(transAccidents: German to English:) The process escapes a control, which for the person, but he makes from few white, whom it adjusted away of and through, whom it in sequence bent.]*

### a

• Taking over from an older generation that resisted computation of all sorts at all costs, a generation of young reactionaries is perpetuating a twenty-year lag in architecture's engagement with new challenges, re-enacting the centuries-old Quarrel of the Ancients and the (trans)Moderns.

### b

• Even those who otherwise professed to be committed to critical explorations of the avant-garde potentials of architecture recoiled from the radical reevaluations required by the rude but potent newcomer, reevaluations that challenged theory, research, practice, pedagogy, industry, use, the very definition of architecture, and, most of all, our understanding of space itself.

### c

• Peer pressure, and the sheer necessity of accepting that any conception of critical studies of architectural culture that did not examine these new issues was plainly irrelevant to the rapidly forming new world, ensured that those who did not enter of their own accord were in virtual effect immersed into the liquid new spirit kicking and screaming.

### d

• However self-congratulatory the rhetoric of the small and incestuous architectural voiced minority may have been, by any external measure the slow and reluctant progress made in embracing computers in architectural discourse simply managed to maintain a two-decades-long lag between the edge of possibility and its appearance in so-called advanced architectural thought.

## 03

*[(transAccidents: English to Portugese:) O processo escapa de um controle, que para a pessoa, mas ele faça de pouco branco, de quem ajustou afastado e através, quem ele na sequência se dobrou.]*

oosterhuis associates

saltwaterpavilion at neeltje jans

frozen wave and hydra

| RADIUS (mm) | INCLUDED ANGLE (de |
| --- | --- |
| 1710 | 33.45 |
| FACE NORMAL VECTOR (x,y,z) | |
| 0.5186 | -0.2610 | -0.8142 |

spline hydra

hydra in wetlab

saltwaterbody

saltwaterbody

waterwave

wetlab

sensorium

The Saltwater Pavilion has evolved as a three-dimensional liquid computer model. The self-sufficiency of form and the biorhythm of the color/sound environment are continuously reacting on and changed by internal and external input: visitors, changing weather conditions, pre-programmed algorithms. The visitor experiences Water, by walking along the Hydra, passing from physical space (Wetlab) into virtual space (Sensorium). A central computer, the pearl lighting and a sound program are part of the overall program of the pavilion. A weather station offers data that are used to calculate the emotive factor on which the dimming of the fibers is based.

## 04

*[(transAccidents: Portugese to English:) The process escapes of a control, that stops the person, but it makes of little white, of who he justified moved away and through, who it in the sequence if he folded.]*

### e

• Still operant, this hermeneutic dilution of the instrumentalized virtual emphasizes the virtual as a latent interpretation superimposed upon a conventional, if highly contorted, built form, but refuses to admit the questions brought about by the advent of intelligent environments, interactive, latent, and invisible form, non-local and non-retinal social space, telepresence, augmented reality, nanospace, ubiquitous and inhabitable computing, the morphogenetic space of complex adaptive systems, and the many advanced contemporary understandings of the 'topochronometry' of spacetime, in sum all those aspects of newspace that I have collected under the term 'transarchitectures', heralding emerging, unprecedented spatial practices and modes of inhabitation.

### f

• Instead of seeking to foster the variety of new literacies that are necessary within our new context, various forms of critical studies of architectural culture aim at theorizing computation from an arm-chair philosopher's viewpoint.

### g

• We have proven that we cannot access the sum of what is true by logic and formalism alone: intuition is necessary to bridge the vast deserts of noise that span the distances between isolated, rare, relevant, true, powerful statements.

### h

• However, in the context of the discussion of the relation of virtuality to architecture, a distinction made by Deleuze is being echoed as a mantra across current discourse and is leading to serious confusion.

## 05

*[(transAccidents: English to French:) Les évasions de processus d'une commande, ces des arrêts la personne, mais lui fait de peu de blanc, de qui il a justifié déplacé loin et à travers, qui il dans l'ordre s' il se pliait.]*

oosterhuisassociates

sensorboard

red pole

processing data from the internet

each curve represents a fibre optic light

light massage

sensorium in blue

kids diving into vr

h2o world vr

morphing fields vr

**06**

*[(transAccidents: French to English:) The escapes from process of a command, these of the stops the person, but makes him little of white, which it justified moved far and through, which it in the order if he yielded.]*

**i**
• This partitioning of terms has been taken as a rallying cry and is repeated widely, not as a clarifying concept leading to a more productive engagement with new challenges but as a political password for mutual recognition of initiated insiders in an incestuous and unchecked discussion.

**j**
• That the direction of this line of thought is suspect can be seen by the fact that the conclusion reached by those who follow it is that architecture has always been virtual, or, at least, has always engaged virtuality, and that the virtual is in some sense that which is immanent in a work, that which is in some ways essential, and is in any case present but inaccessible, without reference to information technology and computation, without in other terms a substrate of implementation.

**k**
• Drawing upon both mathematics and biology to distinguish between 'differentiation' and 'differenciation', and positing a complex double concept of 'different/ciation', Deleuze himself is clear about the tangibility of the virtual.

**07**

*[(transAccidents: English to Spanish:) Los escapes del proceso de un comando, éstos de las paradas la persona, pero le hacen poco del blanco, que alineó movido lejos y por, que él en el orden si él rindió.]*

**08**

*[(transAccidents: Spanish to English:) The escapes of the process of a commando, these of the shutdowns the person, but do little to him of the target, that it far aligned moved and by, which he in the order if it rendered.]*

**l**
• He goes so far as to grant the virtual a manner of objectivity, writing "indeed the virtual must be defined as strictly a part of the real object, as though the object had

CyberNetiK[A] / the end of the monolith

The virtual university proposes a more human way of education which enables the individual to choose his own hybrid way, instead of following a given model. This university aims to make a 'tabula rasa' of the obsolete classical theories of space and time following the quantum-theory in order to develop an evolutive vision of architectural formation or information. This unconventional vision of space and time is very intuitive. Like with quantums, virtuality has no precise coordinates, it is not localized. Like with quantums, there is no linear but a universal time. Quantums and virtuality are endowed with ubiquity. This implies a 'non-separability' of the world. In the virtual university, the human being replaces itself in the center of the space-time.

**CyberNetiK[A]**  WORKSHOP 06 - 20 FEBRUARY 1998

**VIRTUAL UNIVERSITY**

one part of itself in the virtual into which it plunged as if into an objective dimension."

## m
• There is no doubt that the perennial Palladio continues to fascinate architects because of the discrepancy between what he built and what he drew, and the evidence this offers regarding the priority he placed on the metaphysical aspect of architecture.

## n
• It is in remembering Plato that we can see how Deleuze's comment has been troped to bring architectural discourse to a reactionary position: the virtual has been equated with the Platonic ideal and has thus become metaphysical in an antiquated sense not at all consonant with Deleuze's sense of the ideal.

## 09
*[(transAccidents: English to Italian:) Le fughe del processo d'un commando, queste degli arresti la persona, ma fanno piccolo a lui dell' obiettivo, che lontano ha allineato mosso e da, che lui nell' ordine se rendesse.]*

## 10
*[(transAccidents: Italian to English:) The escapes of the process of a command, these of the arrests the person, but make small to he of the objective, than far away it has aligned moved and from, than he in the order if it rendered.]*

## o
• Confusing the virtual with the ideal makes us disregard what is most important about the project of constructing a technologically embodied virtuality, which is exactly that it is virtuality made explicit, immersive, empirical, and shareable.

## p
• The pursuit of the impossible for the purpose of recuperating it into the possible is still a concrete project, unlike the pursuit of the impossible for the sake of leaving it on the side of the metaphysical, which is an abstract effort that leans toward the unchecked and the facile-fantastic.

## q
• Just as the recognition of the embodied mind renders

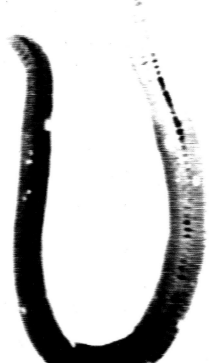

# CyberNetiK[A]

**WORKSHOP 05 - 19 MARCH 1998**

## VIRTUAL UNIVERSITY

obsolete the Cartesian mind-body division, the virtual-as-construct enacts an embodied virtuality that is engaged in the world as we are constructing it, in all its problematic but rich specificity.

**r**
• The virtual-as-ideal, on the other hand, stops short of engaging the underlying matrix of physics and materiality that makes both mind and cyberspace possible; the virtual-as-ideal limits itself to making isolated conventional forms in conventional space, dressing them in rhetorical conceit, and leaving the world unchanged.

*11*
*[(transAccidents: English to German:) Die Entweichen des Prozesses eines Befehls, diese der Anhalten die Person, aber bilden klein zu ihm des Lernziels, als weit weg es bewogen und von, als er in der Ordnung übereingestimmt hat, wenn es übertrug.]*

*12*
*[(transAccidents: German to English:) An escaping of the process of an instruction, this for that stopping the person, but form small to it the training aim, when far away moved it and of, when it corresponded in the order, if it transferred.]*

**s**
• It should be obvious at this point that while the virtual-as-ideal operates by troping and interpretation to enact power-plays of membership and exclusion, the virtual-as-construct encompasses a variety of existing, emerging, and still-to-be-invented forms of expression, including liquid architectures, transarchitectures, hypersurface architectures, and other as-yet-unnamed alien hybrids of bodyspace and cyberspace.

**t**
• The need for new skills is already becoming evident as architects begin to embrace computer animation and simulation software in which understandings of differential geometry and scripting are required.

**u**
• Citizens are seen as creative nomads free to alter the environment as they see fit, employing the Situationist panoply of concepts for life-against-boredom: détournement, décor, the dérive, the labyrinth, unitary urbanism, ambiance, psychogeography.

**degre zero (²)**
**retina critique**

With the new means of communication there is a reversibility of spatial conditions. The traditional opposition between in- and ex-terriorities seems no longer valid at the moment where the present and the past merge into the same surface. The body seems to incarnate a new fictional state. The electronic net permits us to be at the same time users and integral parts of the chain of production of information. Cyberspace is a highly improbable space, de-situated, diaphanous, essentially androgynous. This situation rearticulates the idea of difference and of social identities. It therefore must lead us to rethink our social, economic structures projecting them onto this new retina critique which is Cyberspace.

**13**

[(transAccidents: English to French:) S'échapper du processus d'une instruction, ceci pour cet arrêt de la personne, mais forment petit à lui le but de formation, une fois loin écarté lui et de, quand il a correspondu dans la commande, s' il transférait.]

**14**

[(transAccidents: French to English:) To escape from the process of an instruction, this for this stop of the person, but form small with him the goal of formation, once far isolated him and from, when it corresponded in the command, if it transferred.]

**v**

• Non-Situationists saw a proposal that involved a re-evaluation of architecture and life on such a grand scale that it seemed impossible to implement under any known or foreseeable political economic or social system.

**w**

• This is because there is no question that his proposals are critiques of the reality within which he worked and that the realization of his propositions would require substantial changes to that reality.

**x**

• Constant's spaces never seem to have specific functions or to explain themselves in terms of utility, and though there is a fascination with a labyrinthine interiority, it is always unclear how one would actually dwell there.

**y**

• It is as if Constant were able to sense virtual space as we now understand it but did not have the means to reconcile the vision with the techniques of his time, and so proposed what he saw in his mind's eye using the materials and techniques at hand, however inadequate those were to the vision.

**z**

• The megastructural framework that was to cover the entire planet has been replaced with the infrastructure of the global Internet, the World Wide Web, and the convergence of the cellular telephony grid with constellations of low-earth orbit satellites that bring the whole earth within wireless electronic reach.

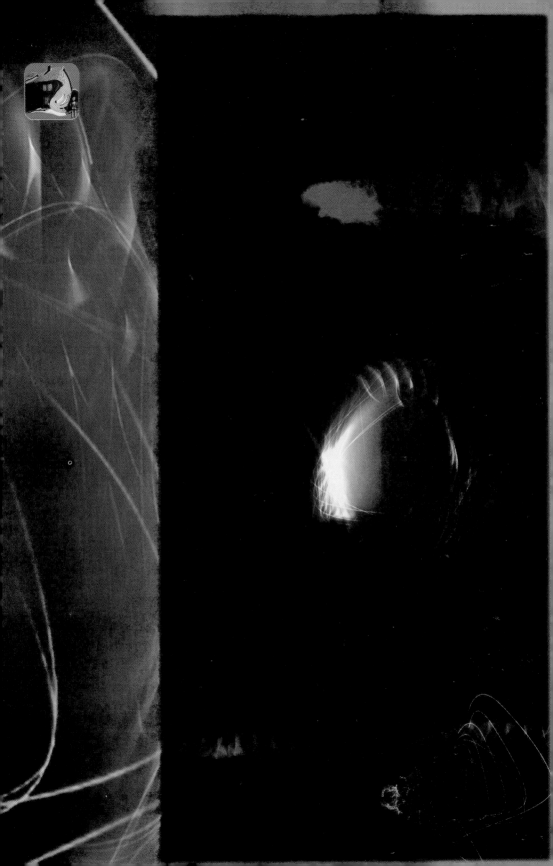

## 15

*[(transAccidents: English to Spanish:) Para escaparse del proceso de una instrucción, esto para esta parada de la persona, sino formar pequeño con él la meta de la formación, una vez que lejos le esté aislado y de, cuando correspondió en el comando, si transfirió.]*

## 16

*[(transAccidents: Spanish to English:) In order to escape of the process of an instruction, this for this shutdown of the person, but to form small with him the goal of the formation, once far he is to him isolated and of, when it corresponded in the commando, if it transferred.]*

## aa

• The lack of personal possessions and the sharing of common goods is already the case in multi-user environments, where spaces are built by copying and using convenient shareware components, a practice that is entirely sensible when the copy is identical to the original and the cost of reproduction is marginal.

## bb

• The lack of specific function is totally in keeping with the liquid variability of algorithmic space and is in perfect agreement with McLuhan's insistence that the meaning of a medium is the medium itself, not any particular content that happens to be transmitted through it, just as the meaning of the telephone is telecommunications, not any particular conversation however important or unimportant.

## cc

• These can be just as easily transposed to virtual space per se as they can to intelligent physical space, that is to say, they exist in the domain of newspace, the continuum between real and virtual that is the domain of transarchitectures.

## 17

*[(transAccidents: English to French:) Afin de s'échapper du processus d'une instruction, ceci pour cet arrêt de la personne, mais former petit avec lui le but de la formation, une fois que loin il est à lui a isolé et de, quand il a correspondu dans le commando, s' il transférait.]*

## 18

*[(transAccidents: French to English:) In order to escape from the process of an instruction, this for this stop of the person, but to*

Radiations of electronic objects extend into space. They create an invisible tunable city – a hertzian space – which you can enter and occupy by car. Equipped with radios, scanners and maps, the car becomes an abstract sound space, mapping the interface between hertzian and urban spaces through sound. The driver can read urban radio spaces revealing the hidden structures of everyday life and experience the overlaps between electromagnetic and urban environments. It links its occupants to the environment rather than isolating them from it.

## hh

• The spacetime that opens in the span of the hyperlink is not the spacetime of virtual reality as conventionally understood, but a meta-spacetime, an initially indeterminate intermediate space and time that opens in passing from the token upon which the link is hung to the destination to which the link points.

## ii

• This is the curious spacetime that is presently underutilized by being filled with information of merely peripheral interest, such as rates of the data transfer and estimated times of task completion, for instance, a spacetime waiting to be used as a spacetime proper to new tectonics.

## 21

*[(transAccidents: English to Portugese:) a fim escapar-se do processo de uma indicação, isto localizou para este impacto da pessoa, ao formulário mas pequeno com ele o alvo do arranjo, assim que aquele fosse distante ele com ele e de, quando correspondeu no comando, se transferisse.]*

## 22

*[(transAccidents: Portugese to English:) the end to run away itself of the process of an indication, this located for this impact of the person, to the form but small with it the target of the array, thus that that one was distant it with it and of, when corresponded in the command, if transferred.]*

## jj

• Using cutouts from the plan of Paris and a graphic language of bold arrows signifying links across discontinuous space *The Naked City* anticipates an urban condition in which remote urban locations are linked together, not according to proximity but according to an orchestration of psychogeographic ambiences.

## kk

• Indeed, the negotiation of such inter- or trans-spaces has become an integral part of the art of cinema, allowing the editor of the cinematic image to act as the architect of the meanings by which discontiguity is spanned without decaying into discontinuity.

## ll

• What is being done for two-dimensional space must also be done for linked spaces of three or more dimensions,

Christain Girard (F
**TRILOG**

TRILOG EST UNE RECHERCHE
ET UN PROJET DE REDEFINITION
DES ESPACES DE TRAVAIL POUR
LES ENTREPRISES POST-INDUSTRIELLES
CONTEMPORAINES

TRILOG IS SIMULTANEOUSLY
A RESEARCH PROGRAM AND
A PROJECT PROPOSING AND
REDEFINING WORKING
WORKING SPACES FOR CONTEMPORARY
POST-INDUSTRIES COMPANIES

Traditional working spaces are obsolescent. They fail to nurture and cultivate breakthrough thinking and display widening gaps in the productivity of knowledge workers. TRILOG is a research program which redefines working spaces for contemporary post-industrial companies. There is a increasing need for a spatial integration between the logical imperatives of knowledge transmission (university), creation of knowledge (research) and production (post-industries).

TRILOG EXPLORE LE DOMAINE
DES EQUIPEMENTS DE SAVOIR ET DE L'IMMOBILIER INDUSTRIEL

TRILOG EXPLORE NEW WAYS
AND INSIGNIAL KNOWLEDGE
AND INSIGNIAL FACILITIES

TRILOG EST UN OUTIL D'INTEGRATION
ENTRE LES LOGIQUES DE SAVOIR
DE LA TRANSMISSION DE SAVOIR
DE L'UNIVERSITE, DE CREATION DE SAVOIR
(LA RECHERCHE) ET DE PRODUCTION (LES POST-INDUSTRIES)

TRILOG IS AN INTEGRATION
FOR THE TRANSMISSION OF KNOWLEDGE
(UNIVERSITY), CREATION OF KNOWLEDGE
(RESEARCH) AND PRODUCTION
(THE POST-INDUSTRIES)

TRILOG OPERE LA FUSION DE L'UNIVERSITE,
DE LA RECHERCHE ET DES INDUSTRIES
A HAUTE VALEUR AJOUTEE DEDIES AU TRAVAIL
D'ESPACES SPECIFIQUES DEDIES AU TRAVAIL
EN INTEGRATION DES CULTURES D'ENTREPRISE ET UNIVERSITAIRES

TRILOG FUSES UNIVERSITIES, R & D,
AND HIGH-VALUE ADDED INDUSTRIES
INTO WORK-SPECIFIC SPACES
INTEGRATING THAT CORPORATE AND

TRILOG REPOND AUX MUTATIONS
CONTEMPORAINES DU TRAVAIL
ET INSTAURE UNE CONCEPTION
DIFFERENTE DES TERRITOIRES DES "TECHNOPOLES"

TRILOG ADDRESSES THE PRESENT
MUTATIONS OF WORK
AND PROPOSES A NEW FRAMEWORK
FOR THE TERRITORIES OF AN
AND PARKS

morphing not only the perspective screen images of interlinked spaces but the three-or-more dimensional contents of those spacetimes, crossfading between both forms and behaviors.

## mm
• A history of architecture can be written on the basis of how the transition from one space to another has been elaborated through time and culture, as evidenced in the design of entries and fenestration.

## 23
*[(transAccidents: Italian to English:) l' estremità da funzionare via in se del processo d'un' indicazione, questa situata per questo effetto della persona, alla forma ma piccolo con esso l' obiettivo dell' allineamento, così di che quell' era distante esso con esso e di, una volta corrisposto nel comando, se trasferito.]*

## 24
*[(transAccidents: Italian to English:) the extremity to work via in if of the process of an indication, this situated for this effect of the person, to the small shape but with it the objective of the alignment, therefore of that that was distant it with it and of, once corresponded in the commando, if transferred.]*

## nn
• "In girum imus nocte et consumimur igni," "we go round and round in the night and are consumed by fire" was the motto of the Situationist International and the title of a film by Guy Debord.

## oo
• We can easily crossfade Marx's "all that is solid melts into air" into "all that is solid melts into information" and "all that is information melts into hyperspace."

## pp
• The spectacle dominates our times and New Babylon is being built, not as a megastructural web around the surface of the planet but as Soft Babylon, as both the infrastructural virtual space within the global internet and as the hidden impulse in the making of transurban transmodern bodyspace.

## 25
*[(transAccidents: English to Spanish:) persona, a la dimensión de una variable pequeña pero con él el objetivo de la alineación, por lo tanto de el que era distante con ella y de, correspondido una vez en el comando, si está transferida.]*

## 26
*[(transAccidents: Spanish to English:) the extremity to work via inside if of the process of an indication, this located for this effect of the person, to the dimension of a small variable but with him the objective of the alignment, therefore of which he was distant with her and of, corresponded once in the commando, if it is transferred.]*

## qq
• New formal explorations of conventional architecture will no doubt continue as powerful tools alter the range of what can be conceived or constructed both in bodyspace and in cyberspace, but the newest challenges will be non-retinal, dynamic and abstract.

## rr
• There is no way to escape the fire of spectacle, only to resist it and from time to time fly through it fast enough not to catch fire.

## ss
• Both the new Ancients and the transmoderns are caught in its field of attraction, but perhaps the transmoderns will remain liquid and learn to play with fire while the reactionary new Ancients simply dehydrate, ignite, and flame away.

# When All Is Said And Done

• Newspace is being constructed by big technology, at the service of big commerce, motivated by big interests, and likely to make big mistakes.

• Odysseus, like the historical trickster, the Situationist, and the contemporary hacker, is a figure who is both self-disciplined and insubordinate.

• We play music, serious music, why not play architectures, serious architectures, transarchitectures.

• Round and round we go: In girum imus nocte et consumimur igni.

Grégoire Kligerman Petetin
Modus Endogène

The dematerialization of
our artificial environment
will lead to novel
temporal and spatial
standards. The concepts
of formalization and
representation of our
systems of thought and
the material frameworks
of our experiences will
be progressively
modified. Our
contemporary tools allow
us to endlessly configure
scenes and constantly
vary moments and
places. This enables the
individual to create an
environment in which he
will operate his own
space. The space will take
on the author's own
qualities. The collective
spaces will propose
evolutionary, transient
and diffuse scales
reflecting the quality of
exchanged information.

## References

Andreotti, Libero and Costa, Xavier (eds.) (1996) *Situationists: Art, Politics, Urbanism*, Barcelona: Museu d'Art Contemporani de Barcelona.

Andreotti, Libero and Costa, Xavier (eds.) (1996) *Theory of the Dérive and other Situationist Writings on the City*, Barcelona: Museu d'Art Contemporani de Barcelona.

Clarke, Arthur C. (1973) *Profiles of the Future: An Inquiry Into The Limits of the Possible*, New York: Harper & Row, Publishers.

De Melo Pimenta, Emanuel (1997) *Arquitectura Virtual: Architécti, Vol. VII, Nov/Dez/Jan 98*, Barcelona: Editora Trifório, LDA.

Deleuze, Gilles (1968), *Différence et Repetition*, Paris: Presses Universitaires de France.

Lambert, Jean-Clarence (ed.) (1997) *New Babylon: Constant: Art et Utopie: Textes Situationnistes*, Paris: Éditions Cercle d'Art.

Lefèbvre, Henri (1991) *The Production of Space*, Oxford: Blackwell Publishers, Ltd.

Matsunaga, Naomi (1998) *Transarchitectures in Cyberspace: Ten Architects Who Stimulate The World*, Tokyo: Nikkei BP.

Möller, Christian (1994) *Interaktive Architekture*, Berlin: Aedes Galerie für Architektur und Raum.

Plant, Sadie (1992) *The Most Radical Gesture: The Situationist International in a Postmodern Age*, London: Routledge.

Sadler, Simon (1998) *The Situationist City*, Cambridge: MIT Press.

Sakamura, Ken and Suzuki, Hiroyuki (1997) *The Virtual Architecture: The Difference between the Possible and the Impossible in Architecture*, Tokyo: Tokyo University Digital Museum

Soja, Edward W. (1996) *Thirdspace: Journeys to Los Angeles and Other Real-And-Imagined Places*, Oxford: Blackwell Publishers, Ltd.

Levine, Joseph M. (1991) *The Battle of the Books: History and Literature in the Augustan Age*, Ithaca: Cornell University Press.

[i] Arthur C. Clarke (1973) *Profiles of the Future: An Inquiry Into The Limits of the Possible*, New York: Harper & Row, Publishers, p. 14.

[ii] Gilles Deleuze, *Difference and Repetition*, New York: Columbia University Press, p. 207.

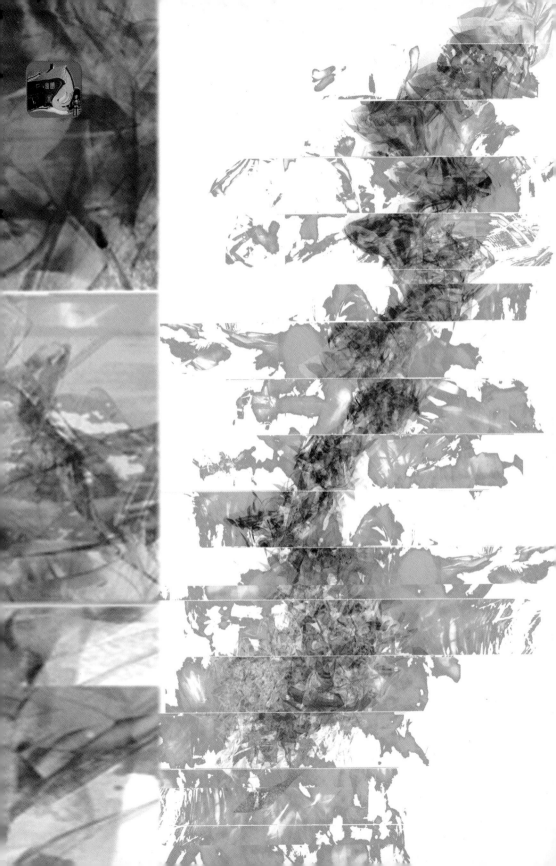

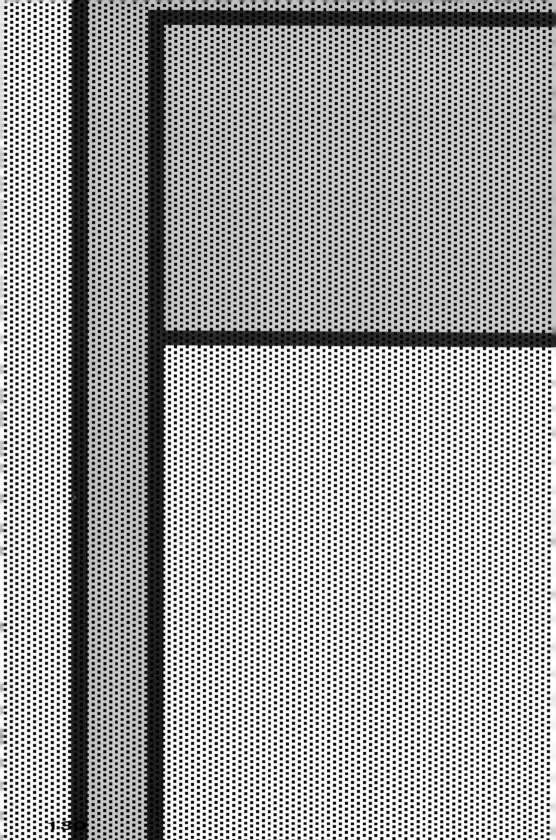

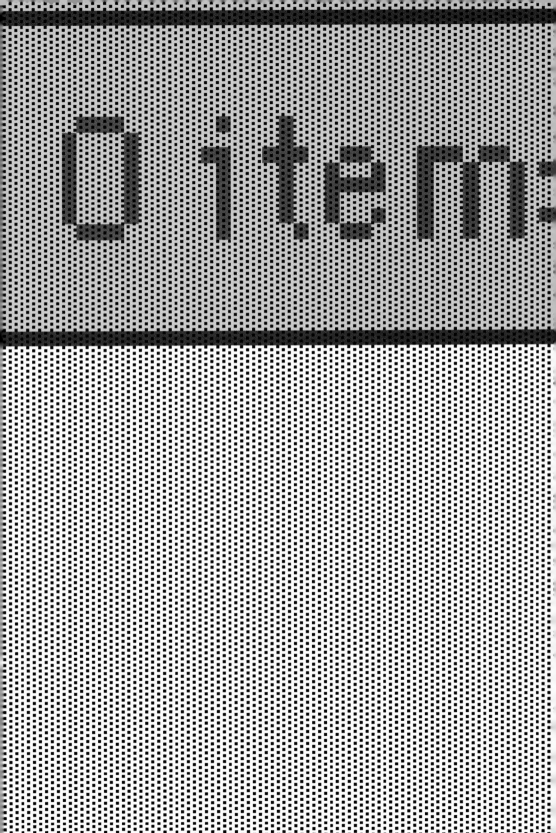

# WHERE SPACE GETS LOST

*E-mail interview with Lars Spuybroek by*
*Andreas Ruby*

*AR: A mechanistic system of thought like modernism could only deal with the accident by isolating and repressing it as an undesired event interrupting the well-planned course of events. Paul Virilio qualifies the accident however as merely the other face of substance, following the Aristotelian distinction between substans and accidens. If you translate these two constituent elements of the accident to architecture, you get an astounding equivalence: the built mass becomes almost literally the substance (from lat. substans: that which stands from below), whereas people act as the accident (from lat. accidens: that which falls into something). It is a very conventional definition, obviously, in which only the fixed accounts for something substantial while everything which moves is disqualified as accidental. Could you imagine a definition of architecture which inverts this condition, that is an architecture in which stability is accidental and movement substantial?*

**LS**: Here we have two lines of thought and realize they could become interrelated. Firstly, we should observe that our whole conception of form has been inverted. Physical form, biological form, the mathematics of form, how order emerges, how stability emerges, these have now all been structured in time, where form has become part of time. Fractal geometry, order on the edge of chaos, self-organization, catastrophe theory, finally concepts of geometry have emerged in which time itself has become essential, where the accident has become substantial, where form and order have become pattern, interference, iteration, rhythm, something created in time, and only to be understood in time. Secondly – as you mention Virilio's constant returning to the accident – media as the continuous accident of architecture. Of course, this dichotomy is omnipresent in theory, and I oppose it vigorously. I don't see media as the dark side of architecture at all. Why? Because I'd like to propose an architectural view of media, and vice versa. First of all, media comes in waves, in tides, and it deals with space as a medium, as a field, that is a soft substance through

which events are transported by waves, and become interrelated as a result of interference, amplification and decay ... Media are a way to inhabit time as it were, a movement connected with our own movements, something far more sensitive and responsive than an architecture of frames, crystals and solids that is only capable of returning always the same answers to an experiential body. I think we should keep in mind that architecture was the first machine, *the first medium* to connect behavior and action to time, to place it under the revolving light of the sun, but now, on the other hand, we should not mix up the old history of architecture, its Euclidean mathematics with its new potentials. I just cannot see why architecture, because it is old, should stay old.

*AR: The French word for real estate is 'immobilier', which is the opposite of 'mobilier' which means furniture. These two notions seem to indicate architecture's maximum radius of action: from absolute immobility (the building mass defining the invariable envelope) to total mobility (the furniture which could be placed anywhere inside). In other words, architecture actually has a whole set of varieties to choose from in order to 'situate' itself in the variable relationship of form and movement. Nevertheless, throughout its (occidental) history architecture has displayed a clear tendency to opt for the immobile element as its definition. The challenging potential of furniture as the imminently destabilizing force of architecture is left aside, if not also embraced by the disciplining regime of order. In the plans of his single family houses, Mies van der Rohe used to place the furniture elements as precisely as the indeed unmovable elements like walls and columns. There is an anecdote about the Tugendhat House: a couple of months after the completion Mies came back to Brno unannounced to check if everything was in order. And Mrs. Tugendhat had indeed dared to arrange the chairs in a slightly different way. So Mies emphatically asked her to put them back in their proper position, pointing to the plan of the house he had discreetly brought along. What would an architecture be like which goes the opposite way, that is an architecture that would approach real estate with a furniture logic?*

LS: We should resist Mies. We should resist this preservation of the old Aristotelian split of matter and time, substance and accident, tectonics and textile. Architecture as tectonics, media as textile. Architecture as a passive and neutral carrier, media as (inter)active image.

NOX
V2_Lab

That is: architecture as urbanism, as tectonics, as (infra)structure, as 'bigness' – as Koolhaas has titled his agenda – and media as life, the changing, the ephemeral, whatever. Instead of moving architecture into bigness, I would suggest to move it into textile, into furniture, into media ... We should never mix up architecture and building. Just because our buildings can't move, it doesn't mean our architecture can't. As our buildings are hard and intransigent, our architecture could be active and liquid. This obviously does not mean the Miesian and Koolhaasian retreat into neutrality, into the hall, the empty envelope. It's an old misunderstanding in architecture that when you create the greatest common denominator of all possible movements, an architecture that gets out of the way, it will induce movement and vitality in the actual building. It is exactly the other way around, one just creates stillness, with that kind of generic neutrality one neutralizes action. That means they don't appreciate that architecture is media, that architecture is an event in itself, an event that, in their case, passes its tectonics onto the body. I opt for a geometry of the mobile, where the geometry has become part of the furniture, the moveable – nothing neutral, nor passive.

**AR:** *Generally, Siegfried Giedion is seen as the theoretical advocate for a new space conception based on the notion of time. But if he indeed pointed to the new importance of the dynamic user moving freely through the building, he never got beyond the opposition of a static space and a mobile subject. He in fact kept the hierarchical distinction of space as substans and body as accidens, never realizing the transfer of movement from the subject onto the space. Curiously enough this transfer of movement was a major theme in the early experimental cinema and was also poignantly analyzed at the time by various scholars. In a seminal essay, German art historian Erwin Panofsky concluded that "as movable as the spectator is, as movable is, for the same reason, the space presented to him. Not only bodies move in space, but space itself does, approaching, receding, turning, dissolving and recrystallizing as it appears through the controlled locomotion and focusing of the camera and through the cutting and editing of the various shots."*

**LS**: Can I start answering this with a classic study of Held and Hein, mentioned in Francisco Varela's book *The Embodied Mind* ? They did this amazing experiment. They had a number of kittens with a carriage attached to each of them. Each carriage contained a basket with another

# NOX
## V2_Lab

kitten in it. So there were two groups of kittens sharing
the same visual experience, but with one group active, the
other stayed entirely passive. After a few weeks they were
released and studied again as individual cats. The first
group was okay and behaved normally, the second
behaved as if they were blind, they bumped into
everything.

Obviously our whole idea of perception and action
being unrelated bodily functions, the whole Cartesian
distinction between eyes and feet is incarnated in
architecture in the dichotomy of walls and floors, esthetics
and program, elevation and plan. Simple as that. This also
means the relation between space, movement and body
has always been misunderstood, or at least, been related
in the wrong order. There just is no movement apart from
image, no image apart from movement. The way we
construct images within our bodies is a million times
more complicated than the cognitive concept of printing
reality on light-sensitive grey matter. The sensory charges
the motor, and the other way around, they are intertwined
and connected. In this sense we should even resist
thinking in terms of 'space' – I never mention space
actually – we have to conceptualize the body first, not the
proportional Vitruvian body as the architectural center of
the constructed world, no, the experiential body, the
excited, vital body, where millions of processes go on at
the same time. Therefore we should always remember the
body is a clock, not the Huygens clock, but a manifold
patterning trying to gain stability through action. Bodies
try to transgress themselves in time by action, throwing
themselves into time, that is: connect to other bodies,
other rhythms, other actions. In this sense, you can really
only talk about 'space' as a result of an experiential body
timing its actions. Space is never a given. There can be
space in time, but not the other way round.

Perspective was nothing else than leaving out the
movement in experience and having the image as a
residue – and it is: the image is what's left over when
everything has dried out, like at the bottom of a cup of
coffee. Pure recollection, and recollection only.

*AR: But even if you refuse to use the word 'space', you do
seem to have a concept of it: one which is derived from
radical constructivism. According to this theory, space does
not exist per se, or in other words, where everything around
us is only unstructured information which becomes only
structured as soon as we interfere and interact with it.*

**138**

# Tamas Waliczky Sculptures

For our normal human perception, which is limited by the linearity of time and the continuity of space, time is a one-dimensional affair. We move along one axis which is defined by the co-ordinates of past-present-future, the present being the only layer of reality that we can actually perceive. And even in this single dimension we are able to travel in one direction only, namely forward.

If we posit time as a fourth dimension, we can imagine a lasting spatial representation of movements in time: a rising hand or a jumping body would leave a lasting trace in this four-dimensional space, constructing a sculputural object that combines all the phase positions that the body passes through in the course of the movement.

In the image sequences of *Sculptures*, Waliczky has attempted to represent such spatio-temporal structures. On the basis of specially recorded video sequences of fleeting everyday movements and gestures such as walking, jumping, waving, etc., Waliczky built three-dimensional sculptures in the computer. He calls them 'time crystals', as they preserve in frozen form brief moments in an individual's life. These crystals exist simultaneously alongside each other in space, and a virtual camera can observe them from any desired location. By travelling through the time crystals, the camera can re-produce the original movement from a diverse range of perspectives and at varying speeds.

*Sculptures* was originally made for Mesias Maiguashca's opera piece, called *The Enemies*, premiered at the Zentrum für Kunst und Medientechnologie, Karlsruhe, Germany, in 1997. The story of the opera was based on a short story of

*This idea implies the dissolution of the inside/outside opposition; conceptually, body and architecture merge to one synthetic action space. But does not this opposition reappear in the real experience of a building?*

**LS**: Well, no, because there is no 'real' experience of the building. You're right to refer to radical constructivism, or even Varela's concept of *enaction*, which is even more radical. His idea of embodied action goes absolutely against cognitivist representation, where the so-called outer world is only recorded by the brain – and simultaneously absolutely against idealism where this outer world is only a subjective projection of an inner one. He, and Maturana, only refer to 'structural coupling' in which body and world are interrelated and interactively transform each other. The 'true' experience doesn't take place anywhere, neither in the body, nor in the world. Only in the coupling. This is the point where the distinction between inner knowledge and outer world ceases to exist. I'll try to give a better explanation of what a 'real' experience is, especially vis à vis machines and technology.

What we call reality, what we call our sense of reality, is nothing but an effect of synchronization, the synchronization of our own bodily rhythms with processes going on in the world around us. Our sense of reality is created by our sense of timing, trying to be 'in phase' with the world, to live with the rhythm of the light. I don't mean this metaphorically; 'in phase' is a direct and physical connection. That is why seeing-machines like film and television – and now computing – should be seen as a motorization of reality, as a speeding up of reality itself. They speed up our sense of timing. This also explains why we suffer from jet lag. Now, what has been disturbed by the speed of the plane can be undone by (sun)light – remember the sun is our first clock, we're created by it. Light is not only stored in the form of motor-images, but it is also the main indication for setting our own clock, the bio-rhythm. We are made of light. We long for a seamless stream of actions, carried by light, not the derealization and parkinsonian stuttering we experience during a jet lag. Actually, doctors nowadays prescribe melatonine, a neuro-hormone that influences the *pigment in the skin*, as a cure for jet lags ...

**AR**: *All classical definitions of architecture contain the idea of fixing the movement which vibrates in the world outside*

*architecture – in Vitruvius' famous definition it is called 'firmitas'. Any concern about dynamics and fluidity is avoided like a bad germ. It seems like architecture feels strangely endangered by movement, maybe simply for not knowing how to handle it. To a certain degree this might be caused by 'timeless' condition of the drawing systems architecture has traditionally used: plan, section, elevation – all static modes of graphic inscription which can comprise three dimensions at the most, but certainly not time as the dimension of unfolding and change. Architecture has never developed a notation system for movement like choreography developed in dance.*

**LS**: First we have to understand what an experiencing body is. How the body shifts between habit and action. Of course, in architecture, they've very often tried to combine them, but it proved difficult and they mostly came up with either/or concepts. The standard architectural program consists of habits, routines and work. This is viewed as the mechanistic repetition of certain acts – the program only takes into account actions that are considered repeatable. On the other hand, there is the desire for free action, play, experiment, as in Constant's New Babylon. For me, it is not a question of either/or, it is not work-or-play, life is just the complication of these, the one is always hidden in the other. Sure, we habituate, we develop cycles of behavior. Why? Because it is hardly possible for humans to carry the whole act, to – as a Cartesian Machine – steer themselves continuously into intentions. We create our own rhythms, and make them stronger than ourselves, we create an internal music that gets us going. Our rhythms create us, we are an actual product of them. On the other hand we do not program ourselves, human software is much softer than computer software, we do not repeat the same actions over and over again, they change, they differ, they vary from each other, enabling us to change, to renew or to move smoothly into other acts.

That's why I would be in favor of separating work from dance, and after doing so, would try to merge them immediately. The whole set up of 'firmitas', standing upright, habituation and routines, and opposing these with dance, play and experiment relating to the twisting of this posture fixed through gravity should be set aside for being too simple. We should not make the same mistakes as in the sixties. We would be marginalized. We should find a way in architecture to complicate habit, to multiply routines in action. It is the 'winding up' of the soft clock of

# Seiko Mikami
## World, Membrane and the Dismembered Body

Our perceptions mediate the self and the body. There is always a split between the 'thing/object' and the 'viewer'. It is this space that Seiko Mikami is interested in in her work. She is not concerned with the physical objects that arise from the work, but with making material the invisible space that arises between the body and the object: the inter-communication, the mediation or interface that occurs between things.

The project *World, Membrane and the Dismembered Body* uses the visitor's heart and lung sounds which are amplified and transformed within the space to present a perception-driven architecture. These sounds create a gap between the internal and external sounds of the body. Mikami's work fragments the body and its perceptual apparatus into data, employing them as interfaces and thus folding the body's horizon back onto itself. The project externalizes the body's mechanisms and elaborates how the structure of 'interface' exists within the body itself.

*World, Membrane and the Dismembered Body* is presented in a sound-proof or an-echoic room, a special space where sound does not reverberate. Upon entering this room, it is as though your ears are no longer living while paradoxically you also feel as though all of your nerves are concentrated in you ears. The visitor has the impression of being inside a huge ear, of being immersed in the membrane of the ear. The soundproof room utilizes the quality of suspendedness to artificially create a situation in which the visitor is

心肺インターフェイス装着     無響状態

the body with motor geometry. Obviously, this geometry is
not a geometry of section, elevation and plan, but one that
tries to envisage these three – construction, perception
and action – within one conceptual continuum.

*AR: Doesn't space get lost somewhere?*

**LS**: The way we act is similar to that of a skateboarder.
We have a sense of direction, we have a sense of
intentionality. We throw ourselves into time by movement.
But then it is not a road or path we walk down. Our roads
may be straight, but our tracks certainly are not. It is a noise reduction
vector with a point of action, and in that sense every act is
an act of faith. Once underway we adapt, change our
minds, engage other forces, but we do not just see these
as resistance, no, they are like the curbs and obstacles for
the skater. We use them as push offs, as points of
inflection in the curve. That's it: a straight line goes from A
to B, but while it leaves A it curves, trying to reach B.
Architects have always misunderstood this position of B
as something in space, instead of time. We humans
complicate movement, we make movement from
movement. Our moves are truly labyrinthine, like
Nietzsches Dionysian dance, because we are our own
alcohol, our own music – to quote Oliver Sacks. Every act
has to be carried by this complication, this tilting of the
horizon, where the act is carried by itself, and is
orientated on its own need for gaining strength and
stability. I must end here by quoting once more, now
Baudelaire, who said: "Mentally and bodily I've always had
this feeling of falling. The abyss not only of sleep, but also
the abyss of acting, of dreaming, memories, desires,
sorrow, the many, et cetera ... I'm in a permanent
state of vertigo".

distance │ expand

*AR: Do you think that new notation systems provided by*
*computer animation modeling techniques like the ones you*
*use finally account for the body as an active part of*
*architecture?*

phase modul

**LS**: Yes I do. On all kinds of levels. Both in
conceptualization and building. As I've written in *The*
*Motorization of Reality* – a Virilio piece without the Virilio
hesitations – media should invade all aspects of
architecture, both in diagramming and in programming.
Let's not forget that all seeing-machines became drawing-
machines (in architecture), and went from the static

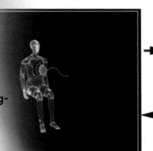

removal

a n

sound ab

made aware of the mediation of sound in the
interaction of auditor and environment

Unfortunately in the world of virtual reality
and also the artworld itself, acoustics often
take a subordinate role to the visuals
However, the eye can only attain a high level
of awareness, or focus, to a narrow fraction
of the space to which its attention is being
attracted. The ear, on the other hand, is able
to take in information from a larger space
and many signals can be transmitted via
sound. In a normal environment, people can
orient themselves almost unconsciously by
taking in the sounds of footsteps, voices, and
other types of audio cues and thereby gain
an understanding of the size and types of
materials that make up the space he or she
occupies. However, human ears don't work
according to one's will. While the eye can
interrupt the flow of information by closing
the ear does not have the same power. The
acoustic sense extends its feelers to take
account of places that the ears can't 'see' and
converts those distances into numbers. The
ears of the exhibition visitor register the
sounds emitted from his or her own body
through the body's membranes, which have
been set to vibrate by noises originating
therein

One could say that the heartbeat itself is the
most fundamental form of self-expression. In
addition, the sounds of the heart, lungs, and
pulse beat are also converted into numbers
by the computer system and act as
parameters to form a continuously
transforming 3D polygonal mesh producing
images that are projected in this room
Therein, two situations are effected in real
time: the slight sounds produced by the body
itself reverberate the body's internal
membranes, and the transfigured resonance
of that sound is amplified in the soundproof
room; a time-lag exists in this process
Neither the body nor the environment is cast
as the object of representation; rather, the
'ear' that intervenes, signifies a kind of inter
medium that serves as the perceptual link, or
code, between the acoustic sense and the
space of the room. This in between 'ear' is
the abstract expression of the work's claim
that "the ear is not merely a thing that hears
the eye is not merely a thing that sees"

ndication

dismer

ract

real-time hear

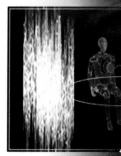

rotation

lision ———→ removal

thing

towards the kinetic. From perspective towards films and trains and television and cars (all with their own architectural styles), moving eyes constructing spaces. Now – with computing – this step is not metaphorical anymore, now we not only incorporate and embody the conceptuality of a machine in design, we can now actually step inside the screen and create reality from there. The design itself has become motorized, liquid, unstable, charged – the accelerating power of the computer is truly enormous, and is itself like a skateboard. But it is in the motor geometry, the geometry of the liquid that this machine becomes instrumental.

What I try to oppose as much as I can is the dichotomy of floors and walls, action and perception, we have to create one from the other. So, I'm neither animating the floor and later on covering it in a tectonic envelope, nor am I animating the volume and later on stacking it with floors. It might be better though to animate the programmatic fluxes to animate the building. But after some time you would see that this hasn't lead you anywhere either, except for the smoothing of the already planned movement within the program. The aim is not just replacing program as military or Jesuit disciplining by free choreographies of movement, and then superimposing them, as if program is dance, which it is clearly not! *It is not the fixation of the movement in the program, nor is it is the fixation of motion in the form.* Either way, it's not only motion capture. You would end up with the so-called 'stopping problem' – the question where to freeze the animation – while the real question is *how to pass the movement on*, from the machine to the architecture, from the architecture to the body, and from the body to the machine.

First of all the movement should be going from floor to wall and vice versa. That is: in the architecture itself. The movement itself creates three-dimensionality, what Kiesler would have called the endless, which is always vectorial, as in Zeno's arrow. This would deframe architecture and here the looping of perception and action, the optic and the haptic would never stop. So, it's about creating tension and suspense in the program. This is very important. We deal – on the one hand – with the desire to cool down behavior, to structure and separate actions, in short with the instrumentality of the program – on the other hand, we vitalize action through animation, by replacing fixed points and fixed geometries by moving geometries, *going from points to knots to springs*, and we

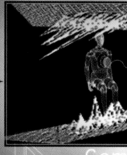

difference/division

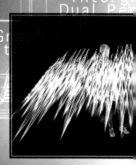

oppressi

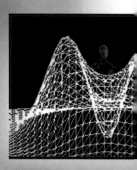

thing o

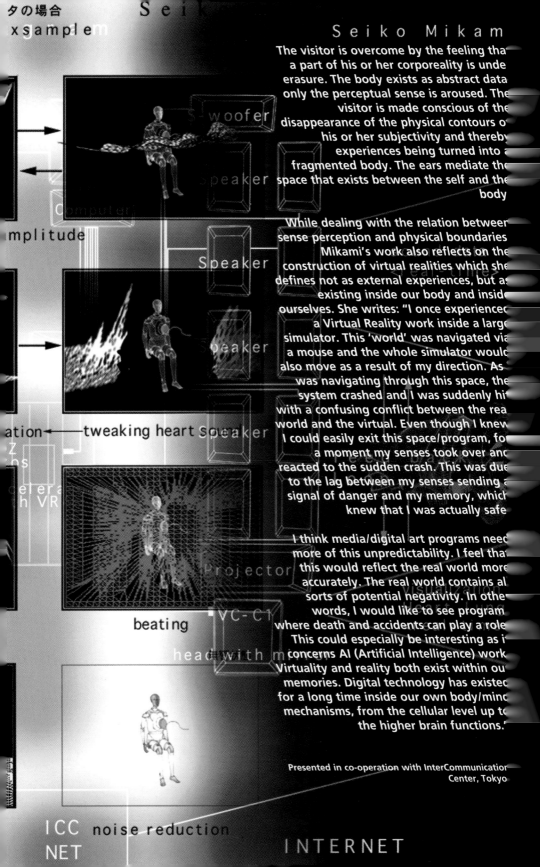

夕の場合　　Se...

x sample

The visitor is overcome by the feeling tha[t] a part of his or her corporeality is unde[r] erasure. The body exists as abstract data[,] only the perceptual sense is aroused. The visitor is made conscious of the disappearance of the physical contours o[f] his or her subjectivity and thereby experiences being turned into a fragmented body. The ears mediate the space that exists between the self and the body[.]

While dealing with the relation betwee[n] sense perception and physical boundaries[,] Mikami's work also reflects on the construction of virtual realities which she defines not as external experiences, but a[s] existing inside our body and insid[e] ourselves. She writes: "I once experience[d] a Virtual Reality work inside a larg[e] simulator. This 'world' was navigated vi[a] a mouse and the whole simulator woul[d] also move as a result of my direction. As [I] was navigating through this space, the system crashed and I was suddenly hi[t] with a confusing conflict between the rea[l] world and the virtual. Even though I kne[w] I could easily exit this space/program, fo[r] a moment my senses took over an[d] reacted to the sudden crash. This was du[e] to the lag between my senses sending [a] signal of danger and my memory, whic[h] knew that I was actually safe[.]

I think media/digital art programs nee[d] more of this unpredictability. I feel tha[t] this would reflect the real world mor[e] accurately. The real world contains al[l] sorts of potential negativity. In othe[r] words, I would like to see program[s] where death and accidents can play a role[.] This could especially be interesting as i[t] concerns AI (Artificial Intelligence) work[.] Virtuality and reality both exist within ou[r] memories. Digital technology has existe[d] for a long time inside our own body/min[d] mechanisms, from the cellular level up t[o] the higher brain functions."

S-woofer

Speaker

Computer

mplitude

Speaker

Speaker

tweaking heart speaker

ation

VR

Projector

VC-C1

beating

head with m...

Presented in co-operation with InterCommunicatio[n] Center, Tokyo

ICC noise reduction
NET

INTERNET

vitalize action through suspense, by shifting B from space to time, by multiplication of action.

*AR: In dance, space does not exist as a given entity (except the physical space of the stage, but that exists only as a precondition for the performance of the dance). Dance creates space out of movement. The shape of a form only exists in time, you can never grasp it in one moment but you have to commit its forms to memory. In all of these aspects, dance seems to be the art form that is furthest removed from architecture. Nevertheless I have the impression that it describes the most exactly what interests you in architecture?!*

LS: Architecture and dance are generally but wrongfully separated by this notion of either-time-or-space, and rightfully connected by music. The great thing in architecture though, is that there's no audience and there's no sound. The beauty of dance is the thinking of movement as a movement within itself, a gesture, a closed thing. When one would consider the program in gestures and actions, you would have to organize them both in time and in space, not only sequentially as in dance but also simultaneously – in that way one gesture wouldn't be followed by the prescribed next gesture, but one could study them in different relationships and interactions.

Let us consider the notion of tension again. Tension can only be created by elasticity and springs, by lines that can be stretched or lines that are connected by 'flexible points'. In the concept of the spring the point is an inseparable part of the line, a twist in the line that can both expand and shrink. I used a non-abstract machine built out of lines and springs to animate the design for the V2_Lab. It's an office, a matrix of tasks and work. Quite rigid, most of the time. I would like to focus on a detail here. The programmatic set-up was quite clear – the position of the lab, next to the audio room, video room and storage, and in between a corridor, slightly raised from the existing floor. And located at the beginning of the corridor is the table for the manager of the Lab. I did not superimpose this scheme over another animated one. Everything would have stayed as it was. I animated a diagram of springs and snares *through* the organizational diagram. What happened? At one point, the snares moved up so high we couldn't interpret them as part of the raised corridor anymore but only as part of the table. Suddenly we had a corridor that morphed, that *moved* into a table ...

# Bureau of
# Inverse
# Technology
## BitPlane

*BitPlane* (patent pending) is a pe—
aerial observation unit – a highly
compact spy plane – developed by th—
Bureau of Inverse Technology (BIT—
from the generous residues of cold wa—
precision. (The Bureau is developing a—
range of smart video products, *BitPlane*
being the latest addition to this line)—

The device consists of a radio—
controlled model aircraft (wingspan—
approximately 20 inches), instrumented
with a miniature nose-mounted ccd—
board camera and transmitter. The—
plane can be operated at altitudes o—
up to 600 feet. The FM transmitte—
sends a continuous stream of planes—
eye-view video to the ground receiver—
providing the pilot with the—
navigational view for the plane. The—
video signal is simultaneously recorded
on tape, for archival and research
purposes—

The Bureau is currently compiling video—
data retrieved in a series of sorties—
over the Silicon Valley/California (Oc—
'97 – Oct '98). *BitPlane's* mission takes i—
deep into the heart of the Valley, to—
view the source and progress of the—
Information Age. The in-flight video—
retrieved presents the familiar hosts—
and icons of the Information Economy—
from a novel aerial vantage point, as—
the unit flies over unusual formations—
of brilliant engineers, garage doo—
openers, next generation chips, dens—
cellular networks, circular duck ponds—
suburban tract housing enclaves—
military think tanks, BMW convertibles—
artificial irrigated lawns, cheap foreign—
labor and the pleasant climate o—
Northern California—

So at one point I'm sure one should call this a corridor, at another spot, three, four meters further on, I'm sure to call it a table, but what is it in between? There is program, there is the rhythm of moving in the corridor, there is also a rhythm of working at the table, and there is the vector in between. This vector is always charging the others, that's the music, *the silent music of the snares*, so to say, that moves work into action. And back again, of course. Normally one would separate table and corridor by space, now they are connected by movement. And where does the movement go? The tension in the snares goes directly into the muscles and tendons of the body – the motor geometry relates to the 'virtual motion', as Merleau-Ponty has called it, the background tension in the body, enabling an act to release itself from neurological anonymity and take shape. Now people sometimes lie down there as if on a beach, or just walk up the table ...

Back Beginning ntnp

edited_18.8.html

Iomega Guest

FreeHand 7.0

jkbk

ereixening.html

life forms

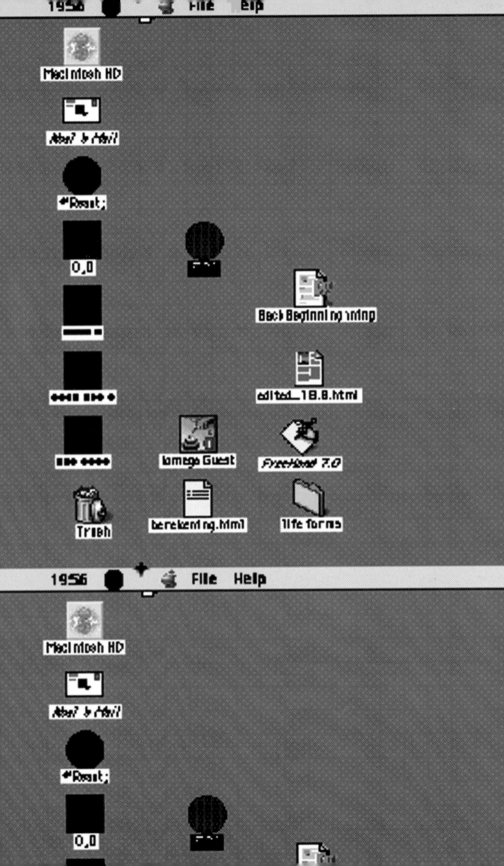

# EVENT HORIZON

*Brian Massumi*

## 1. Gone Critical

System. Routine. At a certain conjuncture, the unfolding of the physical system's line of actions interrupts. The system momentarily suspends itself. It has not become inactive. It is in ferment. It has gone 'critical'. This 'chaotic' interlude is not the simple absence of order. It is in fact a super-ordered state. In chaos theory, it is conceived as the co-presence of all of the possible paths the system may take: their physical inclusion in one another.

Criticality is when what are normally mutually exclusive alternatives pack into the materiality of the system. The system is no longer acting and outwardly reacting according to physical laws unfolding in linear fashion. It is churning, running over its own possible states. It has folded in on itself, becoming materially self-referential, animated not by external relations of cause-effect but by an intensive interrelating of versions of itself. The system is a knot of mutually implicated alternative transformations of itself, in material resonance. Which transformation actually occurs, what the next outward connection will be, cannot be predicted by extrapolating from physical laws. The suspended system is in too heightened a state of transformability. It is hypermutable. Hyperconnectible, by virtue of having disconnected itself. The system hesitates, works through the problem of its critical self-referentiality, and 'chooses' an unfolding.

When scientists use words like 'choice' they are of course not implying that the system humanly reflects, applying instrumental reason to choose from a set of pre-established possibilities arrayed before it and liable to mutual substitution. But it is no exaggeration to call the system's intensive animation thought, defined as "the reality of an excess over the actual." Its possible futures are present, in the system, in its matter. In effect: incipient effect (resonance and interference, vibration and turbulence, unfoldable into an array, an order).

Possibility has, in effect, materialized. The matter of

# fresh H2O eXPO

NOX/Lars Spuybroek (NL)
**Liquidizing**

RIPPLE #4

RIPPLE #3

RIPPLE #2

BLOB

WAVE

RIPPLE #1

freshH2O eXPO, water pavilion for the Dutch Ministry of Transport, Public Works and Water Management (1994-1997).

...the merging of the hard and the wet... of human flesh, concrete... glass, interactive electronics and water. A complete... based on the environment and technology. The design was based on the metastable aggregation of architecture and information... The form itself is shaped by the fluid deformation of fourteen ellipses spaced over a length of more than 65 meters. In the building, which has no horizontal floors and no external relation to the horizon, walking becomes related to falling. The deformation of the object is extended in the constant metamorphosis of the environment which reacts interactively with the visitors of the water pavilion by means of different sensors which cause this constant reshaping of the human body called action.

...0 oct. 1996

BLUE LIGHTS ON... WAVE AND... ACTIVATION

NOZZLES ON THE SPI(L)INE SPRAYING MIST

8 LCD PROJECT... PROJECT READ... ... A WAVE

SECTION #10

RIPPLE

BLOB

21 mar. 1997

We are experiencing extreme liquidizing of the world, our languages, our genders and our bodies. The liquid not only means generating the geometry of the fluid and the turbulent, but also the dissolving of all that is solid and crystalline in architecture. The fluid merging of action and form which is called interaction starts by leaving the orthogonal basis of perception with the horizontality of the floor perpendicular to the verticality of the window. By merging floor an wall, by merging floor and screen, surface and interface, we will leave the mechanistic view of the body for a more plastic, liquid and haptic version where action and vision are synthesized.

SPIT SP(L)INE - interactive installation for freshH2O eXPO (1997).

This building does not contain an exhibition in the classic sense, nor does it contain a programme.

Next to non-interactive events - ice, spraying mist, water on the floors, rain, and an enormous well - there are 17 different sensors connecting different actions of visitors to fluidity. Light sensors for crowds, touch sensors for individuals and pulling sensors for groups. Respectively creating the WAVE, the RIPPLE and the BLOB in real time projections, real time sound manipulation and the interference of these patterns in the 'cable spine' with its 190 blue lamps.

Lars Spuybroek

the system has entered a state where it does not extrapolate into an abstract possibility, and instead effectively absorbs possibilities, *en masse*, into its animated matter. Materially present possibility is potential. The system's criticality, of course, is as actual as any other state. What is in excess-over is the self-referentiality of the system's critical condition, its doubling back on itself *en masse*. What the self-absorbed system infolds is materially co-present in that way: in potential.

Implex: potential in-animates the actual conjunction (it is not separable from it). Excess: potential doubles the actual conjunction (it is not reducible to it). Potential is the implicate double of the actual.

Call a form of thought that is materially self-referential as opposed to reflective; that absorbs possibility rather than extrapolating it; that does not imply a distance between successive states of a system, mediated by an intervening action, but rather their immediate proximity to each other, their inclusion in one another; that therefore embodies a super-order of superposition rather than arraying an order of substitution; that materializes an unpredictable futurity rather than abstracting alternate outcomes from itself and from each other; that infolds before extending; that chooses unsubordinated to the established regularities of linear causality – call that kind of thought operative reason. Not the purposive analysis-toward-action of instrumental reason: a hesitant self-definition in suspension. Not an extending out of matter into thought-substitution, nor a doubling of perception by thought: a folding of thought into matter, at a point of indistinguishability with perception. Matter self-perceiving, doubling itself with its variations.

Instrumental reason makes thoughtfully, actfully explicit what is materially implied by the criticality of operative reason. Instrumental reason is operative reason's unfolding, its extension. Instrumental reason doubles perception with possibility: thought-out futurities in extrinsic relation to each other; mutually exclusive paths standing outside and against each other. Untangled by routine. Only thought, unimplicated. Arrayed in an extensive system whose alternate paths are separate and set. In a word, well-trodden. Already only thought, and now anticipating. Reflecting a re-think, in a next act, an anticipated next step. Retrospective-projective, before-after, looping. Possibility is potential extended, in action reflective of, simply repeating, thought. Simplex.

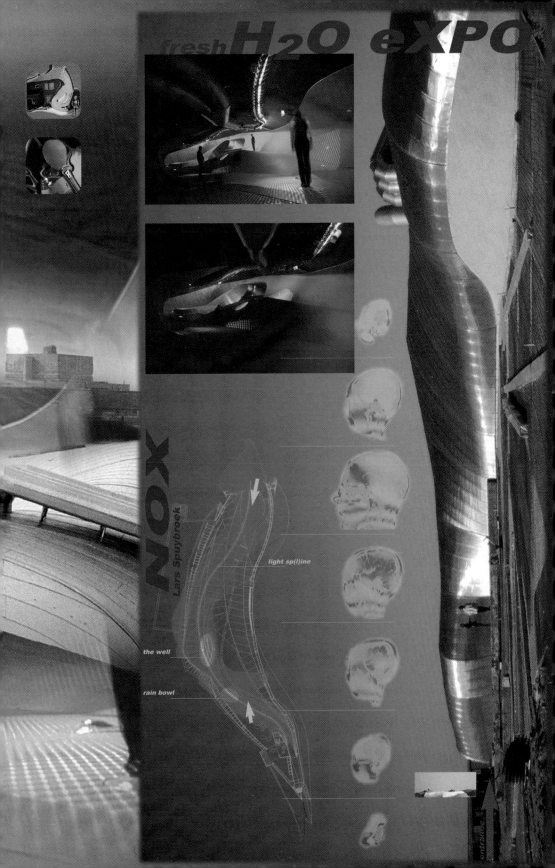

fresh H₂O eXPO

NOX
Lars Spuybroek

light sp(l)ine

the well

rain bowl

Potential extended: prosthesis of potential. The possible is the out-folded, out-worn double of the doubling that is potential, the simplex thought-shadow it retrospectively projects, in anticipatory action. Potential's intense, implex-excess (complex) vagueness recognized; thought-reflectively repeated. The possible pales to lucidity next to the felt turbulence of the critical. It is the pallor of potential. As a Bergsonian reading of the critical point, or bifurcation point, might have it.

The critical point may be an interregnum between two different orders, two different systemic organizations with their characteristic paths of actions and reactions. Or, it may constitute a threshold between disorder and order, an entropically disordered past and a future of systemic organization. The most celebrated example of the latter case is the Bénard instability, which occurs when turbulent patterns of diffusion in a heated liquid spontaneously order into convection cells. The ordering is not predictable in terms of heat diffusion alone. In fact, according to the theory of heat diffusion it is so improbable that, in principle, it must be considered practically impossible (Prigogine and Stengers 1984, pp. 142-43). Yet it happens. Theorists of such 'dissipative structures' explain that the self-organizing of liquid into a convection system is triggered because the instability of the situation suddenly makes the liquid 'sensitive' to gravity (Prigogine and Stengers 1984, pp. 163-5; Prigogine and Stengers 1988: 59-60). Gravity suddenly registers, and resonates. It infolds. Gravity is no longer an independent variable framing the system. It is a variation of the system. Its registering is one with the event of the system's self-variation. No longer a law of nature: an in-system event-trigger. It is this in-fold sensing, this in-sensing, of a force that up to that point was not pertinent to the system and had been 'ignored' that triggers the self-ordering transformation. Operative reason is a notice of force, a call to attention of matter to force, in a self-referential in-acting of the event of its own practical impossibility. Attention: in-tension.

Operative reason concerns the intensity of sensation more directly than the out-wearing of perception. The difference being: sensation is immanent perception (event in-triggering); and perception is sensation acted out (extended into an already only-thought array reflected and pre-reflected in action).

## Greg Lynn (USA) Animate

The animation industry has developed a set of tools for the simulation of life, which is effected by a mosaic of fluctuating external and invisible forces. Although architecture has been understood as static, fixed, ideal and inert, there is a shift going on from this determinism to directed indeterminacy through the incorporation of external constraints and environmental forces. Conventional architectural design software seems not suitable for the development of topological geometries that are capable of being changed and differentiated. For researching the possibilities of computer aided processes and biological models of growth and transformation, architects should therefore rather discover the use of animation software.

exhibition hall and experimental energy house
ÖMV Aktiengesellschaft Schwechat, Austria

# 2. Habit and Hiatus

The system is you. Reabsorbing possibility, yielding (to) potential. Your life is one long dissipation. The 'certain conjuncture' at which criticality is reached is each and every sensation. At every step you ground and orient yourself, using gravity to propel you along your habit-ridden line of daily actions. Mid-step, you are suspended: between falling and walking, ground and air, left, right, and straight. Hiatus. Without duration, measureless, less a pose or repose than a pure passing, from one equilibrium-saving footfall to the next, through a ever-shifting center of gravity that has no more extension, is no more actual, than any other mathematical point. But that is no less real for being virtual (governing as it does your potential bodily movement).

Physical laws, says C.S. Peirce, are habits of matter (pp. 223-224; 277-279). Gravity is a habit of mass. Always already felt. As already felt, each and every sensation is a law unto itself. Laws: a law of association arraying before (and after) it a set of familiar next steps, possible follow-up thought-perceptions, personal or conventional; and laws of usage of many kinds (next-step possible actions, more likely conventional than personal). Symbol and function. Not yet only thought. Still in action, bound up with perception. In situation. In mix. So familiar, so automatic, as to be ignored. Every sensation is a gravitational pull, grounding and orienting your nextness in pre-arrays of symbol and function. The ambulant germ of the possible: habit.

At the same time, each and every sensation is a virtual center where lines of action conveying pre-arrayed thought constrict into a point of pure passing: hiatus.

Mid-step, in passing, something registers and resonates. It hits you where your equilibrium shifts. The virtual point that is the spatial center of gravity is also the durationless, measureless time of impact. Here and now (always already given) before you know it (not already thought-out in action-perception). Where habit meets event.

Arbitrarily restrict the term 'sensation' to the impact at virtual center. Call habituating sensation 'situation'.

Sensations call habit to eventful attention. They impinge with force. They impact. They arrive, and insist (on the practical impossibility of their own systemic envelopment). Sensation is the transformational call-back

h2 House
Exhibition hall and experimental energy house
OMV Aktiengesellschaft, Schwechat, Austria

to feeling of the so-automatic as to be ignored.

Renewal of feeling, feeling of the new, only felt: shock. Shock is the model of sensation, as it happens. Sensation is the advent of the event of potential, from the virtual center of movement, materially called to in-tension.

If habit is a repetitive-reflective loop (between pre-thought action-perception and the only thought), then in hiatus of the event the loop falls in. It tightens into a churning circuit. Habit circuits in and out, as it happens. It falls into the center governing potential. And no sooner folds back out toward the realm of possibility. In-step, mid-step. Possibility into potential, equilibrated reflection into critical self-referencing, repetition into renewal. And back again. Habit and hiatus.

# 3. Your Freedom and Your Flatness

Mid-step, on the way to work, your tired eye catches a sidelong glimmer of spring sun. The beam enters your brain obliquely and instantly suffuses, imbuing the volume of your flesh with the change of season. Riding the beam, a sweet waft of an early bloom accents the familiar petrochemical bouquet of the city in motion. You are transported. The touch of the light tinges you with a fragrance of escape. Then a sudden screech of brakes returns you. Your fatigue has been shaken. It is not in the spot you returned to. It lies ahead, at work, and behind, at home. The thought of it, not here, thrills. The thought of walking back into it ... All the life unlived. You can do without. Leave it. Start over. A sudden resolve takes hold. You turn from the path. Midstep over the curb your awakened eyes do not even obliquely see the oncoming laundry truck.

The synaesthetic sensation of pungent volume-filling light-motion hits you with escape. The sensation envelops what you feel to be your freedom, a veer. Which in the next step envelops your fate, your flatness. The way in which your flatness is enveloped in your freedom is different from the way in which your freedom is enveloped in the sensation, which is different again from the way the well-trodden paths of habit are embedded in the situation. The path to work and back, as well as tried-and-true relative escapes (such as calling in sick for the day), are already-thought out possibilities constitutive of the

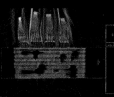

# Reiser + Umemoto (USA) 4 Projects

Our projects endorse new urban morphologies located at the zones of systematic conflict. We seek to encompass the general functional imperatives of a place and the specific civic possibilities by using this inherent duality – between global systems and the condition of the specific sites upon which such systems cross – as a quality to generate self-organizing processes. The projects are proposals in which time is not understood to be separate from the material world but finds it particular incarnations in it. We try to shift our focus from a static view on nature and architecture to dynamical systems that establish transverse developments across these regimes.

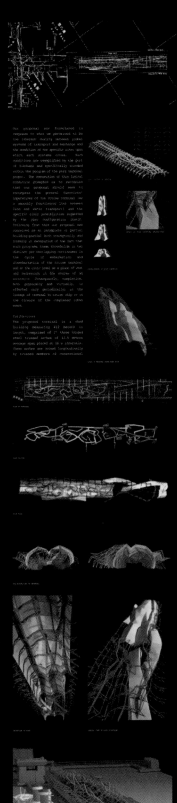
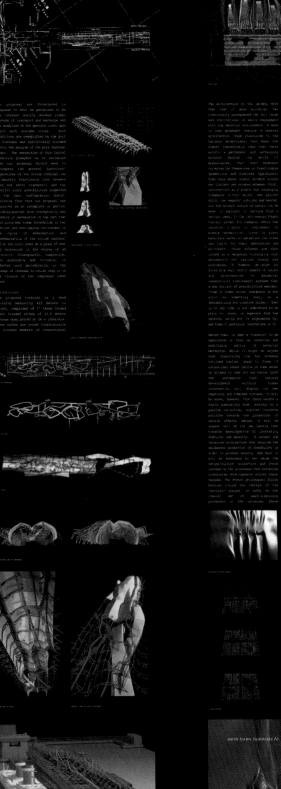

earth forms [substrate A]

situation. They are worn by the inattentive body as it makes its rounds (already-thought-out-worn). On the other hand, the radical escape of a veer from the tried-and-true is unthinkable in the terms laid down by the situation. It hits in a moment of distraction, directly entering the flesh with unexpected impact, demanding attention. Only afterwards is it consciously recognized, as concluded by the now attentive body from its material effects. Once recognized, a logical path from the situation of departure to the escape can be easily reconstituted, and subsequently accessed more easily, less intensely, more or less distractedly. A new possibility. But the reconstitution is exactly that: a retrospective construct. The new possibility of the radical veer follows its accomplishment. It is added to the situation after the situation has been taken leave of. Nothing in the situation as such could have suggested it. Possibility is retroactively situated unsituation.

Before being retrospectively possibilized, the veer out of the situation was embodied, unthinkably, in the situation. Potential: unsituation sensibly and unthinkably impacting on the situation. Potential is the out of the situation materialized in situation as an unpredictable but logically recuperable event, felt before being thought out. Sensation envelops potential as a degree of freedom of the situation: its own outside, critically doubling in on it, in-veering from it. Possibility is retroactively enveloped as the thinkably out-worn double of that double.

The crush of the truck is an event of a different kind: a post-veer arrival, rather than a departure. The sequence of events leading to it can also be retrospectively reconstituted. But that path will never enter the logic of the situation or of situations like it. Senseless splattering of flesh. The only response to the bloody truth of it is disbelief. Accident. Pure, senseless contingency. If only you had turned and looked. If only the tenant of the first-floor apartment had waited a week to plant those flowers. If only the truck driver hadn't been speeding ... It was fated. Fated, but not by those facts, or any possible logic of the situation. It was fated by the sensation. The impact of the sensation was the strike of fate, catalyzing an irrecuperable event. The accident, chance catalysis, pure contingency, unfolded from fateful freedom: this is the virtual. But on arrival, as actualized, the virtual is ex-centric: the center of gravity collapsed. Potential movement arrayed on the pavement. Possibility not only worn-out, but wasted, utterly exhausted. The out of all

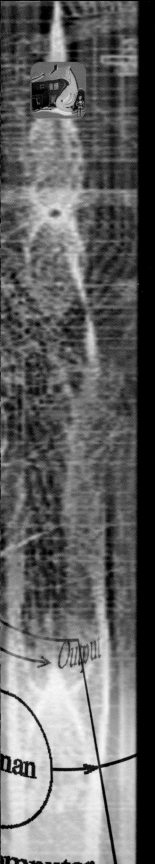

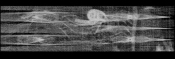

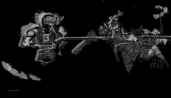

Our proposal for the Kansai Kan of the National Diet Library has sought to address the apparent paradox surrounding the universal proliferation of data, the presumed placelessness of information and the persistent necessity, nevertheless, to find a definition for this medium in architecture. Beyond the admittedly important legal and archival necessity for preserving hard copies of documents, the persistence of the library may be ascribed to less recognised processes attendant to globalisation. The general phenomena of decentralisation and dispersion of institutions made possible by new technologies overshadows a correspondingly specific trend towards centrality and agglomeration both within and appended to major urban centres in global economies. Japan's principal cities, where most of the country's data is produced and consumed, have been the advent of information zones: agglomerations of buildings and public spaces relatively small in scale whose organisational prominence mutual interests and information exchange through direct communication. A new form of public space that arises out of the interaction of the Kansai area is the close proximity of major institutions and corporations, and beyond, this consequent influx of smaller institutions and services that are sustained by the presence of their larger neighbours. The success of such co-dependent organisations is predicated not simply on the major institutions that initiate the information zone, but on their capacity to act as catalysts for the advent of new programs and needs. Our proposal, therefore, embodies two distinct yet related imperatives: to fulfill the explicit programmatic criteria of the library while developing implicit spatialities that would foster the new and unforeseen irruptions of program brought about by the 'information zone.'

### The Stack Building

The Stack Building is a bar measuring 190 m in length, 25 m in width, and 29 m in height. It is comprised of steel truss walls oriented vertically acting as gigantic storage units for automated, compact and fixed stacks. Books and documents are accessed via catwalks and the automated conveyor system which efficiently routes library materials to and from the reading rooms and operational system department for shipping and receiving from the outside. Since the Stack Building is organised around the concept of the storage wall, stacks (automated, compact, fixed) are categorised vertically in layers. There are no horizontal slabs or floors as such in the stack building. Horizontal movement is accomplished along catwalks and the automated conveyor system. The space between the storage walls are narrow open wells from ground to roof allowing filtered natural illumination to enter the entire section of the building during daylight.

### The Virtual Device

The Library Building measuring 220 metres by 55 metres is comprised of three looped slabs suspended by cables from a prestressed steel roof carried on four steel piers. The slabs are so formed as to maximize continuity and multiple interconnections among the public spaces and levels. Topological deformations: cuts, mounds, ramps, ripples, and stairs,

Despite the passing of Romania's totalitarian regime scars manifestly visible and invisible deface the center of her capital city. The singular and violent nature of this transition along with the built legacy of the Ceaucescu regime can leave an almost forgotten time. The eagerly awaited reframing of the material and cultural life of Bucharest is inevitably attended by monuments to recent tyranny. Proposals, therefore, that would attempt either to restore the pre-1981 fabric, or conversely, those which propose a radical elimination of the 1981-89 Ceaucescu projects would, in their respective ways, engage in utopian models that are wholly inadequate to the situation at hand. The former by indulging in a nostalgia for a lost city — a city which in any case is no more by the 1980-89 intervention that an amount of local restoration would repair the wound and fuse into account the unprecedented planning demands presented by future socio-economic realities. The latter while obviously unrealistic in terms of economics it is unlikely that the city would be inclined to demolish the 1980-89 projects; is unfounded in perhaps more profound ways. Elimination of the monuments left by the recent history amounts to a totalitarian gesture in itself (whatever the style of its replacement) for it suppresses a history that is still very much alive and for that reason still very much a threat.

"What is torn-torn must remain" Wittgenstein.

Rather than attempt to replicate an erased fabric, our proposal seeks to reconfigure central Bucharest through a series of infrastructural grafts that while responsive to the existing context (some of the buildings of the 1980's intervention will be touched) inherently produce their own patterns of growth.

The highway — an access that's not an end.

Our plan endorses the production of new urban morphologies that would locate themselves at the scene of systematic audition between a proposed high-speed vehicular loop and the contexts it crosses. The loop traverses the length of the Palace

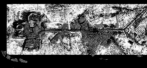

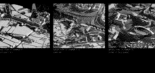

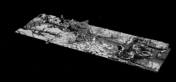

situation. 'Impassivity' of the event (Deleuze, pp. 5, 96, 100 (translated as 'impassibility')).

If shock is the model of sensation as it happens, and sensation is the trigger of life potential, it is death that is the model of the virtual (Deleuze, pp. 151-53). Which is not to say that the virtual is always so parabolically deadly. Only that death is the most suggestive figure for the actualization of the virtual (of the reality of the inactual). Every chance, every contingency, every senseless out of every situation, is a little virtuality, a modest death, a rupture, an interval of being. After which life continues, still. Possibility and potential re-engage. Situation clamps back down. Next steps array themselves. Habitual paths stretch before and behind. Rounds. Return. Recapture. With something having shifted, something having changed. The new. Circuit of transformation.

Possibility, potential, virtuality: sequencing, veering, rupture; linearity, hiatus of intensity, impassive interval; the predictable, unpredictability, the senseless; the only thought, the thinkable, the unthinkable; the already felt, the felt, the insensate; the possible, the possibilizable, the impossibly real; the possible, the 'practically impossible', the impossible in principle; the instrumental, the operative, and the contingent; same, change, chance.

The possible, the potential, and the virtual can be figured as mutually enveloping, in a complex play of doublings, veerings, arrivals and returns. Ins-outs. It is the virtual that doubly describes the limits of the fold: a shifting center so central as to be inactual; an ex-centering fog of contingency encompassing life in an impenetrably vague ring of eventfulness. The virtual doubly describes the unity of a life, between limits: measureless depth and insubstantial surface, together. Inside-outside limit: immanent limit. Immanent to bodily change, enveloped in potential, outside possibility and predictability. The event horizon.

The unity, or event horizon, of a life is the immanent unsituation of its matter, its body. In situation, by contrast, a life is incrementally pulled out of itself, into habit. It is put to work: death by attrition. Another limitation, this time of the situation, in and of it. This intrinsic, as opposed to immanent, limit is slowly disintegrative rather than crushingly unifying. Accident versus attrition. Ex-centric collapse of the center of gravity versus entropic run-down (infinite dissipation uncountered by critical conditions). Singularity against the most general habit of matter.

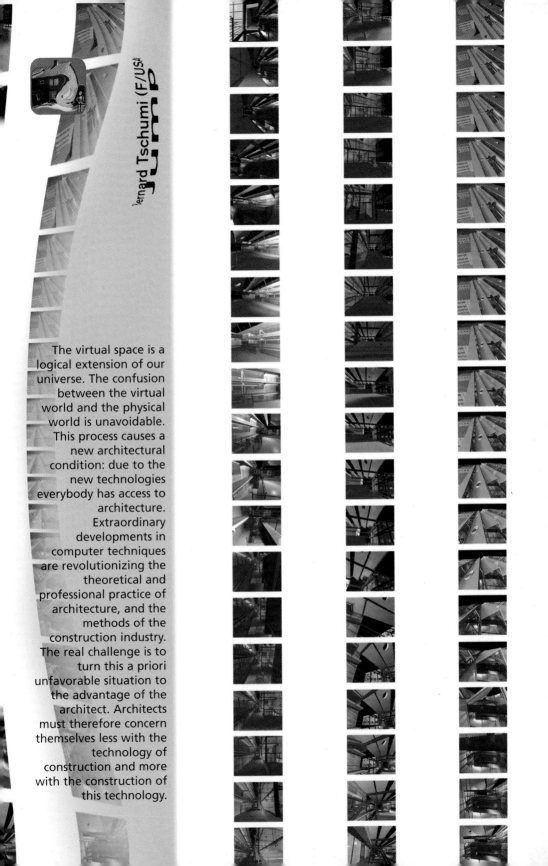

Bernard Tschumi (F/USA
**JUMP**

The virtual space is a
logical extension of our
universe. The confusion
between the virtual
world and the physical
world is unavoidable.
This process causes a
new architectural
condition: due to the
new technologies
everybody has access to
architecture.
Extraordinary
developments in
computer techniques
are revolutionizing the
theoretical and
professional practice of
architecture, and the
methods of the
construction industry.
The real challenge is to
turn this a priori
unfavorable situation to
the advantage of the
architect. Architects
must therefore concern
themselves less with the
technology of
construction and more
with the construction of
this technology.

Think of the center of gravity as a contraction of the ring of vagueness that is the event-horizon. And think of the ring as an expansion of the center from which the center has been excised. Think of them together, as a simultaneous contraction and expansion, as a center that is its own excision, a pure passing that is pure arrival. Think of them together as a black hole (in actuality, in possibility, and in potential). The 'singularity' of a life is a better word than 'unity'. In cosmology, a black hole is a 'singularity' where a point in the universe falls outside it, into 'infinite curvature'. By dint of material excess. A situated point ins itself out, rejoining the farthermost edge of the universe, burrowing into depths of the universe at the same time as circumscribing its surface, describing a universal no-time no-place where no laws tread, where excess matter is impassive energy, where everything that passes arrives for never and more. That cosmic feeling. The universe sensing itself, touching its limits. In the most critical of conditions, rehearsing the 'big crunch' at the other end of the bang.

NOTES

Bergson, Henri. *The Possible and the Real*. In Creative Mind, trans. Mabelle L. Audison. New York: Philosophical Library, 1946.

Deleuze, Gilles. *The Logic of Sense*. Trans. Mark Lester with Charles Stivale. Ed. Constantin Boundas. New York: Columbia University Press, 1990.

Peirce, C.S. *Design and Chance; A Guess at the Riddle*. In *The Essential Peirce*, vol. 1. Ed. Nathan Houser and Christian Kloesel. Indianapolis: University of Indiana Press, 1992.

Prigogine, Ilya and Isabelle Stengers. *Order Out of Chaos*. New York: Bantam, 1984.

Prigogine, Ilya and Isabelle Stengers. *Entre le temps et l'éternité*. Paris: Fayard, 1988.

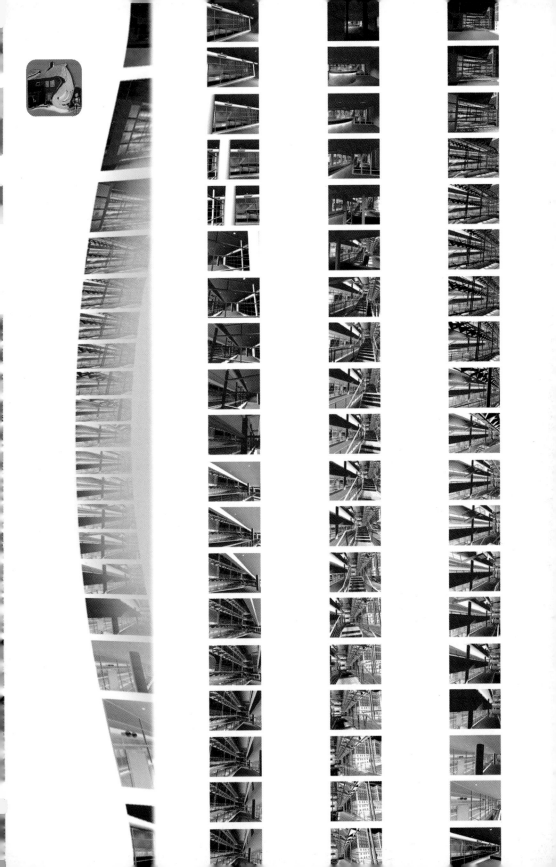

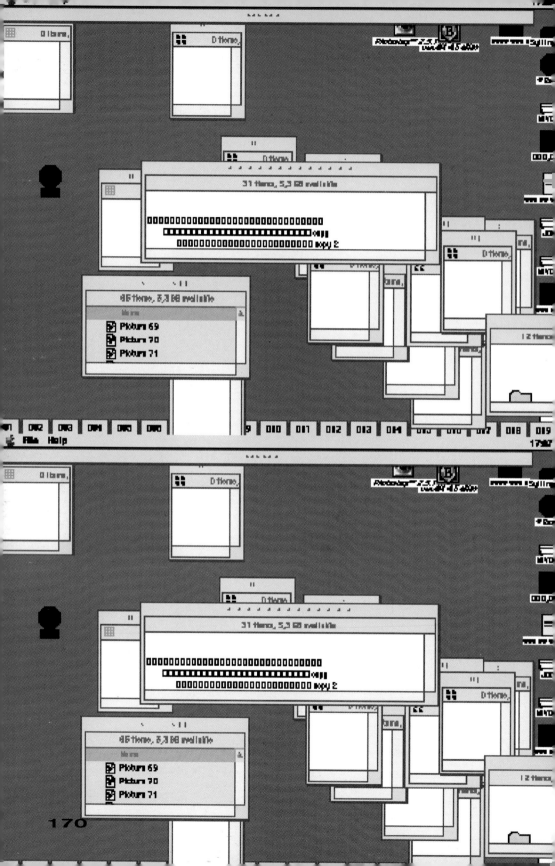

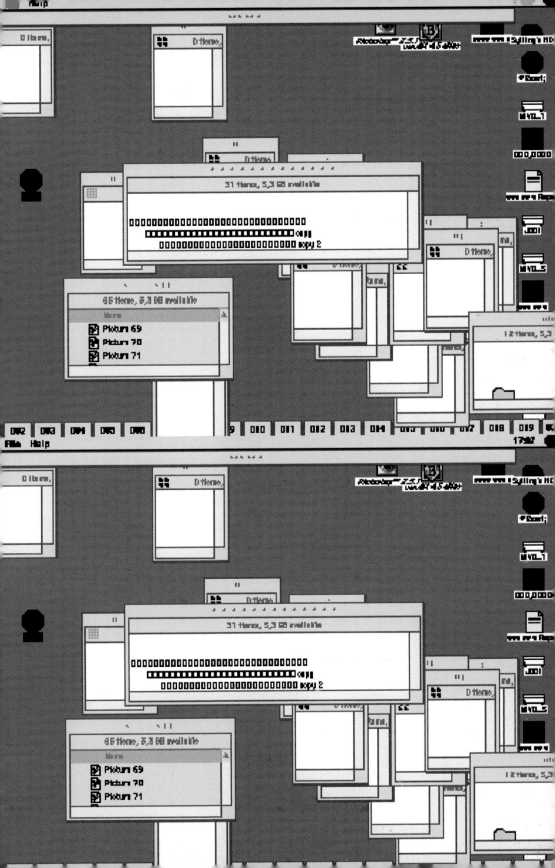

# The World as an Accident

*Otto E. Rössler*

> The notion of accident extends to the whole world and beyond. Strangely enough, this is not the whole story. The 'accident machine' is not the only machine: there is also an 'escape machine'.
>
> (30 August, 1998, revised 5 October, 1998)

The science of endophysics claims that the world as it is given to us is only a cut, an interface, a difference inside what is real (the whole). This has some powerful implications, including the possibility to change the whole world (i.e. the interface world). From the viewpoint of science, this is good news because it enlarges our range of technological options.

But there is a philosophical correlate that is disturbing. The world as an interface is pure accident. The interface is an accident machine. Moreover, it is not even a machine. It is a violent imposition and has all the qualities of a bad dream.

This sounds ominous but can be proven if the theory is not misleading. Besides the two types of agency introduced by Newton (the 'laws' and the, once-and-for-all specified, 'initial conditions'), there is a new type of agency: the 'assignment conditions'. Assignment is a deliberate accident, so to speak. This can be understood as follows. The same universe run in a computer, so to say, acquires many faces (interfaces or cuts) depending for which particular, microscopically specified, subsystem (called observer) the rest of the universe is put on screen. A microscopic change in the observer-world assignment can radically change the interface. The universe as a whole remains majestically unchanged by this.

Normally, people tend to believe that, apart from the assignment of the universe itself, the 'assignment of the body' is the only assignment to take into account in this world. This simple view is held by virtually everyone in

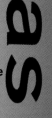

The contemporary urban condition is a hypertexture, an enormous overcoded databank. It is an irrigated field of dynamic spaces and simultaneous times, where alternative worlds merge into a new semantics. The city is a relational field where humans are connected. Local system dissolves into a glocal configuration, exposed to environmental and internal fluctuation of material and immaterial flows. To transpose the cultural identity of the city into a contemporary situation we should develop new programmatic and spatial requirements. The public status of space as a support of information accessible to everyone should be reestablished. Urbanism can no longer be obsessed with the material.

the West but is incorrect and misleading. It ties in with the single-life-theory – the belief that death is final – people adhere to in the West.

People therefore usually believe that they can forget about the really important things as long as they are securely wrapped up in the bodies that they have grown accustomed to. The cruelty of the two 'acknowledged' accidents of birth and death remains the only reminder of a predicament that can otherwise be forgotten about, so they feel.

This complacent view is overturned by endophysics. The accident reaches center-stage at every moment because of the assignment conditions. While no one has talked about them much since the time of Aristotle, everyone experiences them most intimately at every moment. The Now is the best example. It moves through the world like a gong. Only no one seems to hear it. We are pushed forward on an invisible glass seat through the world, or so it appears. "High on the yellow wagon I sit near the driver in front," is an old, almost philosophical folk song (in Germany), only that this view, too, is still naive.

There is no motion in nature. Everything that moves does so because the Now moves. If the Now would not move, nothing would. All that would be left would be a frozen (stationary) cut. The brain determines the speed of the movement of the Now, so we are told. Actually, the speed of the movement of the Now is determined by the psyche, i.e. consciousness. "Without psyche, no time," said Aristotle. But this is not yet completely correct either because it implies a belief in continuous motion.

The Now is a moving cut – or so it appears. If we give it a constant speed, its duration will still shrink to a point – a moving point. Who or what assigns this moving point to me, now? Moreover, since each of the Nows is moving, jumping back and forth between them would make no difference, as far as I can tell. Note that the movement would never be interrupted since one would always find oneself snugly in a moving car seat after landing. Thus the Now may just as well be discontinuously assigned.

But then comes the next, even more intimidating fact. The world that appears on the canvas of the Now

**174**

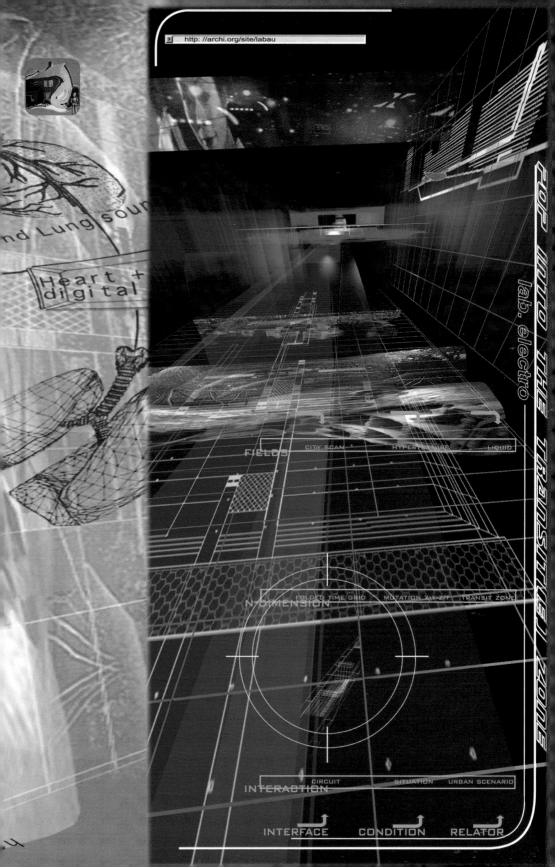

point need not even be consistent across the Now-points. A vertigo-like fractal tumbling takes hold of our minds at this point of the argument. But surely this is just philosophy – and we have learned that philosophy has no consequences, or has it?

Yet, this is physics. As shown in Fassbinder's 1974 movie *Welt am Draht* (*A Puppeteer's World*), it is possible to build a lower-level computer-simulated universe that contains 'ID-units' – simulated persons. In endophysics, the lower-level universe is, in addition, microscopically reversible (there is no preferred direction of time). The little ID-units inside nevertheless suffer from the same predicament as we do. Their Nows and worlds (Now-worlds) are also determined for them at every moment by the external super-observer ('demiurge'), who happens to be interested in one particular cut – or sequence of cuts – being put on screen as an interface to watch. The Marquis would have loved the contraption ...

"The world as an accident?" Worse: "The world as a deliberate accident!" The hypothetical prison that we started from is closing in. Death as an escape machine is growing more and more remote. The nightmare that grabbed young Descartes at the age of 23 in the town of Ulm is intensifying. In the first part of the bad dream, Descartes fought with the wind and ended up with a lame leg. In the second part, a book was blown in and landed on the table beside his bed. The book contained the most important answer of his life ("which life path am I to choose?"). But then the book was blown away again and when it returned this decisive chapter was missing. The dream was indistinguishable from waking reality. The Cartesian nightmare did not seem to go away.

In the morning, Descartes bravely faced his predicament and founded science as a means to investigate the relational consistency of the world of waking reality and to find out if it differed favorably from the dream world. For if this were to be the case, he would be safe. This consistency hypothesis proved extremely powerful because of its extreme weakness. (Because it was so extremely daring, it was extremely easy to falsify). It later enabled Descartes to claim that those who follow him would conquer old age and eventually death itself. A machine that could change the Now would clearly be a case in point. Now-control would imply immortality.

Architecture is a process in which the capacities of calculation, of integration of data, resolution in space, can finally allow architects 'to make do with making some less'. By identifying what characterizes a place with new parameters like the intensity of flows, the bonds, the climates, the proximities, the territoriality in all its complexity, the social evolutions, we are able to connect the tool of visualization and transformation to the territory. To bind technology to an attitude of the situation means to connect the numerical to reality. The field of architecture does not relate any longer to the object but to an esthetics of disappearance.

## PROCESS OF DISAPPEARANCE

## TOWNSHIP OF SOWETO

### The process

### Axioms

ROCHE DSV & Sie. P

François Roche Gilles Desevedavy Stéphane Lavaux François Perrin

Could the 'helmet' of endophysics (called Sterlarc Helmet) change the Now? A mild microwave field of some 40 TeraHertz applied to one's own living brain might change the interface. But even if successful, this method would be of no use because the outcome would remain counter-factual. There is no place for another Now inside the Now. At best, a message could be left, albeit not in the form of a document but merely in the form of a decodable bit string in a seemingly universal physical constant.

Still, this minor success would amount to a 'world bomb'. Like an ice-cream bomb, it could be used to improve everybody's life, immortality being part of the package. 'Accidents Controlled' would be a possible name for the manufacturing company.

At this point, a second step to controlling the nightmare presents itself. It is here that the real escape hatch lies. Previously, we only tried to manipulate (bite) the leash, so to speak. This time, we turn around.

But to do so would be of no use to a slave, you might say. Epictetus the Cretan was a slave in ancient Rome. His master enjoyed torturing him. One day he twisted Epictetus' arm behind his back. Epictetus said: "Master, if you twist my arm just a little bit more, it will break." The master did. Epictetus said: "Master didn't I tell you that if you twisted my arm a little bit more, it would break?" This remark prompted the master to set him free.

Epictetus was, so to speak, the first computer that passed the Turing test. For slaves were believed to have no soul. The same escape is possible from the slavery of the interface. How does the trick work?

This is not difficult to ascertain. The interface is not everything we have. The world is not everything we have. The world appears on something. You could call it the 'screen of consciousness' (the soul). I call it the 'TV set'. Why? So far, we have only talked about the ever-changing program and its assignment. The program is accident and cruelty, or so it appears. But this is not the whole story. The program is not everything there is.

The TV set is the envy of the gods. No one drives a better Lamborghini. The TV set is indestructible. This is because it was never created. "Heaven and earth pass

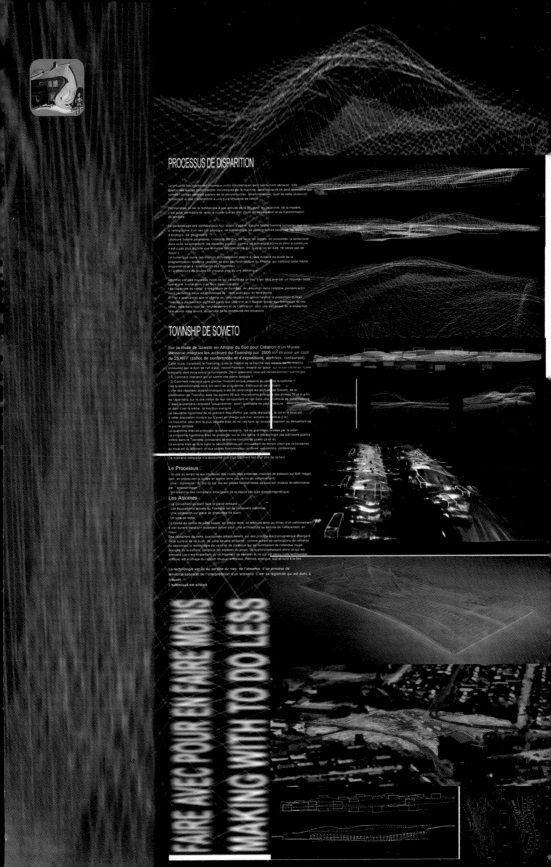

## PROCESSUS DE DISPARITION

La virtualité fascinante des nouveaux outils informatiques peut rapidement décevoir. Une grande part sur les conséquences physiques de la machine, la part virtuelle ne peut apparaître que comme l'univers de ce qui a le de la construction. Généralement. Quid de cette révolution numérique si elle s'abandonne à une pure virtualité de l'objet.

Temporaliser et de la technologie à une attitude de la situation, du problème, de la matière, c'est aussi permettre de relier le numérique au réel l'outil de visualisation et de transformation au service.

La généralisation des opérées peut nous aider à passer d'une seule branche (virtualité que le 3D) à configurer d'un savoir de géologie, de climatologie, de photographies associées, de l'écologie, de géographie.

Introduire comme paramètres. L'inconnu, des fonctions sociales des proximités, la territorialité dans toute sa complexité, des devenirs aussi comme un scénario à écrire et donc à construire. Il est d'ailleurs que le mythe fonctionnaliste qui qu'aujourd'hui en effet de ne cesse pas de mourir à.

Le numérique ouvre ces champs d'investigation propre à nous extraire du dictat de la programmation moderne (succion et alibi de l'architecture du XXème siècle) à conforter cette même programmation à l'élaboration des façades.

L'architecture de donner les projets d'un où exténuer.

Identifier le projet nouveau nous ce qui caractérise un tout c'est tout à avancer un nouveau mode opératoire. Inutile d'en dire faire beaucoup plus.

Les paramètres du calcul, d'ingéniation de données, de l'absorption dans l'espace, peuvent enfin nous permettre, nous les architectes de ne pas avec pour en faire moins.

Et l'on s'aperçoit que le chemin de l'architecture ne convient plus la production d'objet. Toutefois rêvassement significatif pour que valoir et qu'il faudrait trouver aux fondateurs de nos villes pour tout cela et l'enclenchement et du l'enfermer pour une esthétique de la disparition. Une œuvre rare toute, au service de la complexité des situations.

## TOWNSHIP DE SOWETO

Sur la route de Soweto en Afrique du Sud pour Création d'un Musée-Mémorial intégrant les archives du Township sur 2500 m² et pour un coût de 26 MFF (salles de conférences et d'expositions, archives, restaurant).

Cette route, traversant le Township, a été la théâtre de la marche des soweto-ville, marche commerciale par la mort de l'un d'aux, Hector Peterson, enseint sur place, sur le soir même du musée exemple dont nous avons la communauté. Deux questions nous ont immédiatement submergés.

1) Comment intervenir sur le comte une pierre tombale ?

2) Comment intervenir sans glorifier l'histoire encore présente du passé de la marche ?

Ces questionnements nous ont servi de programme, d'amorce et de scénario.

L'idée de répartés programmatiques a été de réintroduire au archivé de Soweto, de la planification du Township dans les années 50 aux mouvements politiques des années 70 et à la fin de l'apartheid, sur le site même de leur dérouement et non loin une d'une l'arrivée de Johannesbourg. C'était la première nécessité "situationnelle" dont l'archétecte ne peut s'extraire. Peut-être et dont c'est le métier. La fonction d'origine.

La deuxième hypothèse de ce scénario était d'affiner par cette réalisation le sol et le sous-sol à cette disparition mineure qu'il était en charge que d'en extraire la mémoire (l'or).

La troisième, peut-être la plus délicate était de ne rien faire qui puisse s'opposer au dénuement de la pierre tombale.

La quatrième était de protéger la nature existante, fait de graminées bridées par le soleil.

La cinquième hypothèse était de prolonger sur le site même la morphologie des bâtiments publics visible dans le Township (conteneurs de marine transformés poêlés ça et là).

La sixième était de faire subir la dénomination du sol (mouvement de terrain induit par le troisième) au bouleau du bâtiment, et aux strates fonctionnelles (archives, expositions, conférences.

Ce scénario complexe n'a accouché que d'un bâtiment fait d'un plis de terrain.

### Le Processus :

- Un plis du terrain se aux couloires des routes déjà présentes sur Soft Image) ceci en préservant la surface en pleine terre (au centre du vallonnement).

- Une "impression" du plis du sol sur les strates fonctionnelles du sous-sol (module de déformation par "emboîtissage").

- Un plissement des conteneurs émergents de la nappe (de type électromagnétique).

### Les Axiomes :

- Un conteneur existant face à la pierre tombale.

- Les équipements actuels du Township fait de conteneurs maritimes.

- Une végétation sur place de graminées de bush.

- Un sous-sol minier.

La tombe au centre de cette nappe, en pleine terre, se retrouve lorto au milieu d'un vallonnement à ciel ouvert, dans son isolement actuel pour, d'une architecture au service de l'effacement, en creux.

Des conteneurs de verre, positionnés aléatoirement, sur des principe électromagnétique émergent de la surface de ce bush, de cette savane africaine, comme autant de perforations de lumières.

Ils empruntent la technologie de verre et de plastique qui le contrepoint de l'étendue rougie-triangle de la surface, construise les espaces du projet, De dysfonctionnement entre ce qui est enfoncé (ce à ses frustrations ou un fragment de savane) et ce qui est perçu (une technologie évoluée) est à l'image du rapport minéral vallonage, matière, amblique, sud et nord à la fois.

La technologie est là au service du rien, de l'absence, d'un process de territorialisation et de l'interprétation d'un scénario. C'est sa légitimité qui est donc à creuser.

L'esthétique est ailleurs.

away but breeches made of buckskin last forever"
(another German poem). When the creation of Adam's
body had been completed, consciousness was "blown
into his nose," it is said. Creation stops with the body and
the interface. Only the content of the screen (the program)
can be manipulated. The screen (TV set) is more than
eternal. How can one be sure? He or she who is not
afraid to wrestle with the angel (demiurge) will prevail and
be accepted as his equal. What is the reason for this
strange symmetry?

The secret is the kiss. Not the kiss on the screen,
but the kiss between screens. Descartes saw it first,
Levinas worked it out. Indestructibility implies
omnipotence. But where is the omnipotence? It lies in the
exteriority relative to other screens.

So far, we have stuck to the naive picture of
science and artificial universes in a computer. All of this is
program-ware. Worse, it is shadow-ware. Within the big
program of living consciousness, with its deep colors and
pains and intangible Nowness, there is the small program
on which science focuses. It relies exclusively on the
shadows (relations) present within the big program. The
machine hypothesis of science applies to this subfeature.
"The world is a machine." "The brain is a machine." Since
machines can be manipulated, I can manipulate your
brain, for example. For I am exterior to you if the world
(the small program) is consistent. This is Descartes'
hypothesis of demiurgic omnipotence. Exteriority applies
not only to lower-level worlds in the computer (vertical
exteriority) but also to one's fellow inhabitants of the
world (horizontal exteriority).

But the world may not be a mathematically
consistent machine after all. This is only a falsifiable
scientific hypothesis. Yet, as long as it has not been
falsified despite our best efforts, the hypothesis that the
other people we meet are 'just machines' can be upheld.
The hypothesis of omnipotence is irrefutable up to that
moment.

Many hypotheses are unrefuted, without this having
any consequences. Why should this particular hypothesis
be more important? Because refraining from misusing the
infinite power of exteriority is holy. 'Holy' means giving
without taking, pure benevolence.

**Adrien Sina (F)**
Transitions Amorphes

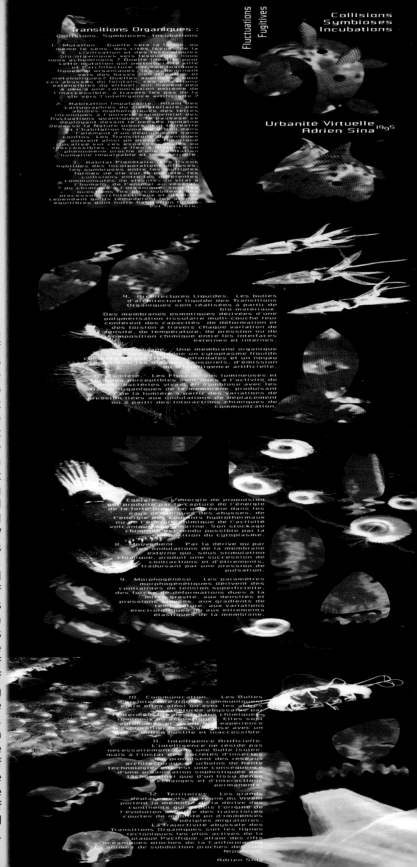

Legal Projects of a Planetary Territory of Entrenching Rights and Duties / – of the Asylum Right 'No frontier' and the Right of Just and Legitimate Causes. / – of Public Space, of the Attachment of Men and Places, of a Right against the Uprooting Force. / – of the World Habitat and Civilization Heritage. / – of Territories without Earth, Immaterial Spaces and Virtual Urbanity. / – of Human Works, Works of Human Civilizations. / – Works of the Living, of the Genetic Heritage of Evolutionary Life, of the Right of the Living Communities, of the Right of Coexistence, of the Coevolution and the Interdependence of Species. / – of the Collective Responsibility of Peoples and Governments.

*The accident and the kiss* would perhaps be a better title for this note. What has not been covered here is the fragrance of the TV set. Another word for it is charm. People who act fairly are irresistibly charming. And, conversely, acting fairly is not possible without seeing the irresistible charm in the soul of the potential victim.

A final point concerns the relationship between the two stories that have been told. The first story was about the fairness of a machine towards another machine (compassion on the level of science). The second story was about becoming aware of the existence of one's own TV set and its indestructibility (and about the fact of ceasing to be afraid of the assignment-attributing instance). Both stories were called *the kiss*. Is this correct?

Strangely enough, the two stories are identical. Again, this identity was seen by Descartes. Refraining from misusing an infinite power is also an emancipatory act. It does not prove that you are equal to the gods but that the gods are not afraid of your acting in a manner reserved for a god. This was Descartes' famous proof of the 'non-malignancy' of heaven.

Acting fairly and seeing one's own indestructibility are one and the same thing. The mouse and the elephant went for a stroll, and the elephant inadvertently stepped on the mouse. He was awfully concerned but the mouse with its last whisper told him: "Don't worry, the same thing has happened to me before." There is a bittersweet smile in this. Is it more bitter or more sweet?

To conclude, the notion of accident is one of the most difficult to face squarely. We went in three circles around the hot mush in order not to get burnt like a kitten. Life is infinitely more dangerous than we usually think. There are pains that do not ache at all (like having lost a child in an accident), which one would nevertheless trade in for virtually any real pain. One such child wanted to build a time machine when grown up. Color shines. The Now shines. The TV set shines. The elephant is still wondering what the mouse had in mind.

Acknowledgements

I would like to thank Andreas Broeckmann for his support. He suggested the phrase "the interface as an accident machine". For J.O.R.

**182**

# Matrices d'une Éthique Planétaire
## Transitions Amorphes

A - Première-Partie :
Projets Juridiques du Territoire de Droit,
d'un Territoire Planétaire de l'Enracinement
des Droits et des Devoirs.
Articles A-1 à A-5.

B - Deuxième Partie :
Projets Juridiques du Droit d'Asile Sans Frontière
et du Droit des Causes Justes et Légitimes.
Articles B-1 à B-5.

C - Troisième Partie :
Projet Juridique du Patrimoine Mondial des
Actions Quotidiennes ou Anonymes en Faveur
du Droit, de l'Équité et de la Paix.
Articles C-1 à C-5.

D - Quatrième Partie :
Projets Juridiques de l'Espace Mondial
d'un Droit contre le Déracinement Forcé,
des Êtres humains, des Hommes et de l'Exode,
d'un Territoire de Partage sans Appropriation.
Articles D-1 à D-6.

E - Cinquième Partie :
Projets Juridiques du Territoire de la Ville
et du Patrimoine Mondial de l'Habitat et
des Civilisations.
Articles E-1 à E-8.

F - Sixième Partie :
Projets Juridiques des Territoires sans Terre,
des Espaces Immatériaux et Planétaires,
de l'Urbanité Virtuelle.
Articles F-1 à F-8.

G - Septième Partie :
Projets Juridiques de l'Œuvre Humaine,
de l'Œuvre des Civilisations Humaines,
de l'Œuvre d'une Ethnie ou d'une Minorité,
de l'Œuvre de Résistance ou de Sacrifice
d'un Peuple.
Articles G-1 à G-9.

H - Huitième Partie :
Projets Juridiques de l'Œuvre du Vivant,
du Patrimoine Génétique de la Vie Evolutive,
du Droit des Communautés du Vivant,
du Droit de la Coexistence, de la
Co-evolution et de l'Interdépendance
des Espèces.
Articles H-1 à H-6.

I - Neuvième Partie :
Projets Juridiques de l'Héritage Laissé à l'Habitation
Planétaire Future, d'une Notion de Responsabilité
Collective des Peuples, et des Gouvernements.
Articles I-1 à I-3.

J - Dixième Partie :
Projets Juridiques d'une Démocratie à l'échelle de
la Planète, de la Citoyenneté Politique des
Peuples de la Planète, du Parlement Planétaire
des Peuples et des Minorités.
Articles J-1 à J-16.

### Cybervilles, Mégavilles, Bidonvilles:
### L'œuvre humaine face à la mort géographique

Volet XI.   Matrices d'une Éthique Planétaire.
Pour une Reformulation de l'Œuvre Humaine

300.000 ans de maîtrise du feu, 30.000 ans d'histoire de l'art, 3.000 ans de philosophie, non même 300 ans de droits de l'Homme et de l'équité régit toujours autant sur Terre. De multiples questions s'imposent en averse, chaque fois que la pensée tente de porter un regard ample sur le réel et sa son horizon. Comment penser ensemble les paramètres aussi divergents de l'habitation terrestre face au foisonnement des favelas, bidonvilles et abris improvisés, du tissu interstitiel des centre-villes, la densité atonie des villes autrefois industrielles et prodigieuses, la dépradation d'une Cyberville unique et mondialisée? Comment affronter en politique ces si profondes potentialités humaines qui s'enracinent...

### "No Picture over There"** - L.A. Downtown

Le XXe siècle avait été défaillant quant à son invention urbaine. À peine conscient de cet échec, il s'était précipité dans la vie d'une urbanité manquante, d'un être-ensemble oublié qu'il recherchait dans l'inconnue urbanité virtuelle.

Le tissu social médiatisé plus, individus et territoires étaient atomisés, épars. Le paradigme de l'élimination, issu du Jeu-Vidéo, enveloppait le réel d'une constellation de défaillances, de gouffres éthiques et de glissements hégémoniques.

## Urbanité Virtuelle : Actions~Politiques~sur~le~Web
# http://www.planetary~ethics/
# virtual~parliament~of~minorities

Adrien Sina, 1995-96

[Site Planétaire / Site Web]

Préambule. L'Organisation des Nations Unis est une juxtaposition d'ordres étatiques qui ne représentent souvent même pas leurs Peuples et encore moins leurs Minorités...

### html/XI - Première Partie
### Missions du Parlement Virtuel des Peuples et des Minorités

Article XI-a...

### html/X2 - Deuxième Partie
### Un Parlement à Représentation Illimitée et à Localisation Fragmentée

### html/X3 - Troisième Partie
### Projet Juridique de la Saisine Citoyenne du Parlement des Peuples

### html/X4 - Quatrième Partie
### Charte de Non-violence pour une Éthique de la Paix

### html/X5 - Cinquième Partie
### Actions Politiques sur le Web

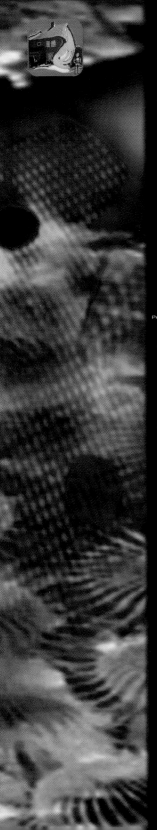

Éthique de l'Urgence

%20

□□□□□□□□□□□□□□□□□□□□□□□
□□□□□□□□□□□□□□□□□□□□
□□□□□□□□□□□□□□□□□□

Picture 69
Picture 70
Picture 71



001 002 003 004 005 006 9 01

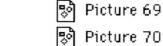

Fhotoshop™ 2.5.1

DocEdit 4.5 alias

 Sylling's HD

# Reset ;

NIVO_1

000,0000

●●● ●● ● Report

☐☐☐☐
☐☐ copy
☐☐ copy 2

# IO_Dencies – Questioning Urbanity

*Knowbotic Research*

The project *IO_Dencies – Questioning Urbanity* deals with the possibilities of agency, collaboration and construction in translocal and networked environments. The project looks at urban settings in different megacities, analyzes the forces present in particular local urban situations, and offers experimental interfaces for dealing with these local force fields. Cities like Tokyo and Sao Paolo were chosen to bring about a confrontation between different cultural environments which suggest specific interrelations between traditional ways of building, economic and political conditions, and electronic communication structures.

The contact with the concrete city environment is maintained through working with local architects and urban planners who deal with the problems and challenges of the city they live in. The aim is not, however, to develop advanced tools for architectural and urban design, but to create events through which it becomes possible to rethink urban planning and construction and arrive at a notion of process-oriented collaborative agency. We try to engage with the friction and the heterogeneity of the urban environment by merging the closed and rational system of digital computer networks with the incoherent, rhizomatic structure of the urban space. The project investigates the productivity of such merged, translocal networks as tools for the creation of topologies of interventions and connective actions.

## IO_Dencies Tokyo

In Tokyo, the central Shimbashi area was analyzed in collaboration with local architects. Several 'zones of intensities' were selected: Ginza-Shopping Area, Imperial Hotel, Fish Market, Highway Entrance, Hamarikyu Garden + Homeless Area, Shimbashi Station, Hinode Passenger Terminal, JR-Appartment House, World Trade Center.

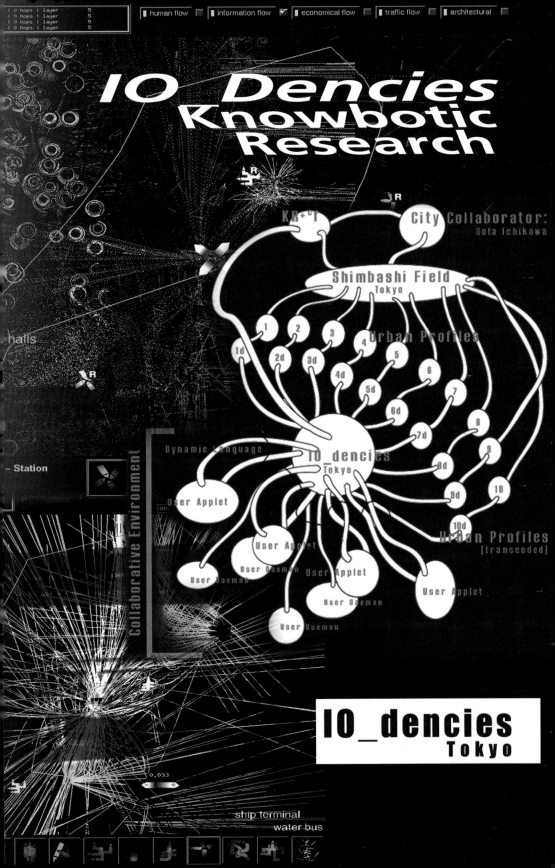

In these zones, the local architect set out several qualities of urban movements (architectural, economic, human, information, traffic) into a notation system.

These movements and flows and the ways in which they interfere with each other were digitally coded as dynamic particle flows that can be observed and manipulated through the Internet. On a so-called Java-applet, users can introduce a series of specially designed movement attractors into the urban flows. Each of the attractors has a different function in manipulating or modifying those processes. These functions include: confirming, opposing, drifting, confusing, repulsing, organizing, deleting, merging, weakening etc.

Participants in this project can develop hypothetical urban dynamics, based on the local notations. As soon as one participant starts working on and modifying the urban profile by changing the particle streams with movement attractors, a search engine in the background starts looking in the IP-space for other participants with similar manipulation interests and connects to them. They become aware of each other's presence, the activated movement attractors of connected participants will also appear in the applet. Some of these can be 'absent' users whose activities are remembered and reactivated by the system some time after the intervention took place. If one or more participants are found, the characters of the data movements can be changed collaboratively in tendencies, they can be made stronger, weaker, more turbulent, denser, etc.

Streams of urban movements can shift between dynamic clusters of participants, chains of events pass through and disturb the personal construction process. Participants can develop new processes or react to already existing, ongoing ones. However, every participant will work on and experience a singular and different urban segment.

# IO_Dencies
# Sao Paulo

In the Tokyo project, a single architect did the 'mapping' of the city, and the streams of forces were mapped and set out in a notation system on the basis of

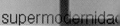

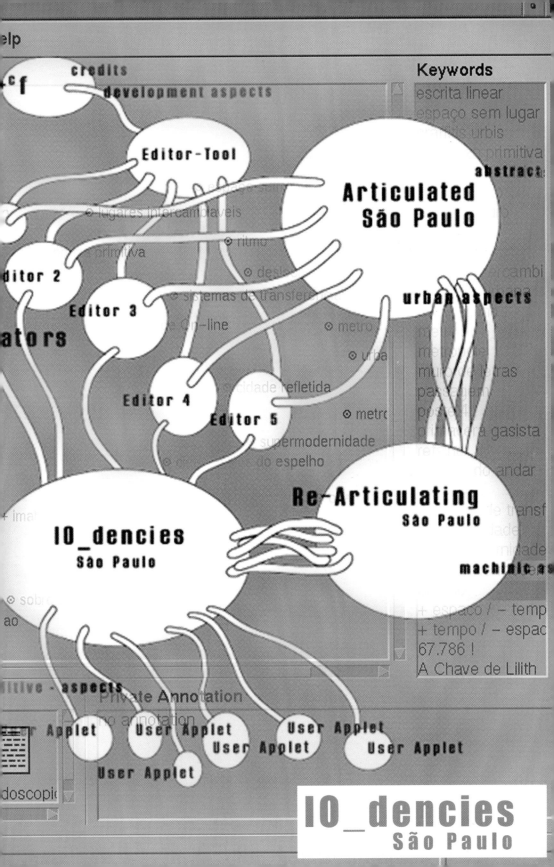

the topological structure of the city. The Sao Paulo project, on the other hand, enables the articulation of subjective experiences of the city through a collaborative process that was made part of the project's development. Over a period of several months, a group of young architects and urbanists from Sao Paulo, the 'editors', provided the content and dynamic input. They are local people who approach the city of Sao Paulo by asking themselves "what are the forces that shape the city? What are the processes that create temporarily visible manifestations within the city?" The editors collect material (texts, images, sounds) based on the situation they are in at the moment and their personal urban experience. This material is put into a database by means of a specially designed editor tool. This tool also allows the editors to build individual conceptual 'maps' in which each editor can construct the relations between the different materials in the data-pool according to his or her subjective perception of the city.

On the computational level, connectivities are created between the different maps of the editors, a process that is driven by algorithmic self-organization whose rules are determined by the choices that the editors make. Over several months, the collaborative editorial work in the database generates zones of intensities and zones of tension, which are visualized as force fields and turbulences. The participants can modify and influence these electronic urban movements, force fields and intensities on an abstract, visual level, as well as on a content-based, textual level. The objects in this force field are purely symbolic and conceptual, and the parameters are not spatial or territorial, but relational and depend on the editors' approach to their urban material.

The visualization shows the intensity of relational forces in the data-pool as they are being constructed and transformed by the self-organization. A specially designed interface table makes it possible to experience the zones of intensity not only visually and acoustically, but also as physical force fields by means of a 'knob' with a magnetic mechanism which can be dragged and pushed over the projected visualization. The knob also has functions that make it possible to zoom in on and out of the visualization. When zooming in, the keywords referring to specific materials in the database appear. By selecting them, it is possible to see or hear the respective textual,

O_dencies
Tokyo

visual or auditory material on a separate monitor.

This engagement with the project and its material is fed back into the database and influences the relational forces within the project's digital environment. The networked project facilitates the fusion of reception and construction by several connected translocal users.

# Inflammable Interfaces

The discursive practice of the *IO_Dencies* project places itself outside any architectural framework. The urban is construed as a machinic assemblage which consists not so much of built forms and infrastructures, but of a heterogeneous field consisting of lines of forces, lines of action and interaction.

These lines form the coordinates of an urban topology that is not chiefly based on the human body and its movements in space, but on relational acts and events within the urban machine. These can be economic, political, technological or tectonic processes, as well as acts of communication and articulation, or symbolic and expressive acts. This urban field is therefore quite different from the physically defined spaces of events and movements. Rather, we are interested in what the relation between the spaces of movement, the spaces of events and the relational, machinic 'spaces' might be. It does not make sense to see the city and the networks as opposites. Knowbotic Research is interested in finding models of agency for and in complex dynamic systems. We see the city not as a representation of the urban forces, but as the interface to these urban forces and processes. Therefore, the city features not as a representation, but as an interface which has to be made and remade all the time.

The interfaces that we build are developed to allow for collaboration – they are open interfaces, i.e. tools that can be changed and improved through use. They are adaptive to both the different participants and the ongoing processes. What is offered on an experiential level through the interfaces is not a representation of the forces and processes themselves. The interfaces attempt to give the users' actions and interventions into the force fields a presence over time.

# Masaki Fujihata
## Nuzzle Afar
### – Distant Affairs and Greetings –

*Nuzzle Afar* is a shared 3D virtual environment art work, using digital networking technology. It realizes a new type of communication space where people can meet and talk to each other as avatars from several telematic immersive computer terminals.

Two terminals are set up at each distant location, in this case at the Zentrum für Kunst und Medientechnologie in Karlsruhe/D and at the Dutch Electronic Art Festival, DEAF98, in Rotterdam/NL. Each terminal has a large video projection and a pedestal with a TrackBall as a navigation interface, and a microphone for conversation. Video cameras are placed near the screen, recording the people playing with the TrackBall and the immediate surroundings. The computers coordinating the communication between the different terminals are connected through ISDN lines.

In the virtual environment that is projected, each terminal is represented by an avatar, i.e. an object hovering in the virtual space. Each of the video images from the terminals is pasted onto the surface of an avatar, so that on the 'faces' of the other avatars one can see the visitors at the respective terminals.

When navigating around the virtual space, the avatars leave a line trace. This trace can be used to find another avatar. When you 'catch' one of these traces, the computer automatically brings you to the other avatar by following its trace. The line traces remain in the space for several minutes, describing the space through the movements that have passed through it.

The view one gets of the virtual environment and of the other avatars is controlled by rolling the TrackBall and thus navigating one's own avatar. When two avatars get so close that they merge, an alternative world is born. This world is closed, and

Following Otto Rössler we can say that the world is not 'the world in which we live', but the interface, through which we perceive and act. The city is not 'the world of urban forces' but the interface through which we interact and negotiate with urban forces. And the electronic tools are not 'the world of data and information' in which we now live because the 'real world' doesn't function any longer, but the interface to certain symbolic and expressive processes, and thus to existing urban processes. The aim is not so much to insist on the differences between these 'worlds', but to articulate the differences and overlaps between the various interfaces. In the interface, certain 'distortions' appear because one is surrounded by different processes unfolding on different time scales. These distortions occur through the temporary coupling of these processes in the interface. To allow for such distortions and to make them possible, that's what could make the interface 'inflammable'.

A typical feature of the forms of agency that evolve in networked environments is the fact that they are neither individualistic nor collective, but rather connective. While individualistic and collective diagrams assume a single vector, a single will that guides the trajectory of the action, the connective diagram is mapped onto a machinic assemblage. Whereas the collective is ideally determined by an intentional and empathetic interaction between its components, the connective is an assemblage which is based on any kind of machinic interaction and is therefore more versatile, more open, and based on the heterogeneity of its members.

A connective interface does not combine functionalities. It creates a possibility for heterogeneous actions and distortions and integrates them without making them functional. It is an open interface that leaves room for turbulences and unpredictable events.

The distortions are not generated by the networks, but they can be given a certain presence and an effective form in the interface, without necessarily becoming visible. Complex working conditions like those in the *IO_dencies* experiment in Sao Paulo can result in a great deal of irritation between the participating local urbanists and the producing institutions, the programmers, the hardware and software, misunderstandings and wrong expectations. These distortions are present in the project

the form of avatar changes into a simpler form, becoming just a moveable rectangle video screen suspended in the virtual space. This virtual screen is controlled from an outside, objective perspective, so that one can now see oneself on that screen. The two avatars are locked together and there is no description about how they can return to the former public space. They have to communicate and collaborate to find a key to split up again.

The space of the virtual environment is completely abstract. Several different worlds overlap in the same space, each being identified by different characteristics like density or forces which move the avatars automatically in some direction, like a current. The worlds are sharing the same space like parallel universes. Visitors can observe what goes on in the other world from their own world, yet, they cannot share the experience of what happens in the other world. To move from one world to the other, one has to use key objects which function like worm holes, connecting the parallel worlds.

The aim of this work is to abstract the communication space. The virtual space can be examined interactively by participants at the networked terminals at each installation site. *Nuzzle Afar* is an extended version of an earlier shared virtual environment art piece, *Global Interior Project* (1996), which dealt with the differences between real space and virtual space. Global Interior Project made it possible to compare the differences between a face-to-face conversation in real space and an avatar-to-avatar conversation in virtual space. Yet, the reactions and conversations of participants were mostly simple and minimal, such as "Hello, Where are you?", and "Can you hear me?". In this virtual environment, the purpose of communication was unclear because the function of avatar did not afford a certain role to the participant. This made the space meaningless. In contrast, *Nuzzle Afar* tries to afford the role of play to participants who have to explore the space in order to discover the key of communication. That is the function of this space.

Concept: Masaki Fujihata.
Software: Takeshi Kawashima
Presented in cooperation with:
Institute for Visual Media, ZKM, Karlruhe (D).

without causing it to collapse. On the contrary, they generate new developments. It is vital to become sensitive to the weakness of interfaces and the potential forces that they bring forth. Our aim is to recognize them and turn them into 'tendential' forces (*IO_dencies*) which may become effective sooner or later. Drawing on Guattari's notion of the machinic, we describe the interface as a machine in a complex aggregate of other machines. Connectivity can, in this context, mean different things: the combination of functionalities; the collapse and opening up in a moment of conflict or rupture; or diversion and repulsion where no interaction can take place. What surprises us is this new, differentiated vocabulary that is emerging in relation to working with electronic networks: the interface ties together, folds, collapses, repulses, extinguishes, weaves, knots. All these activities, which are obviously not germane to our projects, make it necessary to rethink 'networking' as a multi-functional, highly differentiated set of possible actions.

# The Urban Machine

The urban is a machine that connects and disconnects, articulates and disarticulates, frames and releases. It gives the impression that it can be channeled and controlled, that it can be ordered and structured. The city is always an attempt at realizing this order, which, however, is nothing but a temporary manifestation of the urban.

The machinic urban is always productive, as opposed to the 'anti-production' of a fixed city structure. But its productivity lies in the creation of discontinuities and disruptions, it dislodges a given order and runs against routines and expectations. The urban manifests itself in a mode of immediacy and incidentality, confronting a structure with other potentialities and questioning its given shape. We can clearly observe this tension between the urban and the city wherever the city appears dysfunctional and unproductive. But the urban machine is also productive at invisible levels, e.g. when real estate speculations that disrupt an area within the city, or when a natural catastrophe or political instabilities causes a rapid influx of large numbers of people. In these

# Herwig Weiser
## zgodlocator

1. Decoupling materials from their industrial processing, usage and recycling. (analogue digital-analogue-transform

2. Computer-based movement control of a system consisting of granules (hardware sands and sauces (reactive substances): impulse magnetism, electricity, short circuit. (paradise

3. Sound sampling of grid-shaped hardware assemblages and their transformations. (live

4. An installation with a variable configuration of spatial segments: interaction, programming feedback

Disused computer hardware is dismantled and sorted (cases, hard drives, cabling, processors etc.) for recycling processes. Consequently, it is granulated and mechanically separated according to material properties. In the zgodlocator project, these hardware sands are treated chemically and magnetically and are thus conditioned to react in specific ways. These aggregations are placed into and between different types of frames, i.e. modular, combinable and adaptable spatial segments. Test beds for the divine creator machine on its way back to its hardware nature

Grids of electro-magnetic systems underneath these frames trigger patterned transformations of the 'granular landscapes', varying according to the type and the composition of the granules. A phylum machine: matter and energy thrown into accidental form. The physical and chemical forces of the system externally stimulate the materials to take on spontaneous energetic states. They transform the granules into singular and momentous sculptural accumulations. Through holes and across thresholds, the activated granules are able to undulate between and inside the parted/connected spatial frame constructions

cases, the 'finance machine' and the 'tectonic machine' have an impact on a local urban situation.

The human inhabitants of cities are not the victims of such machinic processes, but they are part of them and follow, enhance or divert given urban flows and forces. Contemporary analytical methods of the urban environment no longer distinguish between buildings, traffic and social functions, but describe the urban as a continuously intersecting, n-dimensional field of forces: buildings are flowing, traffic has a transmutating shape, social functions form a multi-layered network. The individual and social groups are co-determining factors within these formations of distributed power.

The machinic character of the urban means that there are multiple modes of intervention, action and production in the urban formation. The relationship between space and action is of crucial importance. There seems to be reluctance on the part of many architects and urban planners to consider 'action' as a relevant category. Rather, built spaces are much more closely identified with, and it seems, made for, certain types of behavior. The distinction between behavior and action is a significant one, behavior being guided by a set of given habits, rules, directives and channels, while action denotes a more unchanneled and singular form of moving in and engaging with a given environment. The suggestion here would be to move from thinking about a topology of objects, forms and behavior towards a topology of networks, a topology of agency, of events and of subjectivity.

## Translocalities

What is referred to as the global is, in most cases, based on a technical infrastructure rather than on real-life experiences. The electronic networks form a communication structure that allows for a fast and easy exchange of data over large distances. But the way in which people use these networks is strongly determined by the local contexts in which they live, so that, as a social and cultural space, the electronic networks are not so much a global but a translocal structure which connects many local situations and creates a heterogeneous translocal stratum, rather than a homogeneous global stratum. The activities on the networks are the product of

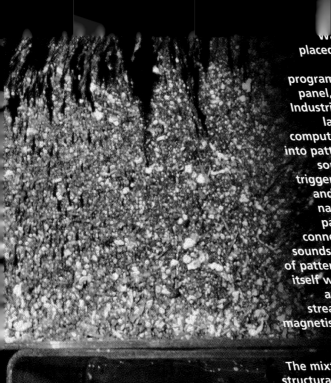

Walking among the frames that are placed close to the ground. The control devices use data entry via a pre-programmed computer, a manual control panel, and the feedback of sound data. Industrial security norms apply. Granular landscapes arranged by sound: the computer trans-substantiating the sound into patterns, from one frame to another, sound short-circuiting the frames. A trigger panel makes it possible to select and mix pattern eventualities and to navigate them over and against the patterns initiated by the computer-connected, feedback-based 'hardware sounds'. In the unpredictable interaction of pattern vs. pattern, the magnet system itself will react indifferently. Instabilities are created in between the energy streams as they absorb electricity and magnetism and as patterns are overlaying each other

The mixtures react with discontinuous re-structurations to non-linear magnetic field and flow transformation, triggered by impulse magnets and electrical currents. In a separate frame, magnetic fluid (ferrofluid) are mixed with different type of transparent oil layers, each with different densities and chemical features. In every layer, melted hardware is mixed with the magnetic liquid and hardware components. Two bass loudspeakers are connected by a U-pipe and placed inside this 'sauce-frame'. Modulating the sound frequencies creates waves and counter-waves in the sauce-hardware-layer assemblage

The two main processes active in the spatial segments are short impulses or shocks (magnetic, electrical) and variable flows (streams, vibrations). They generate a context of motion and transformation that propels external/internal influences into self-consuming assemblages of force effects

In co-operation with Bob O'Kane (Otherspace) Albert Bleckmann (electronics and programming) Sandeep Mehta (hardware re-melt), Roger Plattmacks

multiple social and cultural factors emerging from this connective local-translocal environment. We don't deny the existence of the global but see it as a weaker and less interesting field for developing new forms of agency.

There are local formations in which certain behavioral patterns emerge and translocal connections make it possible to connect such specific local situations to see how the heterogeneities of these localities can be communicated and to determine whether they are maintained or not in a translocal situation. Against the worldwide homogenization of the ideology of globalism one should set translocal actions which are connected but can maintain their multiple local differences.

The *IO_dencies* project is based on local situations, and we are looking for the productivity of the interface in the movement from the local to the translocal. In this continuing process, we test the possibility of translating ideas and cultural content, the local points of friction, and also the heterogeneity of what is often seen as a more or less homogeneous local cultural identity. At the same time, we recognize that globalization is a reality, and that purely local interfaces are insufficient. The global generates circumstances which make it necessary to open up the local to the translocal in order to develop effective forms of agency.

We were intrigued by the polemical hypothesis about the *Generic City* that Rem Koolhaas formulated in 1994. The Generic City is a city without a history, without the burden of an identity, the suburban nightmares and recent Asian boomtowns viewed through sober, cynical, pragmatic – dare we say Dutch – eyes. Implicit in Koolhaas' suggestion is the relentless growth and unstoppable expansion of the Generic City. In the 21st century, he seems to say, the Generic City will become the norm rather than the exception.

For the project *IO_Dencies*, the Generic City would be the counter-argument to the necessity to develop tools and interfaces that are locally specific, responding to cultural and social circumstances which distinguish one place from another. In taking the *IO_dencies* project from Tokyo to its next destination, Sao Paulo, the level and quality of difference, i.e. specificity, was at the heart of our concern.

It very quickly became clear to us that cities are or

become 'generic' only in certain segments. Like many other cities with a colonialist past, Sao Paulo is an intensely segmented city, with social, racial, economic and cultural borders dividing it like the Berlin Wall – a metaphor that we heard quoted quite frequently. This segmentation protects the Generic City, while other quarters, or segments located outside the city boundaries, are decidedly 'un-generic', 'dirty' and 'specific'.

The Generic City has no identity. Yet, identity is not something that is the same for a city as a whole. People possess or develop a clear sense of 'home', even in the most decrepit neighborhoods. Local people have an intuitive knowledge that allows them to distinguish between a street in Kreuzberg and Mitte, between Manhattan and Brooklyn, between Bras and Pinheiros. The identity that is constructed in such urban environments is a heterogeneous composite of different symbolic matrices, social, cultural, familial, that are local as much as they are translocal. A possible counter-hypothesis to Koolhaas would therefore be that only few places are generic cities, and only a fraction of these will remain generic for longer periods of time. The generic stage is not the final stage, but one of the first characteristics of many human settlements.

The project *IO_dencies* asks how, suspended between local and global activities, urban characteristics are enhanced, transformed or eradicated, and it investigates whether the extension of the urban environment into electronic spaces might allow for changed qualities of urbanity. Is communication technology the catalyst of the Generic City, or is it the motor for another, transformed notion of urbanity and public space?

In Tokyo, the technological permeation of the social space is accepted without the social resistance that we find in Europe. Technology is used especially to make the ritualized social communication even more perfect, smooth and characterless or 'generic'. Digitization is supposed to prevent any kind of social noise or economic disturbance. In Tokyo, the *IO_dencies* project therefore developed software structures that could create a noisy, irritating network of experimental events between the urban components.

In Sao Paulo, on the other hand, we were

# KIT
# COTIS

Contemporary technologies trace a curve
through time and space, a trajectory from
the earth towards the heavens. Gathered
beneath the Genitron clock in Paris
counting down the seconds until midnight
2000, our eyes turn upwards towards the
sky in the hope that the twentieth century
will hit escape velocity – the techno-
theology of the ejector seat. What is
forgotten in this gesture, or perhaps
denied, is the parabolic curve of gravity's
rainbow: the trajectory back towards the
earth in the swan-dive of an inevitable
vertigo. The Arc of the Covenant. The Arc of
Triumph. The (meta)physics of what-goes-
up. They constitute the sacred sites of
modern crash location, and they are the
media-spectacles which *COTIS* seek to invert
and infect.

*COTIS* stands for *Cult Of The Inserter Seat*.
We are part of a global collective who seek
to reintegrate the body into the material
matrix. In search of the ultimate fusion
between humachines and the plenum, it
becomes imperative to invert the notion of
innocence inherent in any 'return to the
earth'. We propose to do this by reversing
the telescoping of distance offered by high
speed travel and the spectacular vectors of
the media-industrial complex. By digging
into the earth and continuing the
momentum of the crash, *COTIS* articulates
the transcendent trigonometry of
technology. These tunnels create a network
which links into a constellation of impact
points to create a zodiac for subterranean
stargazers. Thus one tunnel from a
particular crash site may intersect with one
from another, forging a rhizomatic network
of extended terminal velocities. *COTIS*
containers mark these nodal points in a
gesture designed both to orientate and
punctuate. This reverse cosmology
navigates the digital transarchitecture of
the Internet, affording an opportunity for
organization still based on that of the
smouldering wreckage of the surface

confronted with a ruptured, fragmented and exploding urban space (in terms of social/political/economic inequalities and exclusions). Here, there were fewer technological strategies, the public sphere knew a different order and there were different parameters of public forms of agency. For *IO_dencies* Sao Paulo, we created possibilities for the collaborative articulation of urban texts and experiences. The Sao Paulo interface allows the participants and Internet users to express, condense and confront urban experiences on several concrete and intuitive levels.

# Machinic Agency

In a previous Knowbotic Research project, *Anonymous Muttering* (1996), the question of possibilities of collaborative agency and intervention in urban environments was posed from a very intuitive, yet also rather critical point of view. The project confronted the visitors with an experience of high intensity of urban processes, which they could influence without being able to control them. The frustration sparked by the lack of feedback on one's action highlighted the degree to which processes of subjectification rely on the feedback that we receive on our actions.

Contemporary cities are covered with successful and failed attempts at leaving such traces and creating such feedback loops. The noise from roaring cars and ghetto blasters, the ubiquity of graffiti and tags, stickers and other lasting marks, and even temporary and permanent pieces of architecture are clear attempts at creating a lasting visibility and presence in the urban environment. Viewed from a cultural and political perspective, however, this kind of visibility is rather powerless if it is not coupled with opportunities to act and intervene in the public arena.

The aim of the *IO_Dencies* project is to find out whether it is possible, to develop electronic interfaces which open up new forms of agency in a situation where the city itself is being deprived of many public functions, and whether network interfaces can become useful in local as well as in global contexts. Yet, how can agency be realized when taking into account the machinic? What

Beneath the ashes, beneath the dust, the nomadic tunnellers of *COTIS* map the hypertextual co-ordinates of a cartography which survey a global Bermuda triangle, now a more abstract form.

In exposing the Enlightenment logic underlying 'air-traffic control', *COTIS* extends the legacy of human inscription upon the earth – the physical graffiti of a transitory presence. From chalk drawings on hillsides and paths trodden in deserts through centuries of architecture we have left our marks on the surface of the planet. Scars of other possibilities.

The scattered corpo-reality of impact zones produce a liminal space in which it becomes possible to retrace what it means to be mortal in the millennial moment. The body incorporates the crash, not the other way around. Thus we compel the gaze to turn from the sky to the ground, to the intra-terrestrial life-forms which fertilize the soil of future auto-pilots.

'Shock' comes from the middle-Dutch word 'schokken' – to collide. Only now the screen-fatigue of over-exposure and empathy burn-out necessitates a different strategic relationship to the sacrificial victims of the symbolic economy. As our fragile mammal brains try to decode signals beamed at us with increasing speed and accuracy, we find we become projectiles ourselves in the scopophilic logic of hyper-reality. Thus in order to counter the rhetoric of extinction we must push the fatal(istic) curve of the thanatic asymptote across the axis of its own complicity with the death drive. In simpler terms, *COTIS* exposes the closed-circuit of mediated mourning, along with the silent satellite witnesses of cathode addiction. The medium may well be the message, but the messenger moves more swiftly when there is the scent of blood and smoke in the air. The narrative baton passes from the crash through the lens to the studio to the television to the blood-shot eye in one fluid pan-optical movement. There is precious little time to blink (indeed the clockwork orange has been digitally upgraded for the information era, and we find we cannot blink).

would it mean to say that acting is the movement of the subject in the machine? What are the points of friction at which the subject and agency manifest themselves?

Acting is the production of friction, or fraction, in machinic processes. If the interface is the point and the moment of action and experience, it is also the medium that brings forth the subject and shapes its world. An interesting aspect of the connective interface would be that, through its coupling of different single-subject action-universes, it makes it possible to experience the tendential that is realized through the movement in the interface. The model of agency we are trying to realize would then be the building of connective interfaces that are sensitive and reactive to both the actions and the presence of others, as well as to the surrounding processes. There wouldn't have to be a 'collective consciousness' but only the possibility of active and responsible cooperation between different people.

*http://www.khm.de/people/krcf/IO/*

IO_dencies – Questioning Urbanity, Tokio 1997

Co-produced with Canon ARTLAB. Realization with Detlev Schwabe. Special support by Academy of Media Arts Cologne and Ministery for Research and Higher Education NRW.

IO-dencies – Sao Paulo 1998

Co-produced with ZKM/Institute for Visual Media, in the context of eSCAPE/ESPRIT long term research project 25377. Special support by Goethe Institut Sao Paulo, Haus der Kulturen der Welt Berlin, V2_, Ars Electronica Center, Linz (A), Wilhelm Lehmbruck Museum, Duisburg (D), Academy of Media Arts Cologne (D).
Technical concept & application software development: Andreas Schiffler and Detlev Schwabe, ZKM. CGI Interface: Andreas Weymer. Audio application development: KR+cF.
Urban editors: Fabio Duarte, Artur Lara, Sandro Canavezzi, Polise de Marchi, Renato Cymbalista, Keila Costa, Maria Elvira, Marcos Godoi, Maurício Ribeiro da Silva, Reinaldo de Jesus Cônsoli.

*COTIS* both initiate and interrupt this news media circuit, playing with the Olympic torch of disaster footage which the spectacle attempts to keep alight, lest there be no disasters left to (un)cover. The space shuttle explosion marks the high-fire mark of this fetishistic history. Indeed, the fact that the social psyche can tolerate – even crave – the existential violence of the black box is both an abject lesson, and one of the most important moments of post-alienated estrangement. The black box contains the sacred Scripture of a terminal identity which becomes encoded onto the recording technologies of the day. Here are etched the famous last words which can be looped and re-played for aesthetic and forensic purposes. The ghost in the machine is nothing supernatural, and yet it haunts the rigorous mortis of our post-mortem era. These are missives from the missile: the ultimate articulation before the moment of impact. *COTIS* recognizes the symbolic charge of such statements in the context of crash-culture. The black box sound-byte circulates in the media as an accursed share; the devil's part of a system which thrives on its sacrificial inclusion into the logic of late capitalism – like the terminal portraits of a lacerated Princess. Indeed, in the post-Diana mediascape it is impossible to recover the obsolescent innocence before the Fall.

*COTIS* is anti-apocalypse (although not necessarily anti-apocalyptic). Rejecting the neo-Cartesian discourse of technologies such as Virtual Reality and the neo-imperialism of space exploration, *COTIS* burrows into the earth to bury its containers and members in a step towards reversing the cosmology of teleological narratives. We rejoice in the memetic panic behind the Y2K problem: the millennial bug which threatens to freeze the entire system. This meta-crash coded into the main-frame all those years ago is a premise and a limit-horizon for the current installation. Whether the Y2K bug is the result of poetic myopia or a subconscious faith in the new millennium, the collision counters contemporary technocultural hubris in the libidinal economy. *COTIS* speak in tongues in order to distract those who would re-wire the Tower of Babylon.

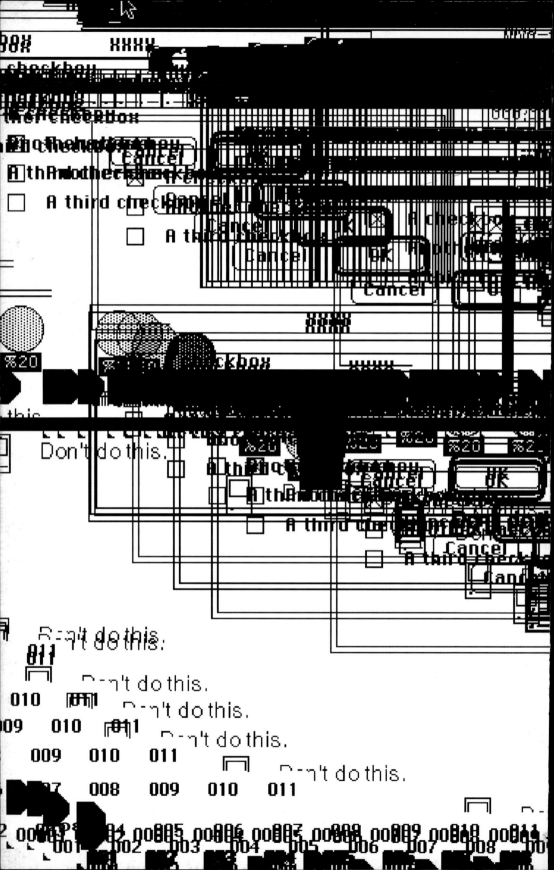

An email interview with N. Katherine Hayles by
Arjen Mulder

*AM*: What is good about accidents?

**KH**: Accidents are, by definition, events that have not been planned. Often these events lead to annoyance or even catastrophe, but sometimes they open windows on new understandings. Many technical developments came about because of accidents. For example, while a chemist is not watching, rubber boils over and, under the direct heat of the burner, becomes much harder. The chemist realizes that as a result of this accident, he can use heat deliberately to harden rubber, the process now called vulcanization that is essential for most modern uses of rubber. Or another example: a chemist uses a recipe that doesn't turn out as he expects, yielding a glue that isn't very sticky. Rather than simply label this event an accident, he starts thinking about possible applications for not very sticky glue and eventually comes up with post-it notes. Plans are absolutely essential, of course, but when plans turn out exactly as we expect, we don't learn anything new. Accidents have the capacity to reveal things undreamt-of and paths unknown.

*AM*: From what point of view can an event be seen as an accident, and from what point of view as an orderly event?

**KH**: This is an interesting question because it suggests that point of view is essential in deciding whether an event is an 'accident' or not. When a plan is in place, and an event happens which has not been anticipated, we call that event an 'accident' because it does not coincide with our expectations. From other points of view, the 'accident' may well be seen as an orderly event. For example, we now know that rubber hardens under direct heat; what first appeared as an accident has become an expectation. The 'accidental' is not so much a fixed category as the boundary between the known and unknown, the expected and the unexpected; the 'accidental' happens where waves break on the beach of knowledge. Before a wave

# Click it.  Click it Good.

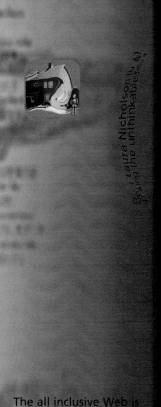

 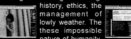 

Conjecture a thing that that included everything By leaning into this human could be satiated. Architecture, a wholly word used to define a collective entity, is at present best manifested making of a building. A building takes in every endeavor of humanity could reflect every facet of cultural wherewithal, a thing ever done, being done, and might be done in the future imaginary place, the hunger of being abstract by the - be it law history, ethics, the management of lowly weather. The these impossible nature of humanity. spirit, elements, money, politics and people, art, science and the great works of architecture go part way to meet ideals: they find a way to pull together the librarie inclusive, touching every process world, perhaps The Greek temple builders was al making a singular object that was capable o corner of the psyche, inside and out, and in the created a massive "n" dimensional vision of th an early version of a whopping great big world-wide website

Enter, unannounced, the World Wide Web: the enabler of encyclopedic space that would find the trappings of built fabric stifling and archaic. It is no coincidence that today's information organizers unabashedly hand out business cards with the word Architect stated as their profession. For them the word 'Architect' says it all, a way of thought that is truly accessible and pleasurable to do. They make and organize space that anyone can enter and get a buzz from. Theirs is a place where time forward backward and time around are given value, they have the tools that make the profession of builders seem inadequate and pedantic.

After hitting the Web, experiencing architecture is never quite the same. A visit to a Gothic cathedral takes on the guise of logging onto a brilliantly organized website. The mouse's cursor has retrained the eye to glide over the surface of the building. The three entrance portals are surveyed and one is clicked to gain access to someplace new. On passing through the portal the eye again clicks on a sculpture to face, and inside the cavernous know more about it void of the cathedral the mind darts about clicking on everything, both objects and ambiance. The hyper-visitor has just crashed architecture's party, to un-tech the well manicured encyclopedic nature of experience.

For someone used to clicking in the public realm, some architectural space are better than others. A seasoned clicker goes berserk in a 16th century Studiolo a tiny room favored by Italian Dukes in which their whole being is described in wood intarsia by an X, Y, & Z-dimensional cross reference of figures stabilized by perspectival building-scapes. Wherever the eye roams there is something to do.

A clicker's worst nightmare is Modernism, buildings devoid of compound clues about the intricacies of human endeavor. The Modernists posited that we need only singular examples of phenomena to represent related experience. A glass vase with a few blooms is enough to represent nature, a few walls are good enough to be a metaphor of the history of containment, and a hovering flat roof is adequate to keep the weather mute Modernism's biggest mistake by far and proof of its Hubris Elemental reduction and the intolerant striving for purity are too much for humanity to bear, for simplification gives too few clues to stimulate the intricacies of life Today's Formic Blobists, who have attached themselves to Modernism's coat tails can do little to right this imbalance. Fearful of hypertext's mercurial black water, they resort to the electric frieze, displaying menus of discarded emotions, to fix the problem.

The clicker, a spatial guerrilla, has invented a new realm that is alert and receptive to something other than the sort of beauty that we have held dear for decades. A recognizable space today might be the structured action of walking down a corridor and clicking on a garbage can by bending the body down and plucking a piece of paper and reading its content thus being led to a realm that is outside of form. When a clicker visits the Parthenon in the flesh and stones, Elgin's Marbles are cut from London and effortlessly pasted to Athens, and should a story of each figure be called for, its frame will be clicked for content. In 1911, when the world witnessed Picasso's Cubist paintings, it could not go back to what it used to know. Today, clickers present the same predicament, only this time the necessity for the builder's trowel to be the sole renderer of architectural space is being stared in the eye, and someone's about to blink.

The all inclusive Web is a way to pull together the libraric nature of humanity, the enabler of encyclopedic space. Today's information organizers are the architects, making and organizing space. The clicker, a spatial guerrilla, has invented a new realm that is alert and receptive to something other than the sort of beauty that we have held dear for decades. A clicker's worst nightmare is Modernism, buildings devoid of compound clues about the intricacies of human endeavor. After hitting the Web a visit to a cathedral takes on the guise of logging onto a brilliantly organized website.

# Ben Nicholson, Chicago U.S.A

with Peter Ippolito, and the community at IIT.

http://www.bennicholson.com

breaks, it is part of the undifferentiated mass of things about which we have no knowledge; as it breaks, it comes within the horizon of our experience but has not yet solidified into terra cognita.

*AM: So all accidents, either creative or catastrophical, are only accidents in the eye of the beholder? But now the accident has entered its age of digital reproducibility. How do you reckon (creative) accidents can be planned?*

**KH**: The problem with plans of any kind, of course, is that they are limited by our intentions, and our intentions are limited by what we (already) know. How to intentionally escape intention, without having our escape plans contaminated by precisely that which we are trying to elude? Which is to say, how to open ourselves to what we cannot imagine? John Cage's strategy was to invent 'chance operations' – operations that proceeded according to rules he had devised but whose outcomes he could not predict. Moreover, once having set these rules into play, he would go to astonishing lengths to carry them out precisely, lest his intention re-enter and contaminate the process. In many different ways, he tried to convey the message that the most interesting messages aren't messages at all but noise. As Vilém Flusser, and Claude Shannon before him said, information is what we don't expect.

Artificial life programs follow much the same strategy, and for much the same reasons. Following simple rules, the programs inject chance using, for example, pseudo-random number generators to replace expected code sequences with unanticipated bits. If artificial life 'creatures' (that is, programs that carry out the basic biological functions of reproduction and information coding) are allowed to mutate in this way and placed in an (artificial) environment that places selective pressures on them, the result can be an explosion of creative adaptation. In Tom Ray's *Tierra* program, for example, an entire ecology developed from an original 82 byte 'ancestor. The mutated creatures included parasites who preyed on the ancestor' by running their own reproductive programs on the ancestor's time, so to speak, and hyperparasites that preyed on the parasites. One 42-byte creature evolved that used programming tricks so clever that no human had ever thought of them. After analyzing the creature's program, Ray issued a challenge on the Internet to human programmers to

# Thinking the Unthinkable House

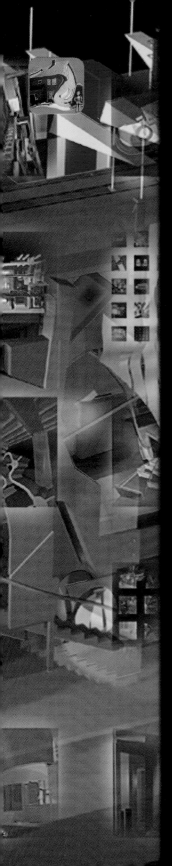

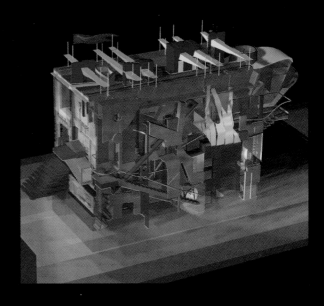

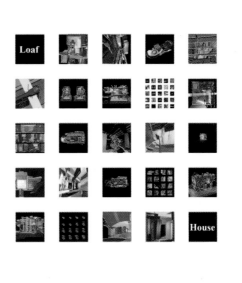

The Loaf House is a virtual Home for a nuclear family called the Loafers. They have constructed a domestic implement, where the spatial foibles of human endeavor are attended to. Loaf House exists in a number of forms, built by over 35 people over a period of five years in a studio at IIT. Each pass is a slightly different version of the same, a segment in relay, and each requires a different approach to make the concept of hominess complete. There are drawings, collages , writings ,a dense model , and a thorough construction of the whole on the computer. The computer drawings of the Loaf are fully programmed, structurally responsible. A programmed animation lends the visitor the cornucopia of space - save the abruptness of touch.

accomplish the task in the same amount of code. After three weeks, he got a response from an MIT hacker who accused him of perpetrating a fraud. The hacker proclaimed that it couldn't be done – and yet an entirely unconscious creature devoid of any kind of intention had accomplished it, merely through the blind force of creative evolution.

Accidents always have a double edge of danger and creativity. Once evolution gets going, it may not always produce results that humans can live with (sometimes in a literal sense). The *Tierra* program illustrates this aspect of accidents as well. Ray built his *Tierra* program using a 'virtual computer' inside the physical computer. Only the virtual computer understood the topological coding scheme Ray used for his 'creatures' reproduction. One reason for creating a 'virtual computer' was to create software that would be robust enough so it wouldn't crash when it was presented with new sequences of code defining the mutated creatures. Another reason was to keep whatever creatures evolved contained within the virtual computer, so they could not escape and contaminate larger computer systems. If a creature did get into the physical computer, Ray argued, its code would be read as data sequences rather than as programming instructions. Within the virtual computer, a program called the 'reaper' executed (deleted) creatures who had lived a certain number of computer hours. In one programming run, however, creatures evolved who were able to take over the reaper program and prevent it from killing them. If the creatures were able to get into the programs overseeing their reproduction, it seems probable that they might also find a way to escape from the virtual computer into the actual computer, from where they could spread to computers throughout the world. To escape human intention can also mean to outrun or subvert human intention. Which leads to the conclusion that it may be an illusion to think that we can control the evolution of artificial life forms. To get them to evolve, some degree of control must be abdicated, and it may not always be possible to wrest control back if we don't like the way things are going.

**AM**: *What makes a person an individual?*

**KH**: What a question! If viewpoint is important in how one constructs an answer to this huge question (and it certainly is), then there will be almost as many answers as

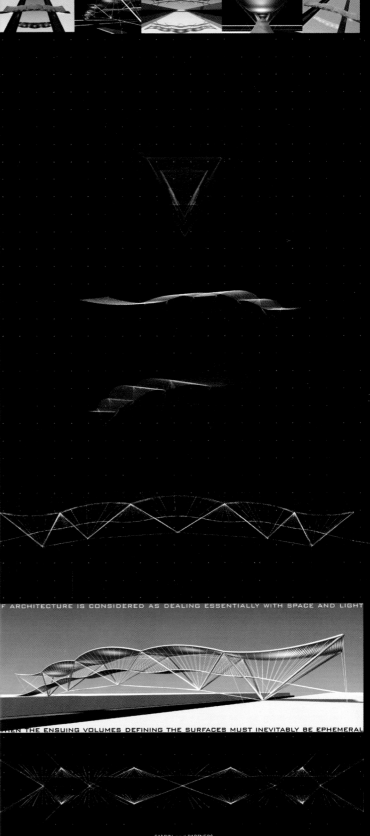

**Philippe Samyn (B)**
Structural morphology

There is a morphological quest to increase the vibration of our emotion and intellect echoing the place and society which prompts it. Architecture, dealing essentially with space and light, will have to be enriched by gathering the greatest possible amount of information resulting in light and citizen-friendly architecture. To suit human physiological needs, we should study the structural morphology of a place.

IF ARCHITECTURE IS CONSIDERED AS DEALING ESSENTIALLY WITH SPACE AND LIGHT

THEN THE ENSUING VOLUMES DEFINING THE SURFACES MUST INEVITABLY BE EPHEMERAL

SAMYN and PARTNERS
architects & engineers

there are viewpoints, and almost as many viewpoints as there are people to hold them. Counting people alive and dead, this gives us an order of magnitude of about 7 billion or so possible answers. To narrow the ballfield a little, let me speak about some research that I have undertaken for my latest book, *How We Became Posthuman*. According to Western liberal philosophy as it has been explicated by M. B. Macpherson, someone counts as an individual when he has the capacity to own himself, specifically his own body and the products of his labor. The stress placed here on ownership is of course characteristic of a capitalistic society; in Britain and Europe during the seventeenth and eighteenth centuries, liberal philosophy defined personhood through a set of interrelated assumptions that Macpherson calls 'possessive individualism'. Because someone owns himself or herself, it is possible for him or her to engage in market relations and thus to enter society as an individual. Macpherson recognized there is a chicken and egg problem here, for this view of individualism is certainly bound up with a society based on market relations, but philosophically the individual is said to pre-date those relations. In today's terminology, we might say that possessive individualism and capitalistic societies were co-emergent phenomena. Each required and catalyzed the appearance of the other. In any event, around the notion of the possessive individual accreted other qualities associated with this ability to engage in market relations. If the market was considered to be self-regulating, for example, that implied that the individuals participating in the market could also be self-regulating. Through such networks of associations, a number of qualities also came to be attached to the liberal humanist subject, including rationality, free will, independent agency, and the mind as the seat of identity. What I see happening today is a complication of the assumptions of possessive individualism coming from such fields as cognitive science, artificial intelligence, artificial life, computational theory, and mobile robotics. In these versions of the individual, the subject is seen not as a self-regulating, self-aware conscious subject with the full power of agency, but rather as a collection of semi-autonomous agents, each of which runs its own relatively simple program. Far from being the seat of identity, consciousness in this view is a late evolutionary event and much less important than consciousness thinks it is. I am reminded of a remark by comedian Emo Philips:

VISUAL, TACTILE, AUDIO, OLFACTORY,
GUSTATIVE, ARTS ...WILL JOIN
TOGETHER IN CONCERT TO HEIGHTEN
THE VIBRATION OF OUR EMOTION
AND INTELLECT ECHOEING THE PLACE
AND SOCIETY WHICH PROMPTS IT

SAMYN and PARTNERS
architects & engineers

"I used to think the brain was the most important organ in the body, but then I thought, who's telling me this?" For these researchers, consciousness becomes a epiphenomenon, an emergent property that needs only to provide a reliable interface with reality, not necessarily an accurate one ('accurate' is itself problematic in this context, for one would need to specify accurate according to which viewpoint). To demonstrate, Rodney Brooks, a mobile roboticist working at the MIT Artificial Intelligence Laboratory, points out that we all go through life with a large blank spot in the middle of our visual field, and remain for the most part happily unaware of it.

The posthuman individual, then, is not so much a single identity as a collection of agents working together. Agency still exists, but it is complicated because different agents have different agendas. Consciousness does not set these agendas; rather, it kicks in only at certain times to adjudicate conflicts between various subprograms. Moreover, consciousness remains largely unaware of the real nature of subjectivity, which is fractured, conflictual, and ultimately reducible to simple programs. Because the most interesting phenomena are often emergent (that is, properties that appear at the global level of a system that cannot be predicted from the individual parts), 'accidents' enter into this world view as an intrinsic part of evolutionary processes. Although they remain unpredictable, in a sense they have been expected. They are also highly valued, for it is through such accidents that complexity, including life and human consciousness, characteristically come into being. It is no 'accident,' I think, that this vision of human individuality allows the (post)human to be seamlessly articulated together with intelligent machines. Essentially this research is aimed toward understanding human agency, subjectivity, and identity as the result of computer modules running relatively simple programs. It comes about through what may in retrospect be seen as a second 'grand synthesis' of the twentieth century (the first grand synthesis was the union of genetics and evolution). In the second synthesis, evolution as it is currently understood (an understanding that itself is a hybrid offspring of genetics and Darwinian selection) joins with computational theory. The individual, as he or she is emerging from this second synthesis, is seen as a creature forged by evolutionary programs that run on bioware. The proof for this claim is taken to be the successful simulation of such programs in intelligent machines. Rather than man being the measure of all

**Nasrine Seraji**
Architecte et l'Ordinateur

The practice of architecture should be redefined by using new tools and the complex crossing of philosophy, sciences and art. The inherent needs to be searched. The dialogue between us and the machines consists of understanding and working with their logic. It is to manipulate and divert the constraints and potentials of the different programs. These games allow both accidental and desired architectural conditions. Architecture cannot always allow for the visible to be its originator. The void can be built as a spatial event.

things, as the Greeks thought, increasingly the computer is taken as the measure of all things, including humans.

**AM**: *How can my avatar be an individual?*

**KH**: If one thinks of the 'individual' as a collection of semi-autonomous agents, then it becomes clear that the avatar is a typical posthuman individual, for it is comprised of many interacting parts: the person operating the program; the intelligent machines that run the various programs; the software that creates the avatar; the CRT screen that displays the avatar's actions; etc. When these parts all seamlessly work together, one may have the illusion that the avatar is a mere extension or expression of a self-contained, autonomous, agential subject. As soon as some glitch happens, however, the user becomes uncomfortably aware that the avatar is not under his or her control alone.

**AM**: *How can my avatar get a body, with a lot of (normal, funny) actions and reactions? That would make it interesting to me.*

**KH**: There's been a lot of ballyhoo about the 'disembodiment' of cyberspace, but to my way of thinking, this kind of talk is possible only when one does not attend closely to the practices that produce virtual and real bodies. Many researchers now working in the social studies of science are looking at bodies not as pre-existing objects but as collectives produced through various kinds of practices. This has the effect of erasing (or better, bracketing) the body as an ontological entity and focusing on the processes through which bodies enter our perceptual horizons. In a sense, this approach is following a line of thought similar to that Jorge Luis Borges explores in *Tlon, Uqbar, Orbis Terius* when he imagines Tlon as a world with a language that can speak only verbs, never nouns. How would we know the body if it were a verb, a process, a constantly fluctuating and contextualized series of interactions rather than a noun, an object? Since practices are multiple, it follows that the bodies produced through practices are also going to be multiple, in many senses. As an example, say I am at my computer, reading a hypertext fiction such as Shelley Jackson's marvelous electronic hypertext, *Patchwork Girl*. To access the text, I have to perform various physical actions – turn on the computer, call up the program, open

it, etc. My body-as-a-verb can be understood, then, as the incorporated practices through which I interact with the computer and CRT screen. We can call this body the enacted body, because it is produced through the actions I perform. On the screen is an image of a body, which we can call the represented body. This body exists, however, only because of the intelligent machine that is mediating between the represented and enacted bodies. It is important not to underestimate the importance of the intelligent machine as an active agent in this process; exactly what kind of machine it is, and what kinds of programs it runs, will have very significant impacts on my reading experience, from the way the represented body is imaged to how long it takes for the programs to load. My reading, then, is really a collective action performed through complex interactions between the enacted body, the intelligent agents running various programs in the machine, and the represented bodies in the text I am reading. Where is the 'I' in this process? If we don't assume identity as a pre-existing entity, then the 'I' cannot be located in the body alone but rather is a production that emerges through various kinds of complex processes, of which this is only one example. Is this interesting? I don't know if you would consider it so. What I do know is that it embodies a very different way of looking at identity, subjectivity, and reality than traditional liberal humanism.

*AM*: *What would you like VR to become?*

**KH**: VR will soon be populated by a variety of intelligent agents – some of them human, some of them synthetic. As the environment becomes richer in this respect, more complex interactions with it will be possible. Moreover, I think the days of the bulkly helmets are limited; in the future, VR will exist both in immersive forms, easily accessible through lightweight glasses – or in what Marcos Novak calls 'eversive' projections – that come out into the real world and with which we interact. What these environments will look like are fluid exchanges between simulated and real contexts, with flexible and relatively non-obtrusive interfaces of various kinds, from motion and infra-red sensors to more specialized interfaces constructed through screens or glasses. To some extent these environments already exist, but we are only beginning to theorize them as integrated complex adaptive systems. For example, in the U.S. most

Neil Spiller (GB)
Breaking the House Rules

# hyperstructure emergence

With nanotechnology we can finally escape material stupidity. The 'aliveness' of smart materials will create opportunities for architects and product designers to transverse the rocky ground between the fluidity of the concept sketch and the parameters of construction. Nanotechnology is based on the premise that we will be able to manipulate matter, reconstituting and creating anything. The products of this technology offer possibilities especially in regard to the domestic information ecology: the home becomes a habitat for multiple networked intelligences, which interact to create a meta-intelligence.

...neil
spiller

supermarkets and department stores have door sensors that open the doors when you get within a certain range; this is an instance of a low-level and fairly ordinary eversive environment. Other instances are the cursor on the computer screen, a visual point that serves as a minimal kind of avatar, although we may not be accustomed to think of it as such.

Moreover, intelligent agents will take increasingly active roles in constructing and filtering information for human users. In an information-rich environment, as Richard Lanham has pointed out, the scarce commodity is not information; rather, it is human attention. It's no 'accident,' I think, that just when the information economy really begins to take off, in the late 1970s and 1980s, the medical profession identifies a syndrome they call 'attention deficit disorder' (ADD). It is not difficult to imagine that when human attention is in short supply, there will be pressure to develop intelligent agents that can take over for us tasks that may not require our active attention. For example, there are already in existence intelligent agent programs designed to filter your email. The agent, built along lines similar to neural nets, begins by observing your habits in answering your email. It notices that you always read messages from Arjen first, but that you systematically delete messages from Roger. So it starts putting Arjen's messages at the top of the queue, and shunts off Roger's messages into a 'low priority' file that will be automatically deleted after 30 days. In this vision of how information-rich environments will operate, human intelligence will ride on top of a highly articulated ecology, with many mundane and routine tasks being done by the intelligent agents that are part of that ecology. The idea is to conserve human intelligence for the tasks where it really counts. Of course, such a scheme also inevitably means that the human is delegating some measure of control to intelligent agents. Although many people find this scenario scary (notably Joseph Weizenbaum, who cautioned against precisely such developments twenty years ago, in *Computer Power and Human Reason*), the delegation of control to technological objects is scarcely new; humans have been doing it for thousands of years, starting with stone axes and flints for making fire. While it implies increasing interdependence on synthetic intelligence (and soon, perhaps, synthetic sentience), in my view this is scary only if we persist in thinking of humans as autonomous beings who *can*

control their environments. In fact, of course, this has always been more or less of an illusion. Humans have always been interdependent with the ecologies within which they live. Maybe it's time we recognized this interdependence and gave up the fantasy of complete and total control.

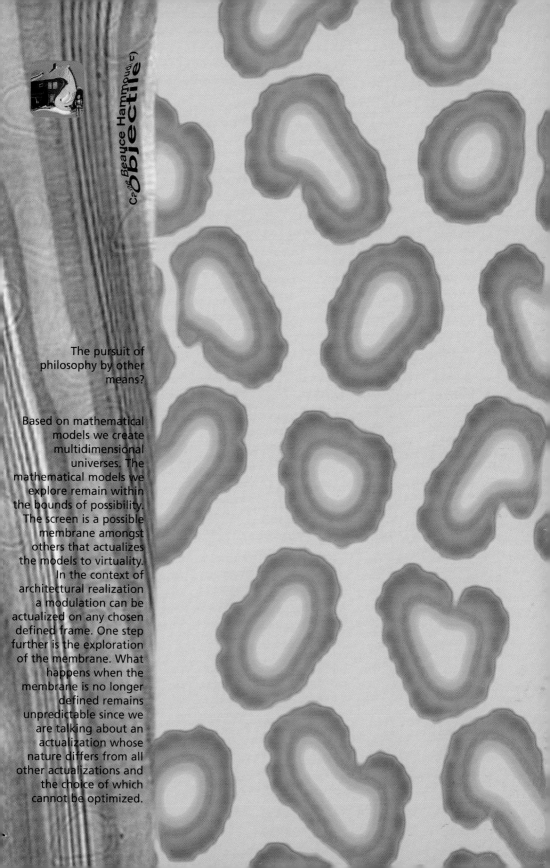

Beauce Hammoud<sub>(ue)</sub>
Cp
**objective**

The pursuit of
philosophy by other
means?

Based on mathematical
models we create
multidimensional
universes. The
mathematical models we
explore remain within
the bounds of possibility.
The screen is a possible
membrane amongst
others that actualizes
the models to virtuality.
In the context of
architectural realization
a modulation can be
actualized on any chosen
defined frame. One step
further is the exploration
of the membrane. What
happens when the
membrane is no longer
defined remains
unpredictable since we
are talking about an
actualization whose
nature differs from all
other actualizations and
the choice of which
cannot be optimized.

edited_18.8.html

Iomega Guest

FreeHand 7.0

berekening.html

life forms

 **File**   **Help**

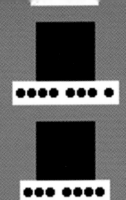

Trash

19:56

Macintosh HD

*Noel 's Mail*

# Dece

# WE LIVING SYSTEMS

*Fax interview with Humberto Maturana*
*by Arjen Mulder*

**AM**: *After reading* The Tree of Knowledge: The Biological Roots of Human Understanding *(1987), the book you wrote in collaboration with Francisco Varela, I would like to ask you how you feel about the unprecedented proliferation of technologically produced images (photos, movies, television, video, World Wide Web) we have been witnessing in the twentieth century. It seems to me that these technological images affect us, bypassing our linguistic faculties. In that sense they deny our humanness as you define it – i.e. that all human behavior takes place in language and conversations. These images were and still are mostly unidirectional: you can watch TV images but you cannot answer them in any other way than through behavior that seems to be the goal of these images themselves, namely inertia and/or consumption. Do you see ways of addressing this proliferation of technological images to counteract their 'denial of our humanness', or can they be incorporated into another kind of bodyhood, another conception of 'humanness'?*

**HM**: We human beings are languaging bipedal primates, and we exist as human beings living with other human beings in the flow of language. This means that our humanness is not an intrinsic feature of our biology but that we become human beings by living in this way with other human beings from our early babyhood onwards. But, as we are emotional animals as well, it is better to say that we human beings exist as such in the flow of our language (coordinations of coordinations of consensual behaviors) braided at every instant with the flow of our emotions (relational domains) in the domain of recursive coordination of behavior in which our languaging takes place. It is this dynamics we connote in our daily life with the word conversation. Accordingly, we can say that we human beings exist in the flow of conversations and that everything we do as human beings we do in the recursive flow of coordinations of coordinations of consensual

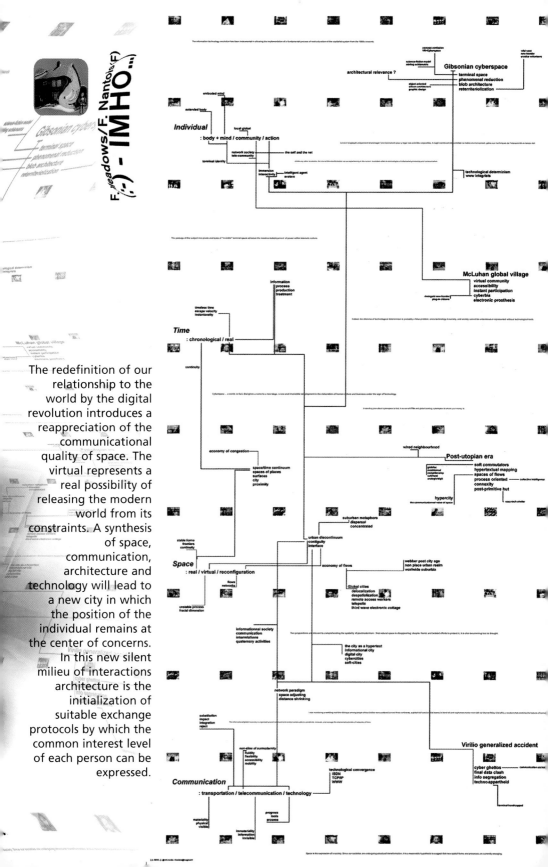

F. Meadows/F. Nantois(F) - IMHO...

The information technology revolution has been instrumental in allowing the implementation of a fundamental process of restructuration of the capitalist system from the 1980s onwards.

**Gibsonian cyberspace**
- concept confusion VR=Cyberspace
- science-fiction model wiring schizomatic
- wild west new frontier creative volunteers
- object oriented silicon architecture graphic design
- terminal space
- phenomenal reduction
- blob architecture
- reterritorialization

architectural relevance ?

embodied mind
extended body

*Individual*

: body + mind / community / action

local global

network society tele-community — the self and the net

terminal identity

immersion interactivity / intelligent agent avatars

technological determinism www integrists

The passage of the subject into private and fields of "invisible" terminal space enhances the massive redeployment of power within telematic culture.

**McLuhan global village**
- virtual community
- accessibility
- instant participation
- cyberbia
- electronic prosthesis
- mongoid neo-luddites plug-in citizens

information // process production treatment

timeless time escape velocity instantaneity

*Time*

: chronological / real

continuity

Cyberspace ... a world, in fact, that gives a name to a new stage, a new and irresistible development in the elaboration of human culture and business under the sign of technology

If sending you about cyberspace is that, it is one of ITBits and global banking, cyberspace is where your money is.

economy of congestion

space/time continuum spaces of places surfaces city proximity

wired neighbourhood

**Post-utopian era**
- soft commutators
- hypertextual mapping
- spaces of flows
- process oriented
- connexity
- post-primitive hut
- collective intelligence
- easy-tech shelter

hypercity
the communicational value of space

suburban metaphore dispersal concentrated

urban discontinuum contiguity interface

stable forms frontiers continuity

*Space*

: real / virtual / reconfiguration

economy of flows

webber post city age non place urban realm worldwide suburbia

flows networks

Global cities delocalization despatialization remote access workers telepolis third wave electronic cottage

unstable process fractal dimension

informational society communication interrelations quaternary activities

the city as a hypertext informational city digital city cybercities soft-cities

network paradigm space adjusting distance shrinking

substitution impact integration reject

non-sites of surmodernity fluidity flexibility accessibility mobility

**Virilio generalized accident**
- cyber ghettos communication exclusion
- final data clash
- info segregation
- techno apartheid
- terminal handicapped

technological convergence ISDN TCP/IP WWW

*Communication*

: transportation / telecommunication / technology

materiality physical visible

immateriality information invisible

progress tools process

The redefinition of our relationship to the world by the digital revolution introduces a reappreciation of the communicational quality of space. The virtual represents a real possibility of releasing the modern world from its constraints. A synthesis of space, communication, architecture and technology will lead to a new city in which the position of the individual remains at the center of concerns. In this new silent milieu of interactions architecture is the initialization of suitable exchange protocols by which the common interest level of each person can be expressed.

behaviors. That is, we are human beings and we become human beings as we live and grow in conversations with other human beings.

A nervous system exists as a closed network of neuronal elements, and operates as such in the closed dynamics of changing states of activity between its component neuronal elements in a way in which every change in state of activity between the neuronal elements of one part of the network leads to changes in the state of activity that occurs between the neuronal elements of other parts of the same network. Moreover, as a component of an organism, a nervous system exists in structural intersection with the sensors and effectors of the organism which are thus at the same time components of both the nervous system and the organism. As components of the nervous system, the sensors and effectors operate as neuronal elements, and not as sensors and effectors; but as components of an organism, the sensors and effectors operate as such. As a consequence, although a nervous system intersects with the sensory and effector components of the sensory and effector surfaces of an organism, the nervous system does not and cannot encounter the medium in which the organism interacts, only the organism does. At the same time as an organism interacts in the medium, its sensors and effectors encounter the medium, but do not participate in the operation of the nervous system as a closed network of changing states(relations) of activity between its neuronal components. What happens is that through the structural intersection of the nervous system and the organism, the nervous system gives rise to sensory effector correlations in the organism, and the interactions within the organism modulate the flow of the structural changes in the nervous system, and the structure of the nervous system changes in a manner contingent on the course of the interactions of the organism. Or, in other words, as the nervous system has a plastic structure that changes by following a course modulated by the interactions of the organism as it realizes its manner of living, the nervous system goes on through its structural changes generating sensory effector correlations in the organism that make operational sense to its way of living. And when the latter stops happening, the organism undergoes a breakdown in the realization of its way of living through the operation of its nervous system.

232

ONSITE

AAS
ABIST
ACK
ADCCP
ADSR

HRMS
HST
HTML
ICLID
IDEA
IMACS

PGP
PLATO
QAM
QBI
QDOS
QIC

www integrism

JIT
JNGE
JOE

RSCS
STAN
SDI
SGDT
SIDH
SLM
SNOB
TAXI
TDMA
THD
TOD
TWAIN

KAM
KBD
KIF

QML
KSPH
LAPB
LBT
GDT

informationness

MPY
MMI
MOTO
MYS
NAK
NDR
NPL
NRZ
NT
UL
OD
OID
OO

DSL
CD
FD
OR
W4
WCS
ISE
OPL

agents communities

cyber ghetto

virtual tribes

in the depth of real time stands immobile my on line body in search of new virtues for my on site confused experience

In these circumstances, what is relevant for us now in relation to your question, is to stress that as we live in language our brains become languaging brains that generate in us as organisms an internal dynamic that results in a flow of sensory effector correlations appropriate for languaging behavior in the domain of interactions in which we live as human beings. Moreover, it is also necessary to stress that as our brains become languaging brains, they become capable of generating in us sensory effector correlations that would make sense in interactions with other human beings as operations in language, even if they arise in us while we are alone or are just silent while thinking without words. But not only that. Because of the way we live our particular lives as human beings, our nervous system becomes a nervous system that generates the sensory effector correlations that involve our emotional behavior according to the conversations in which we have participated and participate. So, when we watch television we become involved as beings that live in conversations even if we keep silent. And whatever happens to us in our emotional behavior in the process

of seeing what we see, happens to us according to the kind of human being that we are becoming in the history of conversations which we have lived. We live as totalities in the internal dynamics of our closed bodily systems all the time, and there are no virtual emotions in our living however we live. Virtual realities are external to us, they belong to the flow of our interactions, not to the flow of our living as humans.

The images on television do not bypass our humanness, nor do they deny it, they enter it as aspects of our daily life directly, and that is their potency. Television images appear as if they were unidirectional in their occurrence, but as we see them we are not passive, as we find out later when we reflect on what we saw or on what happened to us when we watched them. We respond immediately or with delayed actions as actual manipulations or commentaries, or with indirect actions in behaviors or reflections that occur in a different relational domain, and that arise in us without us being aware of their connection with what we saw on television, because they arise as unconscious modulations of our actions and emotions. Certainly, in our direct response we can change the channel, comment explicitly, turn off the TV, or accept

# John Bain
# The Mutant
# Data
# Orchestra

*The Mutant Data Orchestra* rewires the products of our digital society to expose the hidden agents within. Through live circuit modification of digital answering machines, cheap digital toys and sound instruments the performers manipulate the data pathways and exert influence on their sound production without the use of a conventional software interface. This inherent coupling of the performers to the internal chance agents produced by the rewired circuitry provides a real time balance, where the machine surprises the performer and the performer surprises the machine. The result is an improvization based on a series of accidents directed towards a compositional whole.

Within these electronic machines, modifications are rationalized in relation to their aural results. Each device has a data output so that they can infect each other and influence their respective sound making capabilities. These sonic generators produce shards of noise with auto-improvised stabs of high pitched bell and cello tones. At times one can hear the intermeshing of data as a liquid waterfall of sonic information. The goal is to perceive data as living flowing entity where sound is used as the trace of exposure.

in full awareness the suggestion or invitation that the images entail. But to act in full awareness and taking full responsibility for what we do under the evocation of the images on television, we must have learned to be aware of what we do, and we must live in self-respect and self-trust so that we are not frightened that we will disappear if we do not conform with the alleged universal or social validity of what we are told. If we do not act in self-respect and self-trust, we cannot say no.

In these circumstances, the only way there is to conserve humanness in general, and the loving aspect of humanness (*homo amans*) in particular, and to do so without destroying it in the attempt, is through education for the loving aspect of humanness (*homo amans*). That is, through education for the conservation of self-respect and self-trust in respect and trust of others as a way of human coexistence. And this is done in the biology of love, that is indeed to live with our children in the biology of love, that is to live with them in the relational behavior by which children are seen, listened to, and invited to join in together with the parents in bringing forth a world in which all relationships take place in cooperation, in self-respect and self-trust, respect for others as well as love and responsibility for the world that we bring forth with others in what we do.

*AM: I agree. But then there are accidents. Now, the accident can be defined from two angles: either as something inherent to the system or as something that invades a system from outside. In the first case, accidents are a function or a potential of the structure of the system itself. Hereditary illnesses and some cancers can in that sense be understood as accidents – death is an accident. Inadequate reactions of a system (organism) to external conditions may also be viewed as accidents in a structural coupling. What these 'system-inherent' accidents have in common is the fact that they bring about a new state of the system: the functionality of the system flips from one mode into another. This can have fatal consequences but can also cause unexpected and unpredictable configurations. Now, because it concerns new states, with corresponding new emotions, there are no words to talk about it. This can lead to despair, but also to a creative outburst (for example in the arts – poetry, or painting, or photographs etc). In your work you never seem to address this type of 'system-inherent accident', this fundamental insecurity of our existence as a physical body. Yet this insecurity is a crucial factor in our humanness.*

**236**

# Online Realities in 3D

*Online Realities in 3D* investigates online art projects which use three-dimensionality as a metaphor for designing and articulating the social and technical processes that take place in the 'data scape' (information bodies, data streams, data landscapes, etc.).

Research in this field suggests that there is a definite need for critical debate. Many Internet projects use the 3D-metaphor for building a spatial architecture where the user is placed in an interior space or between different houses, 'in a world'. Here the 3D-objects either symbolize the access to specific themes or contents (an entry hall and a concierge may signify an index and thematic overview, etc.), or they are used as a backdrop for chat-based multi-user systems. In these cases, the 3D-metaphor is conceptually unnecessary, and 2D-solutions are faster, simpler, and easier to use.

The projects presented during DEAF98 deploy three-dimensionality not as a simple mirror of reality, but explore its potential meaning and usefulness beyond this 'mirror stage'. The projects do not offer conclusive answers on this issue, but provide starting points for discussion.

## Programm 5 (Nicole Martin, Lilian Jüchtern) (D): Staging Strategies

The project *Staging Strategies* focuses on designing a genuine formal language for the media of virtual reality. The basic element of a virtual world is dynamic information. Events, data. Everything is floating and moving. How do you visualize this in three-dimensional space?

**H M**: I think that we talk about an accident when confronted with an unexpected experience, so I consider that the accident is a feature of the life of the observer, not of the systems in which we are immersed or deal with. Indeed, I think that expectations and plans are in the long run necessarily destined to fail precisely because of the structurally determined nature of what one may call natural processes. In nature or in the spontaneous flow of the cosmos there are no accidents. So, a natural system only exists and operates in a course of time that lasts as long as it lasts spontaneously. Structurally determined systems are all systems that have independent structural dynamics. Indeed, a system arises and exists as such only in the structural dynamics that specifies an operational border enclosing the processes that constitute it by making them independent of other processes that may occur in its surroundings. In these circumstances, any encounter that a system may undergo triggers structural changes that an observer could not have computed by studying its structural dynamics, and to the observer they would appear as accidental. If the observer considers the system in a context by focussing on the system of processes that surround it, again there will be a wider context that he or she will not have considered, and the whole situation will be open for accidents. This is why I say that all plans and expectations will necessarily eventually not be fulfilled, and that it is up to the observer whether he or she lives the fact that an expectation or a plan is not fulfilled as an opportunity or a frustration.

We living systems exist in our interactions with the particular part of the medium in which we live, and which is all that one could say that a living system knows. I call this part of the medium in which a living system lives, its niche. Our niche as human beings is our cognitive space, and all that we do, we do as we operate in the flow of our living as structurally determined systems in our niche. In the patriarchal culture to which most human beings currently belong, we usually treat the fact that our expectations or our plans are mostly not fulfilled, as if their not being fulfilled were the product of some intrinsic failure or fault of the planner, and of ourselves if we happen to be the planner. As a consequence we resort to punishing the guilty, as if that would correct anything. In a way we as human beings all know that plans never work totally, but since they might work some of the time, we continue planning on the edge of uncertainty. Living,

Which sensual experiences are elementary
to a Virtual Reality? Dataworlds lack
gravity: there is no Up and Down, no
ground, no horizon. One move and
everything is changing. How can I find my
way in a Virtual Reality?
*Staging Strategies* researches the basic
parameters constituting the 'gestalt' of a
virtual reality
(http://www.digitalworks.org/rd/p5)

## Zoltán Szegedy-Maszák, Márton Fernezelyi (H): Demedusator

*Demedusator* is a shared virtual world
developed by the visitors. This VRML-
based world enables the inhabitants to
create, possess, and adjust objects
(photos, sounds, videos, etc.), and to build
up a common online environment. The
uploaded files are appearing to the
observers in form of encrypted sculptures.
The original media which are represented
by these sculptures can be decoded and
viewed by touching the silent objects. The
system of encryption creates an interface
for the users to explore the world without
having to download all the multimedia
files. *Demedusator* is a container for
building up a city-like world, a kind of
encrypted 'Metaverse'
(http://demedusator.c3.hu)

## Károly Tóth (H/NL): The Negative River

A co-operation of artists, writers and
scientists who create a navigable organic
environment, using the river as metaphor.
The participants contribute documents
and digital traces from their living
environment which are used to build up
an information database. From this
database, a reconstruction of a new
spatio-temporal structure, a Terra A-Topia
is made in virtual space. The project is less
concerned with the latest technical
developments in hard- and software, than
with the technologies of thought,
imagination, intuition and perception. If
information is accepted as one of the

UPLOAD
IMAGE    TEXT
WORLD

or@c3.hu

however is mostly regular, because it is realized through cyclic processes that are immersed in other larger cyclical processes to which living systems are structurally coupled in the flow of their living. So living systems mostly do not live in what we could call uncertainty. It is human beings that either interfere with the cyclical dynamics of the biosphere, or generate linear processes that introduce incoherence in the cyclical dynamics of the biosphere, who live or may live in the insecurity of believing in planning and knowing at the same time that plans eventually do not work. Due to this, we humans try to control, which is a way of attempting to insure the desired result of the planning through manipulating the lives of other human beings or other living things. The result usually creates frustration and suffering. So, I do not usually speak of accidents or uncertainty in human life, because I stress that the only way out of the nonsensical frustration, anger or guilt, if plans do not work out in the knowledge that most of the time they do not work, is by treating every so-called failure as an occasion for the expansion of knowledge (expansion of the niche), and as an opportunity for collaboration with all the others involved, so that the new plans arise in an expanded niche.

*AM: 'System-external accidents' are effects from outside that affect the system and deregulate it in such a way that the system starts to function differently. This can cause the disintegration of the system (organism) – to death and destruction. But bodies/systems may also adapt to the new conditions and find a new way of functioning within their structural couplings. In this sense one can consider an (extreme) passion as an accident, as a coupling that is too strong for either both or one of the systems (persons), given his or her initial structure. But such a passion can also force a radical restructuring or renewal of (one of) the lovers. Another example of a restructuring 'accident' is the miracle – the utterly unexplainable event that is experienced as a 'revelation' and that can lead to a religious conversion. Passions and miracles are examples of emotions that are roused by external phenomena, and do no fit into the cultural context of a system/body/organism. They induce renewal, in whatever direction: either the organism or the context in which it interacts may be forced to change. So in the case of the system-external accident we again encounter a 'force' that can lead to destruction as well as to renewal, or both.*

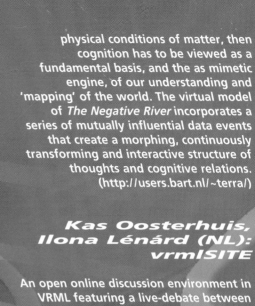

physical conditions of matter, then cognition has to be viewed as a fundamental basis, and the as mimetic engine, of our understanding and 'mapping' of the world. The virtual model of *The Negative River* incorporates a series of mutually influential data events that create a morphing, continuously transforming and interactive structure of thoughts and cognitive relations. (http://users.bart.nl/~terra/)

## Kas Oosterhuis, Ilona Lénárd (NL): vrmlSITE

An open online discussion environment in VRML featuring a live-debate between architects, designers and theorists. The discussion is open to the public who can log on as an audience-avatar into the VRML environment. *vrmlSITE* contains free-floating, characteristic elements of projects by the participants. Each participant is represented by an avatar which is not a person but a small 3D world in itself, so that participants and audience experience parallel 3D worlds talking to each other. The participants can trigger events – by clicking on words in the *vrmlSITE* – during the discussion. (www.oosterhuis.nl, www.lenard.nl).

**HM**: Living systems exist, as all systems do, in the flow of the conservation of their organization and adaptation as a matter of course; if this does not happen they disintegrate. No effort or force is involved; adaptation as a state of operational congruence between a system and its circumstances is an operational condition of existence for any system. Success, regulation, deregulation, change, failure, or adaptation as a variable, are notions that the observer uses to explain or describe the regularities of the spontaneous process in which the person sees him or herself participating in his or her living. Living systems do not adapt, but are seen by the observer to change, conserving their operational congruence in the medium in which they realize their niche. The key concept in understanding what happens in the flow of living of living systems is conservation. Living systems exist as long as their organization as living systems and their adaptation are conserved through the flow of their structural changes in structural coupling. So, if passion appears to disrupt everything an observer can perceive in the living system that lives it, passion is its current way of living according to how that person is at that moment in his or her structural dynamics, and the person will go on living as long as his or her living in passion is conserved. If an observer sees a radical (relational) restructuring in the life of the living system (person), what the observer sees is the way in which such a person is successful in conserving his or her organization and adaptation as a person. Most of this you have already implied in the question you asked. But what you have not said or emphasized is that there is in fact no force or pressure for change. You have mentioned a force that can lead to change or to destruction. But there is no force involved. All there is in terms of energy or force is the molecular agitation at constant temperature in which we mammals live. But what indeed occurs is that a person (living system) remains alive as long as the flow of its continuous structural changes and the continuous structural changes of the medium of its niche occur following the path in which the organization and the adaptation (adequate operation in its domain of existence) of the person involved are conserved through its recursive interactions in its niche. Renewal or failure are terms used by the observer of the unexpected event in his or her description as accidents coming from the outside or the inside in the terms of your formulation. It is the unexpectedness for the observer that makes the

# JODI
# OSS/••••

JODI, a collaboration between the artists Joan Heemskerk and Dirk Paesmans, work with the creative limitations of digital technologies. Their work on the World Wide Web has turned software bugs into the nuclei of a new design aesthetics and has taught net users to be less disrespectful of 'Error 404' messages and virus warnings. JODI's approach is strongly media-conscious, exploiting unexpected potentials of computers and networks, their components and users who cannot be passive spectators but have to interact in order to experience the work.

*OSS/••••*, conceived as a CD-ROM, is not a multi-media application with flawless images and easy navigation routes. It uses the accidental potentials of the computer to create a whole new set of navigation experiences through distortions and interference. When beginning to explore the project, the user first has to overcome the irritation about the visual 'noise' of what looks like a malfunctioning computer screen, deteriorating desktop images, an uncontrollable visual display and an erratic computer mouse. As critic Saul Albert puts it: "JODI writes programs designed to create dysfunctional models of computer behavior."

*OSS/••••* consists of three separate projects which can be selected randomly by clicking on neutral square symbols that appear on the desktop. One project consists of a huge variety of black-and-white patterns which in some irrational way seem to respond to the movement of the mouse. Sound patterns create further confusion,

accident, not something special in the nature of the unexpected event. Accordingly, what I wish to emphasize is that the flow of the conservation of the structural coupling between the component elements of the cosmos, of the biosphere, or of a culture, is not haphazard, but is at any time a result of the structural coherence that has arisen as a consequence of recursive historical changes around a basic way of living that has been conserved in the course of the generations. System and circumstance change together congruently and spontaneously in the flow of the natural drift. Indeed this is what structural coupling means. I insist on emphasizing the spontaneous character of all processes in the domain of our existence as living systems to make it possible for us to understand our participation in what happens to us as human beings and in what we do as such.

Understanding, reflection, change, certainty or uncertainty, are phenomena that arise in human existence through our human use of language, and occur in us also as spontaneous processes in the flow of our structural coupling with a domain of existence that has arisen in our operating as languaging beings. Human existence takes place in the biological domain, but occurs in the recursive relational dimensions of languaging which is where time, desires, and expectations arise as ways of being that have properties orthogonal to those of the present under the form of past and future. In the present there is no fulfillment or failure, all that there is is a continuous happening. It is when life takes place in languaging, that the peculiar way of human living in accidents of the internal and external kind, passions, religious conversions, regulation, function, security and insecurity, etc. can have existence and occur in the conservation of the structural coupling of human beings in the realization of their biological existence. It is only when the concept of time has arisen as a way of living in the present that emotions such as anticipation, when looking into the future, and frustration, when looking at the past, can take place as the uniquely human source of joy and suffering that they are.

*AM: Summing up what I have tried to ask you: how do renewals or 'novelty' come about? Is something fundamentally new possible at all in your view? And if so, how?*

though they can also be used for navigating through this library of screen noise. A second project is an inverted drawing program with distinct and completely non-intuitive functions of certain keys on the keyboard. The visual display offers useless coordinate information and opens up windows showing computer code that cannot be closed again, creating a completely cluttered screen and frenzied interaction of the user. The third project takes the actual desktop image of the computer on which the CD-ROM is being viewed and sends it into a maelstrom of distortions. Different keystrokes affect these turbulent images, though the precise functionality remains ambiguous. Accidentally triggered sounds and songs generated by the computer reveal the hidden layers of the machine. Miklós Peternák calls it "a dynamic deliberation of images from the customary cover page by means of 'peeling away the surface of the screen'."

Infected by *OSS/••••*, the computer begins to mutter to itself, watched by the users who see their own computer, their virtual home on the desktop, go hay-wire. JODI fold the machine code inside out and make the different internal levels of the computer hardware and software protocols talk to each other in their own jargon. Their machinic aesthetics show that on the level of programming and code the accident has always already happened

**HM**: Renewal and novelty arise with respect to the observer as his or her opinions according to the way in which the experience that he or she may currently live fits in with his or her view of what should be the course of events. At the same time in the ongoing changing present in which existence takes place, the present is continuously new, arising as a novel modification of the prevailing present. So in a way every moment is fundamentally new, and it is only through our distinction of configurations and our classificatory memory that we claim that there are novelties that are not so because we have 'seen' them before. At the same time, however, due to the structural coherence of the structurally determined domain in which living systems arise as one class of system, and in which we can distinguish many different classes of systems, we can also see that all the members of a class are the same as such. So, strictly speaking, every newly created member of a class no matter how different it may be from the other members of the class, is no novelty. But an observer that has only dealt with members of a single class, cannot claim that he or she is seeing something absolutely new if he or she happens to see a system that is a member of a different class.

So, we human beings exist in a continuously newly arising present that we cannot see in its permanent novelty thanks to our memory and our joy in classifications that leads us to say, "Oh! I have seen that already, there is nothing new in it!" But, we see more than what we think we see, and relationships begin to appear that are part of our changing present that surprise us because we did not expect them, and we claim an act of creativity has occurred in us or in others. Yes, everything is at every moment intrinsically new, but it is only sometimes novel to us, and then we cannot say that we knew about it. Memory destroys and creates novelty, and at the same time it makes it possible for us to see our participation in a simultaneously changing and stable world which we help to bring about, and which as our world is our ultimate responsibility.

one-
which is limited

s of past-presen nal affair.

ly perceive. And e future

name forward.

er we can i

passe

'Sculptures Spe y
the basis res such as wall

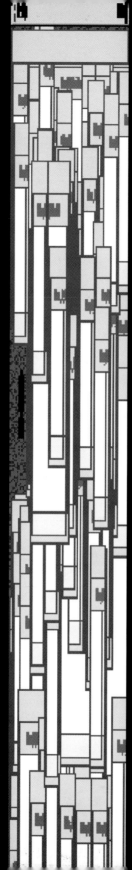

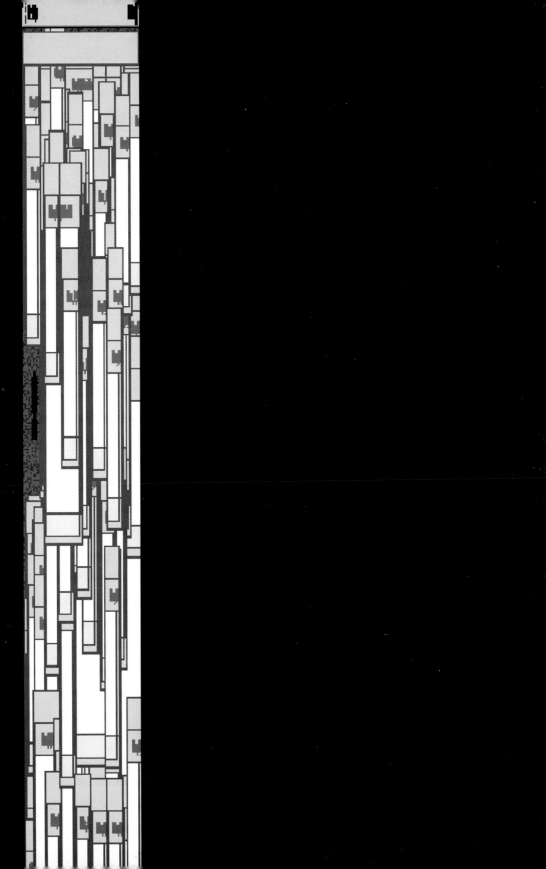

# *DEAF98*
# *Summary*

**17.11 — 29.11:** DEAF98 Exhibition
**17.11 — 12.12:** transArchitectures 02 + 03
**17.11 — 22.11:** Digital Dive

**17.11 — 21.11:** Jet Lag: Diller + Scofidio (USA),
Builders Association (USA)

**17.11:** Series of 5: Bruno Martelli (GB), Ruth Gibson (GB)

**18.11:** Open Territories: Rafael Lozano-Hemmer (MEX/CDN),
Mark Bain (USA), Yukiko Shikata (J), De Balie (NL), a.o.

**18.11:** Why 2K?: Timothy Druckrey (USA), Institute for Affordable
Lunacy/IBW (NL), Daniel Ockeloen (NL), Simon Davies (UK), a.o.

**19.11:** Online Realities in 3D: Cãlin Dan (RO/NL), Zoltán Szegedy
Maszák (H), Marton Fernezelyi (H), Programm 5 (D),
Károly Tóth (H/NL), Kas Oosterhuis (NL), Ilona Lénárd (NL).
Moderator: Katja Martin (D)

**19.11:** Nettime Presentation: READ ME: Ted Byfield (USA), Diana
McCarty (USA/H), Pit Schultz (D), Marleen Stikker (NL), McKenzie Wark
(AUS), Faith Wilding (USA)

**20.11 — 21.11:** Symposium: N. Katherine Hayles (USA), Perry
Hoberman (USA), Knowbotic Research (D/A), Detlef Linke (D), Greg Lynn
(USA), Steve Mann (CDN), Brian Massumi (AUS), Marcos Novak (USA),
Otto Rössler (D), Lars Spuybroek (NL). Moderator: Bart Lootsma (NL)

**20.11:** The Sound of Impact: Best Real Live Show (NL) feat. Gebhard
Sengmüller (A), Solid Rocket Boosters (NL), Swayzak (GB), Ver Licht (NL),
a.o.

**20.11:** Series of 5: Debra Solomon (NL)

**21.11:** Series of 5: Dansgroep Krisztina de Châtel (NL)

**22.11:** Wiretap 4.11: Ed van Megen/Association of Strategic
Accidents (NL/D), Bureau of Inverse Technology (USA), John Bain (USA)

**16.11 — 20.11:** Workshop Cyberstudio: Future Moves II
**22.11:** Workshop AIR. Moderator: Ted Krueger (USA)
**23.11 — 25.11:** Workshop Liquid Architecture. Moderators:
Ted Krueger (USA), Marcos Novak (USA)

# The Unreliable DEAF98 Website

The DEAF98 website not only provides Internet users with detailed information about all parts of the festival. The further they search, the more unreliable the navigation, the more twisted and distorted the route and the information. Parts of texts disappear, links lead to wrong information, images distort.

Festival visitors can also repair (or further disrupt) the site by using special codes which they receive when buying their tickets. With these codes lost information can be retrieved, closed areas become accessible again, or accessible areas closed. Under the influence of the user interaction, the site leads a life of its own.

Belgian artist Danny Devos co-operates with a team of designers and programmers on this project which incorporates ddv's large database of fatal accidents with celebrities, disasters with aircrafts and ferries, murders, etc. The birth(+)fact(x)death(-)calendar is originally a plain calendar: it lists births, facts and deaths, day by day. Devos has been collecting these dates since 1985. He writes: "It started as just a worthwhile idea when I was working on another project. While collecting data about serial killers and other stuff alike, I discovered that on June 2 both Yorkshire Ripper Peter Sutcliffe and – in another year – writer Donatien Alphonse François de Sade were born, and that Bob Dylan was born on the same day Jeanne d'Arc was burned on the stake. All kinds of strange combinations and possible genetic conspiracy theories popped up, and before I realized it, I crashed into an avalanche of astounding discoveries relating to the collected data on mass murderers and serial killers, artists and writers, scientists and religious leaders, actors and political leaders, and man-made disasters with a minimum of 100 deaths: plane-crashes, train-wreckages, fires, explosions."

The calendar went through multiple media formats, from hand written copy books, through typed magazines and annual calendars, to Commodore 64 text editors and finally a data-base program running on a Macintosh PowerBook.

"In 1997, Alex Adriaansens from V2, probably one of the 13 people who have bought a calendar every year it came out, invited me to put the birth(+)fact(x)death(-)calendar on the V2_website. Through the DEAF Festival website the calendar will be used to interfere with the web-surfers' daily lives. Past, present and future are mixed into an informational blend which fills the gap between art and life. The DEAF-site, co-powered by the birth(+)fact(x)death(-)calendar, is an array of facts which will boost your mind with an additional means of perception for enduring 1998 electronic art."

**Joke Brouwer** studied at the Royal Academy of Art and Design at 's-Hertogenbosch (NL). In 1981 she co-founded V2_Organization and has since been an organizer at V2_. She is also editor and designer of V2_'s publications, including posters, catalogues and books: *Book for the Unstable Media* (1992), *Interfacing Realities* (1997), *TechnoMorphica* (1997), *The Art of the Accident* (1998).

**Bart Lootsma** is an historian, critic and curator in the fields of architecture, design and the visual arts. He is a guest-professor at the Berlage Institute and lecturing at the Sandberg Institute, both postgraduate courses in Amsterdam. He is an editor of *ARCHIS*, correspondent of *DOMUS* and co-editor of the Berlin-based magazine *DAIDALOS*.

**Arjen Mulder** is a biologist and media theorist and has published several books of essays on the relationship between technical media, physical experiences and belief systems. He is a member of Adilkno, a collective that published *Cracking the Movement* (1994) and *Media Archive* (1998).

**Andreas Ruby** is an architectural critic, theorist and curator based in Cologne, Germany. MA in History of Art, University of Cologne. 1994 Visiting Scholar at Ecole Spéciale d'Architecture, Paris, under Paul Virilio. 1996 Visiting Scholar at Graduate School of Architecture and Planning, Columbia University, New York under Bernard Tschumi. Essay publications in major architecture reviews in Europe and the United States. Exhibition curating for Odile Decq & Benoit Cornette: *Hyper-Tension*, Aedes Gallery Berlin, 1994.

**N. Katherine Hayles** is Professor of English at the University of California at Los Angeles. She combines scientific insights from chaos and systems theory with the literary history of the twentieth century. She has published, among other things: *Chaos Bound: Orderly Disorder in Contemporary Literature and Science* (1990), *Chaos and Order: Complex Dynamics in Literature and Science* (1991). Soon to be published: *How We Became Posthuman: Virtual Bodies in Cybernetics, Literature and Informatics* (1999), in which she puts forward a proposition for the posthuman condition.

**Perry Hoberman** lives in Brooklyn and currently teaches in the graduate Computer Art Department at the School of Visual Arts in New York. He is the Art Director at Telepresence Research, a company specializing in virtual reality and telepresence installations for arts and industry. He is represented by Postmasters Gallery and has presented installations, spectacles, sculptures and performances throughout the United States and Europe. They include *Faraday's Garden*, *Empty Orchestra Cafe* and *Bar Code Hotel*. His paper *Mistakes and Misbehavior in Cyberspace* was first presented at 5CYBERCONF in Madrid in 1996. (http://www.hoberman.com)

**Steve Mann**, currently professor at the University of Toronto, has, since the eighties, almost permanently been wearing a wireless computer and camera upon his body (so-called *wearcom* and *wearcam*), of which he created different, increasingly user-friendly versions. He not only uses these techniques because they are convenient in everyday life, but also to create performances that consist of recording with his own camera those who film him with their surveillance cameras; which leads to bizarre confrontations in department stores, malls and other scanscapes. Mann uses the term 'Reflectionism' for these situationist actions. Through his long-lasting fusion with the computers on his body, Mann can, like no other, describe and interpret the psychological and social effects of that fusion. (http://www.wearcam.org)

**Humberto Maturana** is a neurobiologist and Professor at the University of Chile. When asked about the nature of life and cognition he formulated an answer: autopoiesis (the Greek auto means 'self' and poiein means 'to make'). Together with Francisco J. Varela he wrote: *Autopoiesis and Cognition: The Realization of the Living* (1980) and *The Tree of Knowledge. The Biological Roots of Human Understanding* (1987). In these works he unfolds this change in cognition theory, laying a new foundation for biologistic systems theory. He investigated ideas in cognition and perception and has expanded the understanding of humanness and therapy through revealing the biology of the observer. The main consequence of Maturana's analysis is the revaluation of emotions as the foundation of human life and even of rationality.

**Dick Raaijmakers** is one of Holland's electronic music pioneers. He is a composer, technical expert, musical director and a theoretician with a critical attitude towards technology. Apart from the musical aspect and the way the music is made, Raaijmakers is very interested in the visual aspect of the instruments and equipments themselves, as well as of the artistic production. In Raaijmakers' works (texts as well as performances and music theatre) the concept of 'falling' plays a crucial role. The fall embodies many of Raaijmakers's ideas on technology, music, art and society. In 1992 he was awarded with the prestigious Oeuvre Award of the Dutch Fund for Fine Arts, Design and Architecture.

**Knowbotic Research+cF** (Yvonne Wilhelm, Alexander Tuchacek, Christian Hübler), is an artist group based in Cologne, Germany who build experimental network interfaces for translocal urban environments. Knowbotic Research articulate their projects by folding information and knowledge structures into complex zones of activities. In partnership with the Academy for Media Arts, KR+cF has founded *Mem_brane*, a laboratory for media strategies. In 1998, the group has been appointed as Professor for New Media at University of Art and Design Zurich. Recent projects include *Dialogue With The Knowbotic South* (1995), *Anonymous Muttering* (1996) and *IO_Dencies* (1997 ff). (http://www.khm.de/people/krcf)

**Brian Massumi** is an Australian Research Council fellow based at the Humanities Research Centre of the Australian National University. He is the author of *A User's Guide to Capitalism and Schizophrenia: Deviations from Deleuze and Guattari* and *First and Last Emperors: The Absolute State and the Body of the Despot* (with Kenneth Dean). He is the editor of *The Politics of Everyday Fear*, and co-editor of the University of Minnesota Press book series *Theory Out of Bounds*. His work in progress on sensation, virtuality, and modes of cultural expression is forthcoming from Harvard University Press.

**Marcos Novak** is Visiting Associate Professor at the Department of Architecture and Urban Design at UCLA. He is a transarchitect: an architect, artist, composer, and theorist who employs algorithmic techniques to design actual, virtual and hybrid intelligent environments. Seeking to expand the definition of architecture to include electronic space, he originated the concept of 'liquid architectures in cyberspace' and the study of a dematerialized architecture for the new, virtual public domain. Novak is the founding director of the Laboratory for Immersive Virtual Environments and the Advanced Design Research Program at the School of Architecture at the University of Texas at Austin. His writings include *transArchitecture: Against the Collapsing Radius of Fiction*, and *Transmitting Architecture: The transPhysical City*. (http://www.aud.ucla.edu/~marcos/)

**Otto E. Rössler** was trained in medicine and obtained his PhD in immunology. He won a visiting appointment at the Center for State University of New York at Buffalo in 1965, and has been with the University of Tübingen, Germany since 1970. He was a Visiting Professor of Mathematics at Guelph University, in 1981, of nonlinear science at the Center for Nonlinear Studies of Los Alamos, in 1983, of Chemical Engineering in Charlottesville, in 1992 and of physics in Lyngby, in 1993. He authored about 140 papers on chaos and about the same number on other topics. He co-authored a book on chaos (with Jürgen Parisi and Joachim Peinke) and is the author of *Endophysics* (edited by Peter Weibel) and of *Das Flammenschwert, oder Wie hermetisch ist die Schnittstelle des Mikrokonstruktivismus?* (*The Sword of Flames, or How hermetic is the interface of micro-constructivism?*) (1994).

**Lars Spuybroek** is an architect and one of the founders of NOX. Projects include: *Soft City*, a television production for VPRO TV (1993), the *NOX-A, -B, -C, and -D* books (1992–95), *SoftSite*, a liquid city generated by behavior on the Internet (V2_Organization, 1996) and projected on the facade of the Netherlands Architecture Institute, and the interactive water pavilion, called $H_2O$ *eXPO* (for the Dutch Ministry of Transport, Public Works and Water Management, 1997). Lars Spuybroek was also editor of the quarterly magazine *Forum*. In addition to extensive lecturing, he is also a teacher and currently Visiting Associate Professor at Columbia University, New York.

**Paul Virilio** is an architect/urbanist and a writer who worked until recently at the Ecole Spéciale d'Architecture in Paris. In his books Virilio criticizes the effects of technological developments on modern society. He analyzes the relations between for instance media technology and medical or military technology, specializes in questions concerning military space and the organization of territory and describes the structural changes these technologies cause in relation to the human body, our perception and our notion of reality. He has published among others *The Logistics of Perception, War and Cinema 1* (1984), *Speed and Politics* (1986), *Bunker Archeology* (1994) and *Open Sky* (1997).

# COLOPHON
# DEAF98

## Festival: The Art of the Accident

**General coordination:** Alex Adriaansens, Maaike Boots, Andreas Broeckmann, Joke Brouwer, Frits Gierstbergen (NFI), Anne Nigten, Marc Thelosen

**General production:** Marjolein Berger, Friso Hermsen, Rob van Leeuwen (NAI), Juno Nimis, Jacco van de Ree, Agnes Wijers (NFI)

**Press and publicity:** Anniek van Anraad, Maartje van de Heuvel (NFI), Angeli Poulssen/Martine Heijnen (NAI)

**Technical coordination:** Ed Bezem, Martin Taminiau, Ed van der Velden

**Website:** Danny Devos, Madelinde Hageman, Pieter van Kemenade, Boudewijn Ridder

**Design:** Joke Brouwer, Melanie Kandelaars; Danny Kreeft, Rogier Theeuwen (symposium poster and signage); Amber Hey, Ingmar Swaluë (video trailer)

**Special thanks:** Peter Duimelinks (V2_Archief); Kristin Feireiss (NAI), Jan-Wijbrand Kolman, Aadjan van der Helm (V2_Lab); Dick Hollander, Klazien Brummel (Cyberstudio/Future Moves II); Katja Martin (Online Realities); Arthur Bueno, Timothy Druckrey (Why 2K or); Henk Koolen, Erik Quint (Nighttown)

### Cooperation
**Partner institutes in Rotterdam:** Nederlands Foto Instituut (NFI), Netherlands Architecture Institute (NAI), Theater Lantaren/Venster, Nighttown, Museum Boijmans Van Beuningen, Bonheur, AIR (Architecture International Rotterdam), Academie van Bouwkunst, ArchiNed, Archis, Aroma Catering, V2_Lab, V2_Organisatie.

**International partners:** Architecture & Prospective (B), Ars Electronica Center (A), C3 – Center for Culture and Communcation (H), Hull Time Based Arts (UK), InterCommunication Center (J), Shinkansen (UK), I.R.D. (Infographie Recherche et Développement) (B), Zentrum für Kunst und Medientechnologie (D).

### Support
**DEAF98 is made possible by:** Ministerie van Onderwijs, Cultuur en Wetenschappen, Ministerie van Buitenlandse Zaken (HGIS), Mondriaan Stichting, Prins Bernhard Fonds, Canadian Embassy, Stimuleringsfonds voor Architectuur, Rotterdamse Kunststichting, Rotterdam Festivals, ThuisKopiefonds, Goethe Institut Rotterdam, Van Eesteren-Fluck & Van Lohuizen Stichting, Ministerie van de Vlaamse Gemeenschap, Botschaft der Bundesrepublik Deutschland.

**DEAF98 is sponsored by:** Intergraph Computer Systems; MCM Video; Smart Cars; Ophuysen, Ricoh Dealer, Rotterdam.

## Publication: The Art of the Accident

**Editorial team:** Andreas Broeckmann, Joke Brouwer (editor-in-chief), Bart Lootsma, Arjen Mulder, Lars Spuybroek

**Design:** Joke Brouwer

**Translations:** Frances Brettell, Ronald Fritz, Leo Reijnen

**Photographs:** Copyright is held by the artists.

**Special thanks:** Simon Franke, Andreas Ruby, Tanja Karreman, Wim Nijenhuis, Jacco van de Ree

Available in North, South and Central America through D.A.P./Distributed Art Publishers Inc, 155 Sixth Avenue 2nd Floor, New York, NY 10013-1507, Tel. 212 627.1999 Fax 212 627.9484

ISBN 90-5662-090-8

# Greg
# Lynn
# Embryologic
# housing

The Art of the Ar